A POLITICAL THEORY OF RIGHTS

A Political Theory
of Rights

Attracta Ingram

CLARENDON PRESS · OXFORD
1994

Oxford University Press, Walton Street, Oxford OX2 6DP
Oxford New York Toronto
Delhi Bombay Calcutta Madras Karachi
Kuala Lumpur Singapore Hong Kong Tokyo
Nairobi Dar es Salaam Cape Town
Melbourne Auckland Madrid
and associated companies in
Berlin Ibadan

Oxford is a trade mark of Oxford University Press

Published in the United States
by Oxford University Press Inc., New York

British Library Cataloguing in Publication Data
Data available

Library of Congress Cataloging in Publication Data
Ingram, Attracta.
A political theory of rights / Attracta Ingram.
Includes bibliographical references and index.
1. Human rights. 2. Autonomy. I. Title.
JC571.I489 1994 323—dc20 94–8692
ISBN 0–19–827901–9
ISBN 0–19–827963–9 (Pbk.)

1 3 5 7 9 10 8 6 4 2

Typeset by Cambrian Typesetters, Frimley, Surrey
Printed in Great Britain
on acid-free paper by
Bookcraft (Bath) Ltd.
Midsomer Norton, Avon

For
Vivienne, Melissa, and Alexander

Acknowledgements

This project was begun in 1986–7 when I was on sabbatical leave from University College Dublin. During spring 1987 I was visiting research fellow at the Centre for Philosophy and Public Affairs in the Department of Moral Philosophy at the University of St Andrews. This fellowship was funded by the Royal Bank of Scotland. I am grateful to UCD and St Andrews for making that research leave possible. I am also grateful to Columbia University, and the University of California at Berkeley, for the assistance and facilities they provided in that year.

For encouragement, comments, and criticism, I would like to thank Maria Baghramian, Ian Cornelius, G. A. Cohen, Gordon Graham, Fergal O'Connor, and several generations of politics students in UCD. I am particularly grateful to Neil MacCormick, Philip Pettit, and Hillel Steiner for detailed comments on earlier drafts. Tim Barton has been a wonderfully supportive and helpful editor at Oxford University Press. I wish to thank the editor of *International Journal of Moral and Social Studies* for permission to use material in Chapter 3 first published in that journal.

John Baker is a very special colleague who deserves special thanks for his advice, friendship, and intellectual support over the years. His penetrating criticisms and suggestions were indispensable for the progress of the work to final form. Special thanks are also due to Ian Cornelius for help with final preparation and for rescuing me more than once from unfriendly aliens in my computer.

Finally, I wish to thank all my families for their love and toleration of a two-timing mother and partner.

ATTRACTA INGRAM

Dublin and Florence
September 1993

Contents

1

Introduction

1.1. RIGHTS: THE ISSUE OF SENSE

This book is about moral rights against the state. Its central
concern is with what may be called the sense of propositions of
moral rights. The question of sense precedes and governs the
answer to the question of what moral rights we have. A theory
of rights which addresses the prior question gives an account of
what in general it is to have a right. What I wish to do is work
out the general underlying principles of valid attributions of
rights. Why is this enterprise called for?

We believe or disbelieve, assert or deny propositions about
rights that humans (and perhaps other sentient beings) are said
to have in justice or morality. These propositions have been
made familiar in our political culture by a stream of declarations
which continues the great eighteenth-century articulations of
the so-called rights of man. Very often, the purpose of these
declarations has been to define the content of (new) domestic
political institutions. More recently, they have been used also to
express the basis for international institutions and alliances
initiated by Western democracies.

While the current code of international human rights law
differs from the great ancestral proclamations in point of detail
and definition the basic content of the documents, the proposition of human rights, remains the same.[1] Thus Article 1 of the
Universal Declaration of Human Rights made in 1948 proclaims:
'All human beings are born free and equal in dignity and rights.'
The specification of rights that follows, continues in form and
content a tradition inaugurated by the representatives of the

---

[1] A useful introduction to the international legal code of human rights,
together with relevant extracts from the main documents is provided in Paul
Sieghart, *The Lawful Rights of Mankind*.

people of Virginia who in their declaration of 12 June 1776 asserted that:

All men are by nature equally free and independent, and have certain inherent rights, of which when they enter into a state of society, they cannot by any compact deprive or divest their posterity; namely, the enjoyment of life and liberty, with the means of acquiring and possessing property, and pursuing and obtaining happiness and safety.[2]

The same sentiments are expressed in the declaration of 4 July 1776 made by the thirteen United States of America:

We hold these truths to be self-evident, that all men are created equal, that they are endowed by their Creator with certain inalienable Rights, that among these are life, liberty, and the pursuit of happiness.[3]

In 1789 the French National Assembly added its contribution to this new political rhetoric in the *Declaration of the Rights of Man and the Citizen*:

The end in view of every political association is the preservation of the natural and imprescriptible rights of man. These rights are liberty, property, security, and resistance to oppression.[4]

Some people think that propositions such as these are nonsensical. This view makes an issue of the *sense* of propositions of rights. The issue of sense raises the question of what propositions of rights should be taken to mean, and in what conditions, if any, they may be properly asserted. When a sceptic challenges our belief in rights we find ourselves having to find an answer to this deeper question. Sometimes we are led to the issue of sense because we are unable to settle some dispute about what rights we have in the absence of a theory of what makes attributions of rights valid. We may be led to the issue also by a philosophical interest in understanding how and why a collection of rights fits together. The job of the kind of theory I am after is to provide a general organizing idea or principle that makes sense of talk of rights and explains how and why certain attributions of rights can be declared valid and others cannot.

[2] See A. I. Melden (ed.), *Human Rights*, for the text of the Virginian Declaration of Rights.
[3] Ibid., for an extract from the American Declaration of Independence.
[4] Ibid., for the text.

Since propositions of rights are a pervasive and contested feature of our political practice, the question of what they should be taken to mean is a central problem for political theory. Whether we hold them to be self-evident truths, or nonsense, or fictions, or something else, we cannot avoid taking some view of their sense if we are to give an adequate account or critique of our political principles and institutions.

1.2. GENERAL AIMS

In trying to answer the question of what a proposition of rights should be taken to mean I have two aims. One is to formulate an account of individual liberty and rights which is appropriate to the practice of pluralist liberal democracy. Accordingly, the terrain of argument is confined to liberal political morality. The ambition is not to present a complete liberal theory of rights. It is rather to elicit a set of principles to form a bridge between the liberal value of individual liberty and the rights we associate with liberal democratic theory and institutions. This project is necessary because the orthodox conception of rights—the libertarian view that rights are a species of moral property in one's person, personal powers, and legitimately acquired external resources—belongs in a theory of justice that fails what is now a widely accepted criterion: justice is what everyone could in principle reach a rational agreement on.[5] This criterion figures as the topic or the background of one relatively self-contained set of debates that has been developing in political philosophy in recent times, namely, discussions of citizenship, community, and democracy. But, as I shall show, the criterion is incompatible with the assumption of rights as proprietary that underlies a second, longer running set of debates, namely, discussions of justice centred on issues of economic entitlement. Arguments about exploitation, redistribution, and talent-pooling have frequently been presented in these debates as turning on different interpretations of the right of self-ownership. But those who accept the liberal criterion of

---

[5] This is Brian Barry's formulation in *Theories of Justice*, i. 7. A great deal of interpretation has to go into making this criterion operable. See Barry, *Theories of Justice*, Chs. 7–9; and Chs. 6–7 of this book.

legitimacy cannot also take questions of economic entitlement as matters of the best interpretation of self-ownership. So I believe that the sense of rights, the kind of claim propositions of rights make, needs to be rethought by liberals to conform to their contractualist view of legitimacy. If rights are not derivable from a master right of self-ownership we need an alternative account of what the master-right is. This is not merely a good housekeeping exercise within liberal theory. It is also a matter of building a bridge between participants in each of the two debates I have mentioned, enabling them to focus their concerns more directly on the nature and justification of rights. This more broadly based discussion is badly needed for fruitful developments in a third set of debates that is getting under way in political philosophy, dialogues about how to honour group identities of various kinds in the framework of federal or multi-national constitutional arrangements.

My second aim is to broaden the appeal of rights. Talk of rights is anathema to many communitarians, both on the conservative right and on the left. I hope that I can persuade them that talk of rights is a valuable part of our moral and political tradition (no less than talk of the virtues); that we need a doctrine of rights because, as citizens of modern republics, we meet as strangers without a common good except whatever we can forge together for the advancement of our diverse ends; that right-holders are not the atomistic, radically unsocialized subjects bereft of communal allegiances that anti-liberals suppose; and, finally, that the form of liberal community that a post-libertarian doctrine of rights sustains is no less worthy of pursuit than the more full-blooded traditional communities of shared ends and intimate personal knowledge.[6]

Traditionally, socialists have been wary of rights, heeding Marx's analysis of rights as the demands of the bourgeoisie

---

[6] The enterprise of restoring the tradition of the virtues is engaged in most notably by Alasdair MacIntyre. See his *After Virtue*, and *Whose Justice? Which Rationality?* Michael Sandel, *Liberalism and the Limits of Justice*, 183, admits that the condition of encountering each other as strangers is not likely to fade altogether and, as long as it does not, justice (and by implication rights, for these are what principles of justice are now taken to distribute) will be necessary. On atomism, see Charles Taylor, 'Atomism'. On why women should continue to talk of rights rather than capitulate to the so-called 'women's morality' of care and communitarian commitment, see Attracta Ingram, 'The Perils of Love: Why Women Need Rights'.

dressed up in the language of rights for all. But the practice of socialism without a space for such 'liberal' rights as freedom of thought and conscience, of movement, of speech and of the press, has not led to domestic success in the states of Eastern Europe. Nor has it presented socialism as an attractive political option for a broad band of people nurtured somewhere inside the liberal tradition. Nowadays, there is increasing willingness among people on the left to have some truck with rights. Many no longer avoid the language.[7] The slide towards deeper implication is unabashed in Tom Campbell's timely study of socialist rights and in G. A. Cohen's observation that 'a defensible socialist constitution must contain a bill of individual rights which specifies things which the community cannot do to, or demand of, any individual.'[8]

But this increasing hospitality to talk of rights should not blind people on the left to the incoherence involved in combining socialist meanings with the libertarian sense that talk of rights currently presupposes. The received view of what it means for individuals to have rights is for each to own all of herself and no part of anyone else. So talk of rights is one with talk of property. As we shall see in the following three chapters this identification of rights and property favours a background system of exclusive property rules in the institutional setting of a minimal state dedicated to preserving proprietary freedom. This cannot be made consistent with socialist freedom and equality. Given the historical identification of rights and property it is no accident that socialist politics has found difficulty in accommodating rights.

Nevertheless, socialists, no less than people from liberal and other political traditions, can identify with that special concern for individuals that rights theories claim to address. They hope to find a coherent political morality which includes respect for individual rights in a broader framework of political values. The present essay makes, at least, a ground-clearing contribution to that project, by detaching rights from their libertarian sense and political implications.

[7] John Baker, *Arguing for Equality* reflects an easy use of the language of rights among egalitarians.
[8] See Tom Campbell, *The Left and Rights*; and G. A. Cohen, 'Self-Ownership, World Ownership, and Equality: Part II', 87.

Many of the important recent contributions to political theory consist in the development of theories of justice understood to be about the distribution of rights.[9] My concern is with the general character of the rights rather than their distribution. The reason for this difference of focus is straightforward. A complete theory of justice includes a doctrine of rights. But its special focus is on principles of distribution, their derivation, general implications, and application. It tells us when inequalities are justified, if at all. The doctrine of rights focuses on the items to be distributed—the liberties, powers, rights, and opportunities that give concrete form to the abstract principles of respect for persons and individual freedom on which rights-based justice is built. The argument of this book will show that the difference between theories of rights is not a matter of which of a range of familiar civil, political, and social rights find a place in each theory. It is rather a matter of different conceptions of the kind of moral power rights confer on their holders. The fact that rights may carry different conceptions of moral power has far-reaching implications for the character of justice, the state, and for the consistency of the set of rights that ensues when a list of civil and political rights evolved under certain assumptions is extended by the addition of a portfolio of social and economic rights evolved under quite different assumptions.[10]

It is not my aim to examine all the issues raised by a theory of rights. I argue against one conception of rights and for another. This book does not say much about what rights we have. It does, however, say how to go about finding rights out, and interpreting their meaning.

My argument remains at a fairly high level of abstraction from concrete debates about rights for two reasons. The first is that philosophical argument of the kind I engage in cannot yield a priori determinate answers to the sort of controversial questions that arise within particular communities at particular times. Philosophical argument can make the case for freedom of

[9] See Hillel Steiner, 'Capitalism, Justice and Equal Starts', 50; also the statement of the first principle of justice in John Rawls, *A Theory of Justice*, 60.

[10] See T. H. Marshall, *Citizenship and Social Class*, for the classic analysis of the relations between civil, political, and social rights. Maurice Cranston denies social or welfare rights in 'Human Rights: Real and Supposed'. Responses are D. D. Raphael, 'Human Rights: Old and New'; and M. P. Golding, 'Welfare Rights'.

expression, for example, on the basis of its relation to the conditions for realizing autonomy, or development and maintenance of a sense of justice. However, more specific issues of free expression, such as pornography, access to the airwaves by supporters of political violence, or blasphemy, cannot be settled by appeal to philosophical argument alone. Such questions are resolved in the context of particular circumstantial knowledge and in so far as the public philosopher engages in those debates, it is as a participant in a practical discussion arising out of a controversy with a particular circumstantial shape. Similarly, debates about economic entitlements are not settled by philosophical argument alone for that remains at the level of the general form of entitlements. Circumstantial variables such as the economic tradition in which the argument occurs and current levels of resources affect substantive questions about, for example, a right to a basic income, or interpretation of the right to work.

The second reason I avoid substantive discussions about rights is that important as these are, my argument should not be seen as gaining validity from its role in more practical deliberations about rights. The case I make for rights as political rather than proprietary depends on their validity being established through the operation of a particular procedure of interpretation and justification.

1.3. THE IMPORTANCE OF INDIVIDUALS

Political morality provides the principles that should regulate political action. When it includes a principle of individual rights it is fundamentally concerned with individuals, taken one at a time, rather than with society as a whole. This does not mean that a political morality which provides for rights must ignore questions of the welfare of society as a whole. It means that those questions cannot be answered in ways that conflict with certain very important elements of individual well-being.[11] These need not be the peculiar interests of a named individual, but ones which each shares with every other. They may be

[11] See Jeremy Waldron (ed.), *Theories of Rights*, 15.

identified in terms, say, of basic survival, sustenance, and welfare, or, more controversially, of freedom, choice, independence, and their prerequisites. For reasons offered below, I favour the latter terms as including the former and accounting for the distinctive contribution of rights to political morality.

But what is so special about persons? Why should any individual interests impose constraints on actions? Although these questions are not the subject of this book, a brief answer is necessary in order to explain its general direction. The idea that individual interests of one kind or another should generate constraints on action is an expression of the principle of respect for persons which prohibits treating one as a means to another's ends. Some version of that principle is common ground among most rights theorists and I shall not be examining arguments for it as an abstract principle although I shall be defending one conception of it as giving the sense of liberal rights.

Now the idea that the separateness of persons deserves special moral consideration, that personal inviolability should never be sacrificed for the sake of satisfying the goals of others, however numerous, is bound up with the idea of respect for individual liberty.[12] And the value thus placed on liberty favours a basis for rights in the active, choosing, meaning-conferring side of human nature rather than in the passive, vulnerable, needy, and dependent side. The emphasis on active human powers, in turn, favours a notion of positive freedom or autonomy, as the ground of claims to non-interference or negative liberty usually thought to be the paradigm claims of rights. At least, that is the stance taken by the theory offered here.

Those who object to this strong ground for rights may point out that human vulnerability to pain and suffering would provide a less contestable ground than autonomy. However, I do not think that a theory of justice and rights can be built up without reference to autonomy. An acceptable liberty-constraint scheme is one that satisfies the justice criterion mentioned in Section 1.2 above of being 'that which everyone could in principle reach a rational agreement on'. That criterion

---

[12] See Rawls, *A Theory of Justice*, 3–4 for the now famous propositions about personal inviolability and its requirements.

is unintelligible apart from a conception of persons as having the autonomy capacities to identify and implement in their lives the principles or rules of justice. A theory of rights that tried to do without autonomy would have to derive from some source other than the agreement of rational moral agents. While I do not doubt that there are interesting metaphysical and theological theories of the bases of rights, I do not think that they can provide a framework for pluralist liberal democracies. The context in which we make rights claims is a society marked by different metaphysical, theological, and moral views. For us to come to reasonable agreement on a scheme of rights acceptable to all, the idea of autonomy has to be presupposed. It is implicit in our recognition that pluralism is a fact of our social and political cultures and that it is no disaster, but a valuable outcome of deliberative autonomy. It is further presupposed by our effort to build social unity in the midst of differences by instituting a framework of justice and rights that is the product of agreement, a possibility that flows from the autonomy capacity to identify and live by self-chosen principles that have the character of social law.

There is a second reason why a theory of rights must be supposed to make the presumption of autonomy. Without that presumption I think that there is no call for theories of *rights*. Let me explain. Consider first a theory which has at its core the idea of the individual's own capacity for framing and implementing conceptions of the good and the just. The specific aim of such a theory is the protection or advancement of individual interests or goods of a special kind—roughly, those connected with liberty and self-determination. What is distinctive about rights, on this approach, is that they are explained in terms of a principle, or complex set of principles, of autonomy. That gives rights a content which fits them to play a leading role in the background morality of liberal democratic politics. The democratic principle of political equality can be specified by autonomy-based rights in a way that respects the heterogeneity of ends and ideals to be found among the citizens of modern pluralist democracies.

By contrast, consider a theory of rights which has at its centre a view of human good in which there are a number of equally fundamental aspects. An example is the list of goods identified by John Finnis: life, knowledge, play, aesthetic experience,

1.4. MISGIVINGS ABOUT RIGHTS

How a government treats its own citizens is no longer its exclusive business, but a matter of legitimate concern for other states also.[18] This is the result of the development of international law to include a code of rights of individuals against their own states. In effect, this has meant that respect for human rights has become an accepted criterion of political legitimacy, in domestic and international politics. Individual citizens can now take their own governments to the International Court of Human Rights. And mutual recognition by states frequently stands or falls on their human-rights records. So we hear a great deal of talk of human rights and there is wide acceptance of their use as standards of appraisal for political institutions.[19]

The new importance of rights in international law and politics has been reflected in renewed theoretical interest in the subject by moral and political as well as legal philosophers. But, as with the earlier doctrines, the new discussions have been accompanied by vigorous criticism of the whole idea of rights. One claim is that rights, at least in so far as they are devised to secure and advance autonomy interests, presuppose an impossible idea of individuals as bearers of selves wholly independent of their attachments and ends.[20] Another claim is that rights protect individuals in their egoistic or selfish existence making impossible the development of the civic virtues necessary for equal citizenship and active support of impersonal political ideals.[21] Still another is that the notion of a right presupposes a system of social rules and since these are historically and culturally specific, there can be no legitimate talk of universal human rights.[22]

Although these objections have been around for a long time their hardiness is surely evidence that important issues are at stake in disputes between advocates of rights and their opponents. Liberals are unsympathetic to the conservative

---

[18] See Sieghart, *The Lawful Rights of Mankind*, p. vii.

[19] See Waldron (ed.), *Nonsense upon Stilts*, 1.

[20] Sandel, *Liberalism and its Critics*, 5.

[21] See MacIntyre, *After Virtue*, 147 and *passim*. Cf. the preface to Karl Marx, 'On the Jewish Question', in Waldron (ed.), *Nonsense*, 137.

[22] MacIntyre, *After Virtue*, 65.

communitarianism and the socialist collectivism that inspires much criticism of rights.[23] Nevertheless, the development of a liberal doctrine of rights as a distinctive political position feeds on the encounter with those opposing doctrines. Pressed in no small measure by socialist success in sensitizing people to inequality, liberalism has faced the problem of reconciling the first two of its ideals, liberty and equality. The current challenge is to bring its third ideal, fraternity or solidarity, into balance with the first two. The communitarian challenge is a timely prod to liberals to develop their distinctive account of solidarity. Of course that is a monumental undertaking, and not my ambition here.[24] Nevertheless, a contribution to that project is the rethinking of rights to meet the common criticism that Marx voiced so bluntly, 'none of the so-called rights of man goes beyond egoistic man . . . an individual withdrawn behind his private interests and whims and separated from the community'.[25]

It should be said too that not all liberals believe in rights. The serious point behind Bentham's ridicule of the idea of a natural right as 'a son that never had a father'—the lack of an account of how the right is made—is a powerful inducement to identify rights with legal rights, especially in the face of bare assertions such as Robert Nozick's bold declaration: 'Individuals have rights, and there are things no person or group may do to them (without violating their rights).'[26] The ascendancy of rights talk in modern politics should not make us complacent about the illusory character of rights if Bentham's diagnosis is correct. To meet his charge, we need to give much more thought to Bentham's question of how rights are made.

1.5. NATURAL LAW AND NATURAL RIGHTS

This book denies Bentham's diagnosis and affirms the existence of moral rights against the state. But it avoids one obvious

[23] For a useful assessment of the different positions from which rights come under fire, see Waldron (ed.), *Nonsense*, ch. 6.

[24] See Attracta Ingram, 'The Empire Strikes Back: Liberal Solidarity in a *Europe des Patries*'.

[25] Karl Marx, 'On the Jewish Question', in Waldron (ed.), *Nonsense*, 147.

[26] Jeremy Bentham, *Anarchical Fallacies*, in Waldron (ed.), *Nonsense*, 73. Robert Nozick, *Anarchy, State, and Utopia*, p. ix.

account of how rights are made, the one associated with the natural law tradition. That account elucidates moral rights against the state in terms of an analogy with legal rights. Just as positive law confers legal rights on individuals, the ancient idea of natural law may be said to confer 'natural' moral rights on them.[27] Sometimes, natural law is viewed simply as a divine command.[28] A better understanding, as provided by the most influential theorists, incorporates the natural teleology of the Ancients. In this outlook, each kind of thing is conceived as a centre of activity which tends towards a certain optimum condition of existence (such as maturity in the case of growing things), which is the specific good or end for a thing of that kind. In the case of human beings the conception is of a nested hierarchy of ends—vegetative, sentient, and cognitive—corresponding to the characteristic human tendencies or inclinations. These fall into a system of principles of organization, development, and change which may be thought of as giving the natural law for humans: how they normally, and how they should, seek their specific goods.

This abstract statement is compatible with different interpretations of what counts as human good, or, at any rate, as the highest good. Hence, the abstract natural law injunction to do good and avoid evil is susceptible of different concrete determinations depending on the theory of human good adopted.[29] But once we are in possession of such a theory, the content of the 'law' is filled in and a schedule of duties (and corresponding rights) can be drawn up. What makes the result a system of natural law and natural rights is the fact that the rightness of fulfilling certain natural inclinations, talents, or desires is seen as a matter of attunement to the natural pursuits through which human excellence is achieved. Thus it can act as an independent standard for the evaluation of conventional arrangements and rules.

[27] For an interesting historical account, see Richard Tuck, *Natural Rights Theories*. An analytical account of a Thomistic version is given by Finnis, *Natural Law and Natural Rights*.

[28] The appeal to divine authority is discussed by Otto Gierke, *Natural Law and the Theory of Society 1500 to 1800*, 88–9.

[29] See Thomas Aquinas, *Summa Theologiae*, 1–2ae, q. 94, a. 2 for the statement of this fundamental injunction of natural law.

Teleological natural law theories of the kind I have sketched are not much in favour among moral philosophers. The reasons for that are not my concern here.[30] But I do want to suggest that natural law should not be seen as a rights-based theory. The common thread in all natural law theories is the idea that there is a natural moral order, independent of but discoverable by human reason. This character is distorted if we think that natural law and natural rights are part of the same idea.[31] The modern doctrine of rights is a set of claims to individual liberties, to spaces within which individuals may pursue their own projects.

Although it was prudent in the seventeenth and eighteenth centuries to insist that various liberties are entrenched in human nature, and fashionable to express this claim in the sophisticated and respected language of natural law, individual rights are better seen as having what might be called subjective rather than objective origins. What this means is only that they are understood to issue from some collective choice procedure such as a bargain or a cognitive agreement, instead of being found in the world along with apples and nuts.[32] This understanding is called for because rights are designed to secure values such as freedom and autonomy, the capacities for which must be developed and exercised through the pursuit of self-chosen purposes. Although in framing and pursuing these purposes individuals inevitably draw on inherited cultural traditions, the special place of individual choice in this scenario runs counter to the idea that individuals must simply attune themselves to a moral reality they discover rather than make. The world of

[30] Many would agree with Onora O'Neill's remark that the natural law tradition is a 'shipwreck'. See 'The Great Maxims of Justice and Charity', in MacCormick and Bankowski (eds.), *Enlightenment, Rights, and Revolution*, 309.

[31] For the view that the doctrine of natural rights is in no way a derivation from the doctrine of natural law, see K. R. Minogue, 'Natural rights, ideology, and the game of life'. The same view is taken by Leo Strauss who identifies liberalism with the idea that the basic moral fact is a right rather than a duty, a reversal of the natural law relationship which gives precedence to duties over rights. See Strauss, *The Political Philosophy of Thomas Hobbes: Its Basis and Genesis*; also 'On The Spirit of Hobbes's Political Philosophy', 13.

[32] For this usage of 'subjective' which I adopt here with some misgivings, see L. W. Sumner, *The Moral Foundations of Rights*, 130. Any determination to act only on a principle that all can act on would be subjective in Sumner's usage. However Kantians among us regard such principles as objective.

naturally given ends that belongs to natural law cannot be fitted
into the world of liberty, autonomy, and choice, that individual
rights presuppose.

Of course, it may be said that this point holds only when we
are thinking of very debatable ends such as Aristotle's intellectual contemplation or Aquinas's knowledge of God. But, the
argument continues, there are obvious and less lofty ends, such
as self-preservation which together with certain natural facts,
such as human vulnerability and scarcity of resources generate a
natural law of minimum content from which we may non-
controversially derive rights.[33] For the reason already given in
Section 1.3 above (the redundancy of rights), I do not think that
a minimal natural law theory will yield anything distinctive
enough to be called a theory of rights. Given survival as our aim
it will indeed yield an account of the protections and benefits we
need from a system of organized law. For the setting of natural
human facts provides circumstances of justice that give a
minimum natural law content to any legal system that is to be
voluntarily obeyed. But it does not make the case for treating
every last individual as an equal that the argument for rights
against utility takes to be the issue.[34] Nor can it accommodate
the idea that rights have a unique normative role that puts them
outside the domain of realist moral theories.

I take it then that if we are in the business of developing a
rights theory to fit the tradition of rights discourse which
accompanies the emergence of the modern concept of an
individual we need something more than those rules which
make survival possible. The discussion of rights is about
conditions for human flourishing far more demanding than
those for mere survival. The latter are, in any case, presupposed
in any account of the former, but our concern is with the terms
of co-operation among beings capable of thought and action and
disagreement on the worthwhile life, not with those needed to
end a war of all against all.

---

[33] The circumstances which lead to a minimum natural law are identified by
Hart as: human vulnerability; approximate equality; limited altruism; limited
resources; and limited understanding and strength of will. See Hart, *The Concept
of Law*, 189–95.

[34] A divine-law theory is better able to argue for individual inviolability than a
purely secular natural law.

The unavailability of natural law as a basis for constitutional rights in pluralist democracies leaves us with the alternative of some sort of constructivism.[35] By that I mean the thought of basic rights as products of agreements reached in a certain well-defined situation. Historically, the constructivist approach was developed by the social contract tradition of the state. Rights were usually seen as antecedent moral constraints on a constructed political order. Their own source was divine law or a restricted natural law of self-preservation. One important strand of argument in this book is that we must be constructivists about rights themselves. If we cannot appeal to natural law, neither can we be content with the assertion of rights as an axiom of political theory. If rights cannot be seen as given they must be made and the job of a constructivist political morality is to show them in the making.

1.6. THE PRINCIPLE OF SELF-OWNERSHIP

So my proposed derivation of rights against the state departs from the tradition of belief in natural 'given' rights. It departs even more radically in another respect. The notion that a theory of rights is to capture—that individuals have a distinctive moral position as self-governors of some sort—is standardly expressed as the principle of individual self-ownership. This holds that each human being is the morally rightful owner of her person and powers. The best known historical expression of the doctrine is John Locke's: 'every Man has a Property in his own Person.'[36] But Thomas Hobbes had held the doctrine before Locke: 'Of things held in propriety those that are dearest to a

---

[35] I am using the terms 'natural law' to cover realist moral theories and 'constructivism' to cover anti-realist theories (though some people may be unhappy about this usage). I take constructivism to be a method of generating principles (e.g. of justice) or institutions (e.g. the state) by reference to choices or consents made in an initial situation defined in a certain way. A 'constructivist' procedure can settle disputes without reference to an independent moral reality because it relies only on initial agreement on the characteristics of the agents of construction. Clearly, different assignments of characteristics define different initial situations or 'original positions'. See Rawls, 'Kantian Constructivism in Moral Theory'; Barry, *Theories of Justice*, chs. 7–9; David O. Brink, 'Rawlsian Constructivism in Moral Theory'; O'Neill, *Constructions of Reason*, ch. 11.

[36] John Locke, *Two Treatises of Government*, ii., sect. 27.

man are his own life, and limbs.'[37] And as Richard Tuck has observed, the identification of rights as a kind of normative property is much older: 'By the fourteenth century it was possible to argue that to have a right was to be the lord or *dominus* of one's relevant moral world, to possess *dominium*, that is to say, *property*.'[38] The thesis appears in James Madison's essay on property of 1792: 'A man has a property in his opinions and the free communication of them . . . in the free use of his faculties and the choice of the objects on which to employ them. . . . he may be . . . said to have a property in his rights.'[39]

And in a striking repetition H. L. A. Hart acknowledges its twentieth-century presence: 'Rights are typically conceived of as possessed or owned by or belonging to individuals.'[40] As the foundational claim of libertarianism it dominates the work of Robert Nozick and of Hillel Steiner.[41] More recently, the view has been supported by Judith Jarvis Thomson who claims that the cluster of rights that people have in respect of their bodies is sufficiently similar to the clusters of rights they have in respect of things like their houses, typewriters, and shoes to justify saying that people own their bodies.[42]

Despite the vintage and contemporary standing of the principle of self-ownership, it is, I believe, a serious error to identify right-holding with ownership. Right-holding revolves round the importance of certain moral capacities to frame and execute one's own plan of life. It is related to being in command of one's own life and so with the idea of being a master or *dominus* which, historically, goes with being the overlord of property. But the identification of dominion and ownership is contingent. Alongside that sense has always run another, according to which having dominion is having a power to rule. Ruling does not entail (although it may sometimes involve)

---

[37] Thomas Hobbes, *Leviathan*, ch. 30, pp. 382–3.

[38] Tuck, *Natural Rights Theories*, 3.

[39] Philip B. Kurland and Ralph Lerner (eds.), *The Founders' Constitution*, i. 598. The identification of rights with property (and with being one's own master) is common enough to appear without critical comment in Kant's *The Metaphysical Elements of Justice*, 43 f.

[40] Hart, 'Are there any Natural Rights?', 83.

[41] See Nozick, *Anarchy, State, and Utopia*, in the light of the interpretation advanced by Cohen, 'Nozick on Appropriation'. See also Steiner, *An Essay on Rights*.

[42] Judith Jarvis Thomson, *The Realm of Rights*, 225–6.

owning.[43] That is the sense I want to develop in this book. It fits intuitively with the idea of autonomy, which is now the favoured way of talking about self-command. But more importantly, it shapes a doctrine of rights to meet the constructivist criterion of justice and rights we must espouse in late twentieth-century liberalism. These cannot be self-ownership rights, or so I shall argue.

The argument of the book may be seen, therefore, as a critique of self-ownership and an attempt to argue for a notion of self-government. Self-ownership is understood as the doctrine that each human being is the morally rightful owner of her person and powers. She may do as she pleases as long as she does not harm others. So what it means to have a right is to have a certain proprietary control over the domain specified as the object of the right. Whether we are talking of our kidneys or our powers of speech, the common thread is the presence of some cluster of proprietary claims, liberties, powers, and immunities.[44] A claim of right is validly made if it can be shown to be contained in, or derivable from, the core system of proprietary projections and benefits associated with self-ownership. The elucidation and critique of this appealing doctrine will occupy Chapters 2–4 and recur as a foil to developments in later chapters.

Self-ownership endorses negative individual liberty, that is, the freedom to do as one pleases as long as one does not harm others. If negative liberty is independently desirable, then unfettered ownership rights may be a good enough conception of the liberty–constraint system we want to describe. But the considerations of Chapters 3 and 4 constantly tempt us to reach out towards a way of talking about being in control of our own lives that is more than the mere formal self-command which a consistent regard for negative liberty permits. The way of talking we find ourselves adopting substitutes self-government for self-ownership and autonomy or positive freedom for negative liberty. Can such talk be made credible? Chapter 5 endeavours to elucidate a conception of autonomy that has

[43] The distinction is brought out by Brian Tierney, 'Tuck on Rights: Some Medieval Problems', 439.

[44] The analysis of rights into the constituents of *claims*, *liberties* or *privileges*, *powers*, and *immunities*, is made in Wesley N. Hohfeld, *Fundamental Legal Conceptions*. For a useful account see Waldron (ed.), *Theories of Rights*, 6–7.

sufficient moral force to be the basis of rights. A central feature of this conception is that autonomy is a matter of shaping one's life in accordance with principles that are self-imposable by all. This has implications for the next stage of argument which is to take us from autonomy to principles of rights.

As I have already indicated, the procedure we need is a constructivist one. Familiar models of constructivist theories of justice represent the procedure as a process of bargaining which ends in contractual agreement.[45] And if autonomy is a matter of identifying and pursuing an ordered set of preferences, the bargaining version of contractualism may be adequate. But, if autonomy is regarded as ordering one's life under the direction of moral principles, the relevant procedure is better seen as a social discourse in which the principles are selected on the basis of reasons that all accept. Chapter 6 examines the idea of social discourse and Chapter 7 devises a scheme of autonomy-regarding constraints on discourse. These define a particular 'original position', a situation in which what is right is to be determined by the force of the better argument, not by the will of the powerful or the uncritical play of prejudice.[46] The doctrine of self-ownership is run through the tests that the constraints provide and is, finally, rejected.

In Chapter 8 the constraints are further developed and specified as a set of principles of self-government. These are devised for the basic social structure of a liberal democracy in which conditions of moral pluralism and civic equality must be met. Thus autonomy, as well as being intrinsically valuable, is justified by its consequences in shaping the principles of political union for diverse and equal citizens. The pragmatic political character of the principles of self-government carries over to the rights, powers, freedoms, and opportunities which further specify them. So in Chapter 9 this political dimension is carried through in an interpretation of rights which I call rights as political after Rawls's similar description of justice as

---

[45] The best known philosophical treatment of justice in game-theoretical terms is by David Gauthier, *Morals by Agreement*. For a very useful discussion of this approach see Barry, *Theories of Justice*.

[46] Rawls introduced the phrase 'original position' in *A Theory of Justice*. See his ch. 3 for his construction of an original position. On constructing original positions with different assumptions see Barry, *Theories of Justice*, ch. 9.

fairness.[47] The answer to the question of sense which starts this project is that rights are political not proprietary claims. It is then time to return to the various challenges to rights noted in this chapter: Is autonomy unintelligible? Are rights connected with separation from the community? Is talk of rights nonsense? Are all rights legal rights? While giving a negative answer to those questions, I will try to show how the good sense in the points made in support of the positions they summarize is accommodated in the theory of rights as political.

[47] Rawls, 'Justice as Fairness: Political not Metaphysical'.

PART I

Self-Ownership: The Proprietary Conception of Rights

2

What is Self-Ownership?

2.1. INTRODUCTION

The most influential view of the sense of propositions of moral
rights holds that they are used to make a species of private
property claim. This view vests everyone with the right to
private property in herself and also in extrapersonal resources.
The latter right will be considered in the next chapter. Here I
focus on the former right of self-ownership. This is the idea that
each individual is the morally rightful owner of her person,
powers, and talents. It is usually taken in a libertarian sense to
mean that an individual is entitled to dispose of herself as she
sees fit, as long as she does not cut across the similar rights of
others.[1] If this is how self-ownership must be understood, we
can hold the thesis that rights are properties only by being
libertarians. If we find libertarianism unpalatable, we have two
options. We can dissociate ourselves from belief in moral rights.
Or, we can develop an alternative to the proprietary account of
their sense. The latter option is my enterprise in this book. But
how plausible is my diagnosis?

Several writers have argued that there is a flexibility in the
meaning of property which allows for a sense of proprietary
rights, or self-ownership, that is non-libertarian.[2] If this view
holds we need not abandon the proprietary rights thesis and an
enterprise like mine is misconceived. So the main task of this
chapter is to refute belief in non-libertarian self-ownership. The
task divides into three. First, it will be useful to explain the

[1] See e.g. Robert Nozick, *Anarchy, State, and Utopia*, 28–35 and *passim*; Hillel
Steiner, 'Capitalism, Justice and Equal Starts', 62–3; G. A. Cohen, 'Nozick on
Appropriation', 89.
[2] C. B. Macpherson, 'Human Rights as Property Rights'; Andrew Kernohan,
'Rawls and the Collective Ownership of Natural Abilities'; John Christman,
'Self-Ownership, Equality, and the Structure of Property Rights'.

notions of ownership in general and private property in particular in order to identify the concept of self-ownership. Second, the libertarian conception of private property has to be outlined and related to self-ownership. Third, the case for favouring libertarian over other possible conceptions of self-ownership has to be shown. Since it is not the ultimate point of all this to affirm self-ownership but rather to make conceptual space for an alternative to proprietary rights, I end the chapter with some preliminary doubts about self-ownership. I will start, however, by giving a brief account of the appeal of self-ownership in order to bring into focus the concerns that motivate the doctrine. This also provides an occasion to explain my strategy in this and the next couple of chapters.

It is not hard to see why people might be reluctant to abandon self-ownership. It is an appealing way of expressing a point about the distribution of power. To say that each individual is a self-owner is to say that the power to control her and her activities is distributed to that individual and not to anyone else. This is a doctrine of limited power. It denies a government or an employer, a parent or a guardian, a right to dispose of you or me or direct our actions in forced labour and the like. Thus, the great intuitive appeal of self-ownership lies in the fact that it responds to fears of unrestrained power, enslavement, and latterly, of spare-part cannibalization of bodies, as well as to ideas about being in control of our own lives, determining and pursuing our own ideas of the good life.

This book offers an alternative response to these basic fears and aspirations. But to see why that is called for we must first examine the reigning doctrine of self-ownership. What does it mean to have what Locke calls a 'property' in one's own person? Why has self-ownership been thought of in the libertarian way? Is it possible to affirm a more limited self-ownership than libertarianism offers? Is self-ownership necessary to identify such injustices as absolute power and slavery? These questions motivate the separate tasks of the present chapter. The case against self-ownership is built up in the following two chapters where I try to undermine its initial appeal by showing that it cannot be reconciled with a host of intuitive beliefs about rights. The strategy is to prepare the ground for an alternative theory of what people need in order to be in control of their own lives, one which is superior to self-ownership in preserving the bulk of our beliefs about rights as well as having independent justification. So the undermining of self-ownership is a lengthy business. Although there may be other approaches to the thesis, there is no more direct assault possible, because it is not incoherent. One cannot get a quick demolition on the ground that ownership is an *irreflexive* relation (so *A* cannot own *A*), or that a 'self' is of the wrong moral type to be subsumed under 'ownership'.[3] The points at issue are precisely the irreflexivity of ownership and the categorization of persons as property.

2.2. WHAT IS PROPERTY?

The doctrine we are considering holds that the meaning of rights is controlled by the meaning of property. Although the latter shifts historically and is shaped by specific local understandings, the concept may be defined in an abstract way to give us some initial purchase on it. The account that I want to use as the basis for my approach to self-ownership is usefully articulated by Jeremy Waldron: 'The concept of property is the concept of a system of rules governing access to and control of material resources.'[4] It is worth observing that Waldron is here using the term property to refer not to things, as in our common-sense use, but to rules that confer rights, a stricter legal use.[5] Property is not a relation between one person and a thing but between persons about things. Second, Waldron's description of property as a system of rules about access to and control of material resources can be taken to cover income, pensions, shares, options, and the like, as well as material objects like land and buildings.[6]

Since rights are individualistic considerations in the sense of being called up to secure interests that persons have as separate individuals, we also need, in addition to the general notion of property, some initial understanding of private property in

---

[3] J. P. Day, 'Locke on Property', 212. See also Richard Norman, *Free and Equal*, 141.   [4] Jeremy Waldron, *The Right to Private Property*, 31.

[5] Cf. Macpherson, 'The Meaning of Property', 3 ff.

[6] Waldron, *Private Property*, 37. See also Macpherson, 'Meaning of Property', 8.

order to grasp the idea of self-ownership. Waldron's way of distinguishing private property from other forms is useful here too: 'In a system of private property, the rules governing access to and control of material resources are organized around the idea that resources are on the whole separate objects each assigned and therefore belonging to some particular individual.'[7] Waldron takes this to amount to the idea that in a system of private property each object is correlated with some named individual who has the final say over its disposal.[8] Following this approach I shall say that the owner of an object is the person who does not require the consent of others to use it and whose consent others must seek if they want to have access to or control of it. Thus, the approach remains faithful to Locke's definition of property 'the nature whereof is, that *without a Man's own consent it cannot be taken from him'*.[9] This captures the core meaning of property, whatever the detailed rules of a particular system turn out to be. In this sense a person has property only if she can legitimately exclude others from depriving her of some right recognized in the local system of ownership. This might be some right to the exclusive enjoyment of something, but it might also be a right not to be excluded from access to common property. Thus one person's having a property in something entails her being in a position of rightful power over others with respect to the object of that property right. This means that the state or society will uphold her special access to or control of the object as assigned by the property right against any challenge by another.

It is important to heed Locke's formal link between property and consent for two rather different reasons. The first is one that James Tully draws to our attention. It is that Locke's definition marks the distinctive turn in the history of rights from the view of them as deriving from duties to abstain from interference on foot of prescriptions of natural or divine law to the modern concept which has them flowing from our own moral sovereignty.[10] Property in selves protects from interference by others, but it does so 'by focusing on the agent's moral power to exercise his consent, his natural right or property, rather than

[7] Waldron, *Private Property*, 38.   [8] Ibid. 39.
[9] John Locke, *Two Treatises of Government*, ii., sect. 193, p. 442 (italics in original).   [10] James Tully, *A Discourse on Property*, 114.

granting primacy to others to perform their negative duties'.[11]
The second reason for keeping Locke's definition in mind is that
its entailment of power to individuals over others helps account
for the tendency to equate all forms of power with ownership,
one disastrous example of which was the political theory of
absolute power which assigned to rulers the ownership of their
subjects as well as of all other resources under their rule.

These definitions enable us to see, in the abstract, the various
components of the concept of self-ownership. First, there is the
background assumption that property rules cover people as well
as other types of item. We need to notice this because not all
systems regard people as possible subjects of ownership.
Second, there is the thought that each natural bundle of human
resources is assigned as private property to the particular
individual named. Call this the concept of self-ownership. It is
the thought of a system of private property rules assigning to
each person the final say over the disposition of the personal
resources in her possession as a natural individual.

2.3. FULL LIBERAL OWNERSHIP

How is the abstract concept of self-ownership related to the
interpretive claim that each self-owner has full private property
in herself and, consequently, may dispose of herself as she
pleases as long as she does not harm others? Employing the
familiar concept-conception distinction, I shall say that the
concept of private property allows of several conceptions of
which the system of unfettered capitalist private property rights
is one.[12] When self-ownership is interpreted according to this
conception it confers freedom to do as one wishes with one's
person and personal powers.

It follows that the usual conception of self-ownership is but
one of a number of possible interpretations of what is involved
in having a property in oneself. To get a better grip on how

---

[11] Ibid. 115.

[12] The distinction between concept and conception is employed by John
Rawls, *A Theory of Justice*, 5–11. See also Ronald Dworkin, *Taking Rights Seriously*,
103, 134–6, and 226. The distinction comes from H. L. A. Hart's *Concept of Law*,
155–9.

these different interpretations might be constructed we need to open up the notion of a private property right. It is not a simple right at all but a complex package of claim-rights, powers, liberties, and immunities. The elements that can go into this package to yield a distinct system of private property have been identified by A. M. Honoré as a set of standard incidents of what he describes as full liberal ownership.

Honoré writes that to be an owner is to have: (1) a right to possess a thing; (2) a right to use it; (3) a right to manage it; (4) a right to the income that can be derived from letting others use it; (5) a right to the capital value of it; (6) a right to immunity against expropriation of it; (7) a power to transfer it to another by sale, or gift, or bequest; (8) absence of term (temporal limitations) on the possession of any of these rights, liberties, etc.; (9) a duty to refrain from using it in a way that harms others; (10) a liability that it may be taken in execution of a judgment for debt; (11) a right to the residue, that is, to the return of all rights in a thing held by others when their term is up or they are forfeit for any reason.[13] These features are compiled from consideration of a variety of systems of ownership. They are neither jointly nor individually necessary for a system of rules to count as a regime of ownership. Thus, the fact that a particular system does not recognize a right of bequest, or limits the use or management of certain things, need not stop us from describing it as a private property system.

The importance of this open character of the concept of private property is that it allows for different conceptions according to the weight given to particular incidents by different actual or postulated systems of rules. Where all the incidents are present we have what is described as full liberal ownership or unfettered capitalist private property rights. But different systems vary the set of incidents and may also fetter them in various ways. For example, a system which denies a right of bequest or restricts the right of sale in the case of objects of cultural or national importance is just as much a system of ownership as unrestrained capitalism. So too is one which fetters the operation of private property for the sake of the public interest. In the terms of the concept-conception contrast

---

[13] A. M. Honoré, 'Ownership', 112–28.

each such system is a concrete conception of the abstract concept of private property.

Clearly, full liberal ownership is what is in question in the usual interpretation of self-ownership. It assigns to each named individual the unfettered control of *all* the elements of the parcel of personal powers correlated with that name. So the rights are full, and their scope is the full complement of resources individualized in each natural human being.

But if private property need not embody all the incidents of full liberal ownership then neither need self-ownership. For example, we can postulate a conception which excludes the right of bequest over one's body or over acquisitions derived from legitimate exercises of proprietary power. Or, a conception which excludes the right to the whole benefit of the use of labour or talents. That would relieve some of the unappealing inegalitarian consequences of full liberal self-ownership. Or, we can frame a conception that permits multiple ownership of individuals, as in Locke's version, where each person's body and natural powers are owned by God, but each may use her powers as she wishes, provided she does not destroy God's property in herself or anyone else.[14] Locke does not scruple to describe the rights we have in ourselves as having a property in our persons even though we cannot rightfully alienate ourselves by taking our own lives or committing ourselves to slavery. The fact that my body is ultimately God's property gives no other *human* being apart from me any rights over it.[15] In somewhat similar vein, it might be argued that society has certain ownership rights in individuals, that, for example, individual talents are assets of society as a whole and cannot, therefore, be directed to the exclusive benefit of the one who possesses them. Note that such an argument would not deny private property in selves. It would mean that a variety of private property rights could be held by different people in the different elements of a single self.

Compare the case where a landlord is the owner of accommodation which is let to a tenant who enjoys many of the incidents listed by Honoré. Something like this is involved in

---

[14] See Locke, *Two Treatises*, ii., sect. 6, p. 311; sect. 23, p. 325; sect. 135, p. 403.
[15] See Waldron, *Private Property*, 177–8.

Locke's idea that God as Creator is the primary proprietor of human beings, but that we have trustee or tenancy rights in ourselves which are inviolable against each other.[16] And the same sort of analogy might be invoked to allege social ownership of talents under conditions which allow society as a whole to benefit from their development and exercise. Of course, less radical versions of self-ownership can be constructed by varying the package of incidents. One example, a self-ownership which does not include the right to bequeath the product of one's own activities, has been mentioned above. Another possibility is a self-ownership that includes the incidents of full liberal ownership except for the right to exploit one's talents by selling their use to the highest bidder. That is replaced by the legitimate expectation of the reward for the exercise of talents assigned by a just social structure.[17]

The property ideas we have been considering allow us to see self-ownership as a concept which brings persons into the domain of private property rules and which is susceptible of interpretation by different conceptions, in theory at least. Why then, is self-ownership standardly given the libertarian interpretation of capitalist private property? This is the question for the next section.

2.4. THE MEANING OF SELF-OWNERSHIP

The problem of how power is distributed arises in any society which has any significant political organization. It is a historical problem the character of which depends on particular political and social circumstances. The principle of distribution used in one set of circumstances may not be appropriate in another. For example, if all power were vested in a hereditary monarch or a religious leader there could be no warranty that it would remain in his hands. He might split it with members of his family, or his friends, or even hand it over to a foreign ruler.

---

[16] I am indebted to Alan Ryan's interpretation. See his *Property and Political Theory*, 29.

[17] For suggestions along these lines see Waldron, *Private Property*, 404–5; and Andrew Kernohan, 'Rawls and the Collective Ownership of Natural Abilities', 26–7.

Or, a principle that distributed power equally might later be upset by the emergence of dictatorship through democratic processes. The costs in civil war of maintaining the operation of the initial principle might be too high to consider. So a political society might have to live for some time with a distribution of power which departed from that sanctioned by its initial principle. This would very likely entail living under despotism. Some would find themselves victims of the arbitrary power of others, having to live as chattel slaves, supplying forced labour under threat of death.

But another solution to the problem suggests itself. This is to vest power equally in individuals but in such a way that it cannot be taken without their consent and they cannot freely transfer all of it to another. This would prevent any rightful development of unfettered central power through prescription or alienation. Suppose we think that self-ownership is the relevant principle of power distribution. Then individual citizens would be free to control their own lives, transferring to a defensive state only as much power as was necessary for them to retain control over their persons and powers. This would avoid the risks to personal security and social peace inherent in life under unrestrained central power or majoritarian democracy. Now this solution to the power problem is quite specific about the character and extent of the power distributed. It is proprietary power and it is only fettered by other such powers. Why should the distribution be one of unfettered proprietary powers? The answer is, I suggest, historical and relative, not perennial and absolute. The meaning of self-ownership has been shaped by its historical role as a response to the doctrines and practices of political absolutism in seventeenth-century Europe.

To see how the response is fed by the character of the particular power problem it addresses it will be useful to outline the main features of the doctrine of absolute power. Its most famous defender was Sir Robert Filmer, whose book *Patriarcha* is the target of the first of Locke's *Two Treatises of Government*. Filmer argued that God had granted to fathers a power over their offspring which was paternal, political, and proprietary. Children are subject to the control of their fathers and they are also owned by them as subjects who may be sold or killed. This unencumbered dominion was first vested in Adam and descended by succession to his heirs who, as monarchs, have unfettered ownership of their subjects and all other things in their domain.[18]

Filmer's aim was to defend the absolute and arbitrary authority of seventeenth-century monarchs. Leaving that aside, the interesting aspect of the enterprise is the identification of dominion with ownership and this with unfettered rights of disposal. Those identifications persist in libertarian self-ownership in the assignment of absolute and arbitrary powers of self-disposal to everyone. Each self-owner is, in effect, an absolute sovereign with respect to the dominion of her own person and faces everyone else on the terms set by their equal sovereignty. Thus each possesses over herself full rights to do as she pleases, as long as she does not harm others similarly situated. This means that she is not obliged to place herself at the disposal of others to the least extent. No one else is entitled to command the use of her talents for their own benefit, however pressing their needs. When libertarian self-ownership is seen in this way as reproducing a doctrine of absolute power, Robert Nozick's claim that taxation for welfare is the moral equivalent of forced labour is fully understandable.[19] So too is the doctrine of the minimal state, that is, of a state with no more power than is necessary to secure people's natural self-ownership and legitimately acquired property in external goods. A more extensive state is not compatible with each person's primordial self-ownership.

2.5. MUST SELF-OWNERSHIP BE LIBERTARIAN?

One reason for thinking of people as libertarian self-owners is that nothing less than this may seem adequate to the identification of the injustices of slavery, serfdom, exploitation, and political absolutism. In the context of self-ownership these are seen as, or as consequences of, rights-violations.[20] The slave-

---

[18] Robert Filmer, *Patriarcha*, 11–12, 16, 38–9.

[19] See Nozick, *Anarchy, State, and Utopia*, 169–70.

[20] Steiner explains the liberal theory of exploitation as a consequence of the use of exclusionary force against a third party named *Blue* (a violation of rights)

owner or exploiter illegitimately claims rights of disposal over a person's services that belong morally to that person herself. Of course, the latter claim presupposes that each individual is born free of full or partial chattel-slave status. That is the reason why the libertarian conception of full self-ownership is favoured over other possible ones. Were a person to be born into slavery or a situation in which others owned part of her, by having a claim on her service, for instance, self-ownership could be neither universal enough nor complete enough to check practices of absolute power or forced labour. So the idea of self-ownership would be ineffectual for political purposes.

But a number of suggestions of a more restricted conception of ownership would deny the hegemony this argument allows to libertarian self-ownership. The first issues from the form of split ownership in persons allowed by Locke. In the *Two Treatises* Locke treats as self-evident the proposition that makers have (ownership) rights in and over their creations. As God's workmanship humans are his property, sent into the world on his business, made to endure as long as he should choose.[21] This is why suicide is a sin. It is an assault on the property of God. It is also why others cannot claim ownership rights in our lives and liberties. As God's property, we can neither alienate ourselves nor be rightfully taken by others as their own property. But while our enjoyment of our lives may be at God's will, we do nevertheless have full rights to be in possession of our bodies and to their exclusive use and benefit. For these are necessary so that we may flourish as God intended.[22] So the split of ownership rights between God and creature does not provide any case for a split of self-ownership rights between you and me. Nevertheless, Locke's example of split rights shows that self-ownership can block the master–slave relationship

to stop her from entering a market for some good of *White's* which then goes to *Red* for a lower price than it would have fetched had *Blue* been bidding. The difference between what *White* gets from *Red* and what she would have got from *Blue* is 'surplus value' and goes to *Red*, who exploits *White*. See Steiner, 'A Liberal Theory of Exploitation', and also 'Exploitation: A Liberal Theory Amended, Defended, and Extended'.

[21] 'They are his [God's] property whose Workmanship they are', Locke, *Two Treatises*, ii., sect. 6, p. 311. For an illuminating discussion of God as maker in Locke's political philosophy see Tully, *A Discourse on Property*, ch. 2.

[22] Locke, *Two Treatises*, i., sect. 41, p. 205.

without being libertarian, provided we regard ourselves as dependent on a rational God who is the source of our natural obligations. If that assumption cannot be made because the desired scheme of rights is one for a secular liberal democracy, then Locke's model of split ownership is no challenge to the libertarian. Indeed the fullness of libertarian self-ownership may be seen as an attempt to work out the consequences of doing without the theological assumption.[23]

Another possibility for a more limited self-ownership is suggested by the idea, noted earlier, that different systems of private property rules might exclude some of the incidents of ownership on Honoré's list.[24] Suppose a system where the rules of property in persons permit most of Honoré's incidents, but exclude the right to exploit the use of natural talents in a free market (an entailment of the fourth incident—the right to the income from letting others use a thing).[25] We could envisage a ceiling on what could be demanded for the exercise of talents on analogy with rent-control for housing. In this latter case, rent legislation restricts the income rights of landlords, but leaves them with a substantial battery of ownership rights. Analogously, it might be thought that self-ownership would be little affected by limiting income rights in the use of talents. The self-owner would be left with a great many ownership rights and would be no less of an owner than the landlord operating under rent-control legislation. Libertarians are unlikely to be persuaded by this proposal to abandon full liberal self-ownership. Under the proposed restriction individuals are prevented from charging what the market will bear for the exercise of their talents. Instead they receive the reward assigned by a social structure designed according to a competing conception of justice such as the one John Rawls provides.[26] Libertarians argue that in so far as this theory and others like it fetter the exploitation of talents

---

[23] Doing without the theological assumption is equivalent to treating persons as independent of found or unchosen obligations. The implication of this was seen but not endorsed by Locke: 'If man were independent he could have no law but his own will no end but himself.' MS *The Lovelace Collection*, c.28, fo. 141, quoted in Tully, *A Discourse on Property*, 36.

[24] See Sect. 2.3 above and n. 17.

[25] This is Kernohan's suggestion. See 'Rawls and the Collective Ownership of Natural Abilities', 26.

[26] See Rawls, *A Theory of Justice*, esp. pt I.

in a free market, they suffer from a crucial defect. They breach individual inviolability. This is the consequence of regarding the totality of natural talents as a collective pool on which everyone has some sort of claim.[27] That view is the acknowledged basis for setting up a social structure in which differential claims to reward for the exercise of talent are permitted only if they also benefit the worst-off members of society. In very simple terms, this means that I can benefit from the employment of my natural abilities (above a certain threshold deemed necessary for survival, and marked, say, by the point at which my earnings attract tax), only if certain others do also. In effect, this gives others a claim on, or property in, some of the benefits of my talents. But however small the extent of claims on my services arising from the exercise of my talents, other than claims I have freely contracted, the result is that I am to that extent in the power of others. Although they cannot conscript my labour, they can stop me charging what the market will bear for my services (by placing a proportional tax on earnings or by some more direct interference with market mechanisms) and in that way give me no alternative but to labour for them if I labour for myself. Whilst this is not as direct an assault on individual inviolability as slavery or forced labour, it is no less a violation of freedom than that which occurs when the hungry proletarian finds herself with the bare freedom to refuse the terms of employment set by the capitalist who is about to exploit her.

Now the situation of involuntary submission to the power or authority of another is precisely what the doctrine of self-ownership is designed to withstand. Its social role is to break any challenge to individual liberty unless that liberty is used to harm the equal liberty of another. For this reason, the possibility of a variety of conceptions of self-ownership is of little interest. Nothing less than full liberal self-ownership is adequate to the social role set for the doctrine.

---

[27] See Nozick, *Anarchy, State, and Utopia*, 228. The dispute is with Rawls whose famous Difference Principle requires any inequalities which result from natural abilities or social privilege to be maintained only to the extent that they contribute to the life prospects of the worst-off group. Rawls holds that the Difference Principle treats the distribution of natural talents as a common asset, *A Theory of Justice*, 101–2.

2.6. SELF-OWNERSHIP: SOURCES OF SCEPTICISM

The conclusion of the previous section should be understood
hypothetically: if self-ownership is necessary at all in order to
rebut slavery, serfdom, and exploitation, then the relevant
conception is the libertarian one. But how useful is self-
ownership in this role? How relevant to us now are issues of
slavery and absolute power? And is proprietary power the only
available power for us to plug into if we are to give content to
the notion of self-command or individual moral sovereignty that
our language of rights is aimed to capture?

In considering the first question we should not overlook the
fact that self-ownership embraces the most important claim of
slavery: that people can be the objects of private property rules.
This is the claim which must be rebutted if slavery is to be
overcome. In fact, the doctrine of self-ownership offers no
challenge to slavery as such. Its target is involuntary slavery.
The point is acknowledged by Nozick who believes that self-
owners are free to sell themselves into slavery.[28] But this throws
into question the major ideological justification for self-
ownership—that it identifies the injustice of slavery and the
like. If slavery by consent is all right, then what is wrong with
slavery is not what it is, but only the use of force to bring it
about. But this means that the case for self-ownership is grossly
oversold if it is represented as identifying the injustice of
slavery, when, in fact, involuntary slavery is all that is in
question. In similar vein, it might be argued that self-owners are
free to consent to the institution of absolute power, the political
counterpart of the master–slave relationship. But it seems
inadequate to represent the wrong of absolute power as merely
the absence of any consent by those subject to it.

The reason the libertarian response to slavery and political
absolutism seems too weak here is that it treats them, in the
absence of consent, as offences against the right to be free when
the more fundamental evil is that the master–slave relationship
they illustrate makes one person the living 'tool' of another, a
mere instrument of the master's ends. Of course slavery and
political absolutism violate the right to be free (on the minimal

---

[28] Nozick, *Anarchy, State, and Utopia*, 331.

libertarian interpretation, in the absence of consent). But what makes that wrong? Surely, the fact that a person needs liberty in order to pursue the ends or interests which she inevitably has as a human being no less than the next person. The underlying value here is not liberty but, to be as uncontentious as possible, equal human worth. For those of us who think in this way, self-ownership offers a very incomplete understanding of what is wrong with slavery and the like.

While the resurgence of institutions of absolute political power and slavery can never be ruled out, they are not a clear and present danger to citizens of modern constitutional liberal democracies. So even the weak case that may be made for self-ownership as a barrier to despotism and slavery is no longer compelling. The best way to defend self-ownership now is to canvas it as the attractive thesis it is in its own right. This is not a Herculean labour for the thesis is already well entrenched in our moral thinking. Who does not favour the idea of being able to do as she pleases without interference by others? Who does not *already* think that each individual has a special moral claim on the fruits of the exercise of the talents and capacities that reside in her? The successful entrenchment of self-ownership in our ideas and institutions is part of the circumstances in which the question of the distribution of power now arises.

But while it is not difficult to feel the pull of self-ownership we also find it has a less attractive aspect. In our society the power question starts from the inequality that inevitably comes about when people enjoy self-ownership. Once people enjoy a system of unfettered private property rights in their persons and powers, they can, through a combination of effort and good fortune in their natural endowments come to own unequal shares of worldly resources. Over time, the operation of the private property system issues in ever larger inequality of holdings of external resources and results in great inequality of condition.[29] People find themselves unequal with respect to their abilities to satisfy their needs and to live the lives they wish for themselves. Those with few or no holdings of their own are entirely dependent on others for their sustenance. Unless they wish to starve or live on charity, they must sell their labour for

[29] I am indebted to the analysis of G. A. Cohen, 'Self-Ownership, World Ownership, and Equality: Part II', 77–8.

whatever it will fetch. Evidently, there is very great potential in this situation for economic exploitation and invasions of moral independence. So the distribution of power cannot be regarded as finally settled by the principle of self-ownership. In addition, self-ownership being itself an egalitarian doctrine with respect to rights to personal resources appeals to an egalitarian instinct that does not naturally shut off in the face of inequality in worldly resources. So despite the fact that right-wing libertarians take pains to show that the liberties of self-ownership are incompatible with equality, the universality of self-ownership has the effect of creating demands for further and incompatible equalities. Must the attempt to meet these demands reproduce the horrors of absolute power and slavery? Can we have a sense of individual self-command, no less powerful than that offered by self-ownership, but more in keeping with egalitarian intuitions?

The developed answer to these questions is lengthy and complicated. But it may be useful at this point to indicate the heuristic idea I am operating. This is that the kind of power we need in order to be in control of our own lives is political rather than proprietary. So our rights should be constructed as political rather than proprietary powers. The conflation of the two kinds of power is much older than its seventeenth-century appearance in the literature and politics attacked by Locke. But it is interesting to note that Locke, while conflating political and proprietary power in his doctrine of proprietary rights, grounds his opposition to Filmer over the dominion of Adam on the defence of different kinds of power: paternal power is different from proprietary power, and both are different from political power. Against Filmer's claim that the absolute power of monarchs derives from their place in an unbroken line of succession from Adam who had such power from God, Locke argues that the dominion of Adam was not absolute. Were God to grant such a power it would have been certain to corrupt men, for human wills are weak. A rational God gives his agents only as much power as they need to fulfil themselves. The dominion of Adam was the right to use nature and direct his children so that they might flourish.[30] Although, Locke's

---

[30] Locke, *Two Treatises*, i., sect. 41, p. 205.

defence of limited dominion is in theological terms, the argument also has an independent philosophical pedigree in Aristotle's discussion of the kinds of power in the *Politics*.[31] This is not to say that the distinction of powers is indisputable— Filmer disputed it in his *Observations* on the *Politics*—but it illustrates the persistence of another notion of dominion running alongside the proprietary one. This is relevant to our current concerns.

If ownership is not the whole of power, it remains an open question whether the kind of power individuals need to secure their self-command is the proprietary power of self-ownership. It seems better then, at the initial stage of a discussion of the sense of rights, to take the foundational right as the abstract right of self-command. Self-ownership may be regarded as one form of that dominion, but if political power is a distinct form of power, we can envisage a political form of self-command also. This, at any rate, is the idea that I intend to work up into an alternative to self-ownership.

2.7. SUMMARY

The orthodox belief that a right is a property is affirmed in the idea of self-ownership, which is standardly interpreted as a libertarian principle. I have tried to show that this standard interpretation is the right one to adopt if self-ownership is to be our response to the practice or the threat of proprietary political power. Thus we have a reasonably clear view of what it is we are disagreeing about when we dispute about belief in rights, or the uniqueness of self-ownership as a conception of their sense. From now on, I shall not distinguish the concept of self-ownership from its libertarian conception. Self-ownership will always have its libertarian sense.

To sum up, the main points I have made are the following. First, the *concept* of self-ownership is the thought of an individual having the final say over the disposal of her bodily resources within a system of property rules. It should be distinguished from particular *conceptions* of self-ownership as

---

[31] See Aristotle, *Politics*, bk. 3.

specified in different systems of property rules. One such conception is the libertarian doctrine. Second, libertarian self-ownership is favoured over other possible conceptions because any partial self-ownership is inadequate to the task of the doctrine which is to deny us *any* ownership of each other. Third, self-ownership is not very impressive in its response to slavery or political despotism. Because it affirms the view that people can be subjects of private property rules, and allows them to do as they wish with their own property, the thesis permits voluntary slavery and subjection to absolute power. Its moral authority is thereby considerably diminished. Finally, self-ownership, the solution to a power problem that is no longer ours, has become the main source of our current power problem—the distribution of effective equal power to be in command of our own lives.

3

Self-Ownership and
World Ownership

3.1. INTRODUCTION

People have rights over their own persons and powers. Do they also have rights to external resources, so-called socio-economic and cultural rights? The idea that people should have access, as a matter of moral right, to a certain welfare condition underlies the provisions of documents like the *International Covenant on Economic, Social, and Cultural Rights* and the *European Social Charter*. They recognize an array of what are commonly described as welfare rights. These include rights to reasonable conditions of work, an adequate standard of living, rest and leisure, social security, cultural participation, and a share in scientific advancement.[1]

Welfare rights are given a certain popular credibility through the legal and political life of such documents. And they also have an initial appeal as responses to a widely shared moral belief that individual interests in survival and well-being are sufficiently important to justify holding anyone who can serve them out of their surplus holdings to be under an obligation to do so. This is the obligation that welfare rights pick out. A theory of justice which runs counter to this belief has to make a very good case for itself as the only credible defence of some baseline value such as individual liberty which, for the purpose of the debate about justice, is not in dispute.

On the face of it, welfare rights cannot belong in a single system with the unfettered private property rights of self-ownership. Welfare rights, it is acknowledged, presuppose a

---

[1] *International Covenant on Economic, Social, and Cultural Rights*, arts. 7, 9, 15; *European Social Charter*, arts. 2, 12; *Universal Declaration of Human Rights*, arts. 22–7.

welfare principle according to which individuals are entitled to
call on the effort of society as a whole to achieve an acceptable
welfare condition for all.[2] On a right-wing libertarian construal,
this welfare principle inevitably leads to the efforts and talents
of the more able members being treated as common resources
and, consequently, as subject, in their fruits, to a principle of
distribution which denies exclusive private property in personal
powers, a clear contravention of self-ownership. Accordingly,
claims to welfare rights are not countenanced by right-wing
libertarianism. Instead, it counsels the state to take what Eric
Mack has described as the 'hard and spare route' of dismissing
the claims of the needy out of hand.[3]

But so-called left-wing libertarianism offers the possibility of
another view of welfare rights. This is developed by Hillel
Steiner who proposes a constitution which unites self-ownership with egalitarianism with respect to 'raw' resources or their
value.[4] Steiner's constitution would give everyone 'equal starts'
in life, and looks a promising basis for a new interpretation of
welfare rights, one which satisfies their intent without prejudicing self-ownership. The success of this project would
greatly strengthen the case for libertarianism by combining the
appeal of equality with the already powerful thesis of self-
ownership. Could it at the same time disarm welfare state
supporters (welfarists) by ensuring sufficient incidental welfare
(that is, welfare contingently associated with equal rights) to
render unnecessary any appeal to a genuine welfare principle?

In this chapter I want to show that welfarists have no reason
to suppose that libertarianism offers either: (1) a compelling case
for dismissing welfare rights; or (2) the possibility of an
economic constitution which is consonant with the underlying
impulse of welfarism.[5] The overall aim of my argument here and

---

[2] Cf. *Universal Declaration*, art. 22: 'Everyone . . . is entitled to realization,
through national effort and international co-operation . . . of the economic,
social and cultural rights indispensable for his dignity and the free development
of his personality.'

[3] Eric Mack, 'Distributive Justice and the Tensions of Lockeanism', 135.

[4] Hillel Steiner, 'Capitalism, Justice and Equal Starts'.

[5] I use the terms 'welfare', 'welfarism', 'welfarist' to refer to the view that
individuals have rights against their society as a whole to certain material and
cultural resources, for example, those laid out as economic and social rights in
the international code. My use is not to be confused with Amartya Sen's use of
'welfarism' for the view that the goodness of a state of affairs depends finally on

in the next chapter is to lessen the initial appeal of self-ownership by showing how it runs counter to well-entrenched moral positions. My present task divides into four. First the various possible types of moral ownership of the natural world are explained in relation to self-ownership and the two best known Lockian routes to individual acquisition of resources are laid out. Then (Section 3.3) the first route is explored by examining what is probably the most cogent union of self-ownership and rights in worldly resources, the one set out by Locke himself, and the reason for its rejection by contemporary libertarians is made plain. Then, we follow the second route as mapped by Nozick. So Section 3.4 examines his theory and points out some of its central defects, thus undermining its authority to dismiss welfare claims. Finally, Section 3.5 considers the rather different approach to be found in Steiner's combination of self-ownership and equal division of raw resources. I argue that its amelioration of the condition of the needy should not blind welfarists to its contravention of the basic welfare belief that no one should be in need when others are in a position to meet that need.

3.2. RIGHTS TO RESOURCES AND VARIETIES OF WORLD OWNERSHIP

Self-ownership is not very interesting unless a person's survival needs are met and she is in a position to exercise and develop her powers. This is impossible without access to the material means of human life, for all vital human activities presuppose material supports—food, water, air, and a location for one's own body. And the exercise of bodily powers almost always requires an implement and material to act upon. So the principle of self-ownership is of little use until it is joined with a principle of rights over material resources. As things stand most of the world's available natural resources are in collective or individual private ownership. So a principle of rights over material resources will operate to validate existing titles to these resources or else sanction some redistribution. Now there are

the set of individual utilities in that state. Amartya Sen, 'Utilitarianism and Welfarism', 463.

two chief candidates for the role of foundational rights to resources. The two are: (1) a general right to subsistence; and (2) a general right to liberty (or equal liberty). The first is associated with Locke, the second with libertarianism.

Whichever foundational right we select we must also have some characterization of our initial moral relationship to the natural world. There are three possibilities here: (1) the world belongs to us in common, which is to say that no one owns it but each of us can use it on her own initiative provided that she does not exclude others from similar use; (2) the world is jointly owned by all of us, which means that what each may do is subject to collective authorization; (3) each person owns a share of the world equal to that of everyone else. (1) is the favoured initial status for Locke and Nozick who go on to derive private appropriative titles from it out of the rights to subsistence and liberty respectively. (2) must be rejected for incompatibility with self-ownership. Under joint ownership the consent of the collective has to be obtained for any individual initiative with respect to naturally occurring substances. This means that an individual cannot act on the world without the permission of others and this clearly jeopardizes the exercise of self-ownership. In Locke's case, joint ownership is rejected for the different reason that a person would die of starvation if he could not appropriate on his own initiative. (3) is the Steiner position. It differs structurally from the other theories in an important respect. While they describe an initial moral relationship to natural resources which is subsequently altered by the exercise of a foundational right, Steiner's theory has the foundational right working from the start to determine the initial moral relationship. Thus the equal right to liberty founds equal share-holding in natural resources. I leave further discussion of the theory until Section 3.5.

With common ownership as the initial *status quo* there are two lines of derivation for individual appropriative titles corresponding to the two foundational rights noted earlier. The first is through the requirements of survival needs. The second is through the construction of the right to liberty as a right to take what one wants provided one does not worsen the position of anyone else. Both derivations have the same basic structure: they are *historical entitlement* theories. They seek to establish rights historically as the outcome of unilateral individual acts. Within this type of theory there are only two ways of acquiring a valid title. The more familiar one is through transfer from someone already entitled to a holding. Transfer gives valid title provided that the title itself derives from an unbroken historical chain of titles. Clearly, transfer can operate only if there is another mode of acquiring a title in the first place. Chains of transfers must end in acquisitions which are not themselves transfers but sources of original titles. Thus the justice of initial acquisitions of holdings is crucial to the historical entitlement story.

Although the two derivations have the same basic structure there is an important difference. The derivation which begins with the right to subsistence constrains all distributive outcomes so as to satisfy at least the pressing needs of all. In recognizing survival needs as a structural determinant of distributive outcomes it is broadly welfarist in character. Thus it could yield an argument for state intervention on behalf of the less well off. By contrast the libertarian interpretation looks to the historical derivation of titles unconstrained by any structural features of their distributive outcomes, because structural determinants such as need (or desert, or the equality of holdings), are said to be incompatible with liberty. Thus the upshot of this interpretation is a minimal state restrained from redistributive activity.

The first (Lockian) derivation is now passed over by libertarians despite Locke's evident inspiration of the thesis of self-ownership. Yet, his derivation of titles in private property from a foundational right to subsistence (via labour) offers the possibility of a union of self-ownership and a general welfare right which must first be overcome if libertarianism is to make good its claim that welfare prejudices self-ownership. In the next section, I think the reason why Locke's position is regarded as untenable will become evident. Locke is working within a theological/natural law framework which gives precedence to duties and which has been generally abandoned by liberal theory. The overall aim of the section is confined to tracing the shape of Locke's argument for appropriation in so far as it highlights a possible way of combining a general welfare right with self-ownership, at the same time as it reveals the features which make it unacceptable to contemporary libertarians. I am not therefore concerned with the validity of controversial arguments such as the labour theory of appropriation or with the basis for particular claims, such as for a general right of subsistence.

3.3. LOCKE'S THEORY OF JUST ACQUISITION

Locke begins chapter 5 of the *Second Treatise* with the claim that everyone has a natural right to the resources necessary for survival. 'Men, once born, have a right to their Preservation, and consequently to Meat and Drink, and such other things as Nature affords for their Subsistence.'[6] Locke's right of subsistence calls for nature to be treated as a common resource. Hence Locke is able to appeal to the general right of subsistence to defeat the suggestion that all the property of a realm belongs to one person, an absolute ruler claiming a historical entitlement deriving from an unbroken chain beginning with Adam.[7] The same general right to subsistence is used to reject joint ownership on the ground that people would starve in the midst of plenty if the consent of all were necessary to any individual appropriation from nature.[8] The thought behind this point cannot be merely the empirical difficulty of getting universal agreement to an appropriation in time to offset death from starvation. That could be settled by a once and for all permission by all. (Since it is implausible to suppose that all mankind could gather in one place for the purpose of making any compact, the relevant permission would presumably have to be tacit.) The point must be that joint ownership authorizes one person, Ajax, to refuse another, Bantam, permission to appropriate. And Ajax has good reason to exercise that veto because he can then bargain with Bantam about the size of the compensation he will get if he gives in and lets Bantam appropriate after all. Ajax is then likely to get a larger amount in compensation for his loss of joint ownership rights than what Bantam would otherwise have given him.[9] Joint ownership's contravention of the right to subsistence is normative rather than empirical.

---

[6] John Locke, *Two Treatises of Government*, ii., sect. 25, p. 327.
[7] Ibid.   [8] Ibid., sect. 28, p. 330.
[9] I have adapted this example from the description of the problem in G. A. Cohen, 'Nozick on Appropriation', 99.

Locke believes that resources cannot remain in common if they are to be of any use to an individual. 'The Fruit, or Venison, which nourishes the wild *Indian* . . . must be his, and so his, i.e. a part of him, that another can no longer have any right to it, before it can do him any good for the support of his Life.'[10] If the point is that legitimate consumption requires an exclusive title to the resources in question the claim is fairly plausible. At some stage in the consumption/digestion process food becomes irretrievably part of the consumer in a way that is incompatible with others having common rights in it. But the fact that the consumption of food is biologically an individual matter does not establish private property in it in the extensive sense that Locke wants. For example, it does not licence taking food from the common stock and storing it for later nourishment or barter. It gives no title to the wide range of discretionary powers that go with having private property in an object.[11] Yet Locke thinks his argument from need generates a system of private property which replaces original common ownership. What reasons has he? One reason may be worked out of the fact that a hand-to-mouth existence can guarantee subsistence only when resources are plentiful. If there is scarcity the only way an individual can ensure her personal subsistence over time is to have exclusive possession of some resources which can be hoarded and defended against the claims of even needy others. This is consonant with the first duty under natural law of preserving one's own life.[12] A second reason is that the duty to preserve others or as many as possible suggests adoption of the most efficient system of property for production.[13] Locke thinks that appropriated land is more productive than land lying waste in common (he does not consider the possibility of collective cultivation). Increased productivity benefits all in several ways. A man who privatizes land to grow corn 'has increased the stock of Corn, which [people] wanted'.[14] Even if he keeps it all for himself, his privatization makes more resources available to others because he feeds himself off less land than was necessary to support him in the common state. 'He, that encloses Land

[10] Locke, *Two Treatises*, ii., sect. 26, p. 328.
[11] Cf. Jeremy Waldron, *The Right to Private Property*, 168, 172.
[12] Locke, *Two Treatises*, ii., sect. 6, p. 311.
[13] Ibid.   [14] Ibid., sect. 36, p. 335.

and has a greater plenty of the conveniences of life from ten
acres than he could have from an hundred left to Nature, may
truly be said, to give ninety acres to Mankind.'[15] Now these are
not very weighty arguments for a system of private property.
The first gives property only in food (and perhaps other
personal items such as clothing, implements, and necessary
household chattels).[16] The second establishes private property
in land (and other major resources) only if privatization
outstrips communism in both production and distribution of the
means of life. Obviously, Locke was in no position to evaluate
the relative merits of capitalist and communist modes of
production, but a contemporary need-based argument from
productivity would have to do so.

Be that as it may, Locke thinks that private property is
necessary for the satisfaction of needs. He thinks he has an
argument which takes us from 'everyone has a right not to be
excluded from using nature' to 'everyone can take parts of
nature for her own exclusive benefit'. So for the sake of
argument let us accept that some story can be told which makes
the connection, or if not, that some quite different case can be
made for the right to private property.[17] Then we can move to
the crucial question: how does private property get instituted
from a position of common property?

Locke's famous answer to the question of how common
resources come into private hands is given in his labour theory
of appropriation, according to which labouring on something,
provided it is unowned, gives title to that thing. Briefly, in
removing what we need from nature we mix our labour with it
and, in mixing our owned labour with what is not owned by
anyone else we make it our private property.[18] (Were this not
acknowledged, others would be free to enjoy the unagreed use
of the benefits of the labour a person has incorporated in an
object thus violating her self-ownership.)

Labour is the most obvious act by which resources come into

[15] Locke, *Two Treatises*, ii., sect. 37, p. 336.
[16] See Waldron, *Private Property*, 168–71 for the detailed analysis of
Locke's argument.
[17] For a brilliant analysis of argument for and against a general right to
private property, see Waldron, *Private Property*.
[18] Ibid. 184–91 contains a devastating attack on the labour theory of
appropriation.

private hands. But some of Locke's favourite examples involve negligible labour: drinking water from a stream; picking acorns; gathering fruit. Another does not involve the 'mixing' of labour with object which is the central justification for the labour theory of appropriation. This is the example of the hare, which is regarded as the property of its hunter during the chase.[19] In these cases what seems to matter for Locke is not so much how the appropriation is effected but whether others are harmed by it.

He that leaves as much as another can make use of, does as good as take nothing at all. No Body could think himself injur'd by the drinking of another Man, though he took a good Draught who had a whole River of the same Water left him to quench his thirst.[20]

All of this suggests that the importance of labour is due to its acceptance as a normal mode of acquisition, but that there may be other normal appropriative acts also. Thus even though the labour theory of appropriation is sometimes contrasted with the theory of first possession, it may be that the latter has a role in generating a conditional title to resources which a would-be appropriator intends to cultivate?[21]

Original acquisition, however effected, is modified by the general right of subsistence, through the operation of provisos, the most important of which is the injunction to leave 'enough and as good' for others.[22] Nozick has shown that this provision cannot be applied literally, under conditions of immediate or even eventual scarcity, without nullifying all acquisitions. Consider the first person Z who finds herself left without enough and as good to appropriate. The last appropriator Y left Z without her previous liberty to appropriate an object from the common and therefore did not leave enough and as good for her. So Y's appropriation is disallowed by the proviso. Therefore, the penultimate appropriator X left Y in a situation where she could not appropriate for X's appropriation ended permissible appropriations. Therefore X's appropriation was impermissible. But then, the

---

[19] Locke, *Two Treatises*, ii., sect. 30, p. 331.
[20] Ibid., sect. 33, p. 333.
[21] See Karl Olivecrona, 'Locke's Theory of Appropriation', 228 for this suggestion about the priority of enclosure to cultivation.
[22] Locke, *Two Treatises*, ii., sect. 27, p. 329.

appropriator two from last *W*, ended permissible appropriations, since she left *X* in this situation. And so on back to *A* the original appropriator.[23] So it seems better to follow the line suggested by Locke's drinking from the river example quoted above of focusing on whether any injury to another follows an appropriation. From what Locke says there we may infer that one person can think herself injured by another's appropriation only in circumstances of scarcity. Even then the proviso does not come into effect until an appropriator has secured her own survival for the first duty of natural law is to preserve oneself. In all of this there is no barrier to appropriating more than one needs when such appropriation does not threaten the survival of others.[24]

Any trouble with Lockian appropriation starts when there are virtually no more natural resources in common because everything has been privatized. Once that situation obtains a general right of subsistence cannot be met from a liberty to appropriate from nature directly. The propertyless can have their survival needs met only if they can make a rightful claim on the holdings of property-owners. In the *First Treatise* Locke is quite clear that there is such a claim based on the law of nature which obliges us not merely to give justice to others but to preserve them.

We know that God hath not left one Man so to the Mercy of another, that he may starve him if he please: God the Lord and Father of all, has given no one of his Children such a Property, in his peculiar Portion of the things of this World, but that he has given his needy Brother a Right to the Surplusage of his Goods; so that it cannot justly be denied him, when his pressing Wants call for it.[25]

Evidently, Lockian self-ownership is fettered by the duty to preserve others which comes into play once a person has secured her own subsistence. And the right to be sustained out of another's plenty is not overridden by the fact that it is undoubtedly the fruit of her own labour or that of her antecedents. This view is supported by the fact that Locke does not argue that the right to subsistence gives a general right to

---

[23] Nozick, *Anarchy, State, and Utopia*, 176.
[24] Cf. Locke's claim that the rule of property 'that every Man should have as much as he could make use of' would not have straitened anyone had not consent to the use of money allowed larger possessions. (*Two Treatises*, ii., sect. 36, p. 335).   [25] Locke, *Two Treatises*, i., sect. 42, p. 205.

private property, that is, a right that there be resources available for each individual to appropriate.[26] For non-appropriators and their heirs the right of subsistence can be met from charity which, for Locke, is a stringent obligation on all those with property surplus to their needs.[27]

So Locke does not anticipate later worries about the impact on self-ownership of people claiming rights in the fruits of others' powers. Clearly, this is because he thinks of the preservation of mankind as a duty under the commands of natural law and scripture alike, a framework which gives duties precedence over rights. Within this framework self-ownership exists to enable us to fulfil our duty of self-preservation. But while that has priority over the duty to preserve mankind in the event of competition the two duties must be compossible in normal circumstances. So the specification of self-ownership is confined by its role in allowing us to preserve ourselves as part of a wider system of duties. In other words, self-ownership cannot be defined in a way which would prejudice our duty to meet the needs of others out of our surplus goods (any more than in a way which would prejudice God's property in us by permitting suicide or self-enslavement).[28]

This explanation also shows why, unlike an orthodox Lockian, a contemporary libertarian finds self-ownership incompatible with welfare rights. Once the theological/natural law framework is dropped, there is no external source of duty to constrain individual liberty. So if individual liberty becomes the baseline value for our theory of justice no antecedent duty of self-preservation let alone the preservation of others exists to fetter it. A right to individual liberty is identical with the rights of exclusive self-disposal of full liberal self-ownership and these are incompatible with rights to mutual assistance, even in the case of need, as Nozick and others have argued *ad nauseam*.

---

[26] For the argument for this see Waldron, *Private Property*, 209–18.

[27] Locke's view of the stringency of the obligation of charity may be gauged from the following: 'He that sells his corn in a town pressed with famine at the utmost rate he can get for it does no injustice against the common rule of traffic, yet if he carry it away unless they give him more than they are able, or extorts so much from their present necessity as not to leave them the means of subsistence afterwards he offends against the common rule of charity as a man and if they perish is no doubt guilty of murder.' (Locke, *Venditio*, 86)

[28] See Locke, *Two Treatises*, ii., sect. 6, p. 311.

We may take it then that the dismissal of antecedent duties which gives life to contemporary rights theories on the liberal spectrum accounts for the libertarian turn against Locke's right of subsistence. If there are no antecedent determinants of justice (like needs, moral desert, or the equality of holdings), original titles to natural resources must be established through historical acts which are limited only by other acts of the same kind. The current powerful paradigm of such a 'pure' historical entitlement theory is due to Nozick.

3.4. NOZICK'S THEORY OF JUST ACQUISITION

A procedure for just initial acquisition must specify the actions to be performed before an object can be deemed to be in private ownership. Does looking at an object suffice? Or occupying it? Using it? Labouring on it? Occupying, using, and labouring are all acts which are held to give rise to just acquisition. Indeed if use and labour give title, it is arguable that first occupancy is a necessary contributory condition on the ground that an act of taking logically precedes using or labouring.[29] But merely looking at something is not a plausible ground of title because of the difficulty of establishing first possession in this case.

Although a procedure for just acquisition is crucial for any historical entitlement theory—no titles can be validated without it—Nozick does not spend any time telling us which methods of appropriation he favours. Perhaps this is because all feasible means of appropriation are open to self-owners. If so, it is unnecessary to focus on how appropriation is effected, and we should look instead at what would defeat an appropriation. At any rate, this is Nozick's outlook, which is why he concentrates on the impact of an appropriation on others. 'The crucial point is whether an appropriation of an unowned object worsens the situation of others'.[30] Thus in so far as Nozick has any theory of appropriation at all it may be described as making the presumption of validity for all original appropriations. We can then treat the following as stating the condition in which the presumption gets defeated. A process normally giving rise to a permanent

---

[29] See n. 21 above.   [30] Nozick, *Anarchy, State, and Utopia*, 175.

bequeathable property right in a previously unowned thing will not do so if the position of others no longer at liberty to use the thing is thereby worsened.[31]

In Locke's case concern with the impact of appropriation on others is in recognition of the general right of subsistence, a motivation which is absent from Nozick's position. So why is he concerned about the position of non-appropriators? Why is it the crucial point? The answer cannot be a concern for the material condition of non-appropriators, for in Nozick's scheme the only fetters on the exercise of self-ownership are the *rights* of others. So we have to take it that 'worsening the position of others' refers to curtailment of their rights. This suggests that at the outset, when the world is still unowned, Nozick vests everyone with original rights in natural resources. These are the rights which have to be observed by appropriators. Now the change that an appropriation makes to the situation of others is that they are no longer at liberty (under no duty not) to use that object. This need not worsen their overall situation. 'If I appropriate a grain of sand from Coney Island, no one else may now do as they will with *that* grain of sand. But there are plenty of other grains of sand left for them to do the same with.'[32] Here the availability of 'plenty of other grains of sand' would, as in Locke's case of the river of water, preclude legitimate complaint. And this is the situation which has to be reproduced in any legitimate appropriation. An appropriation must leave others with no ground of grievance. This is Nozick's version of the Lockian proviso. It can be met by privatizations which do not worsen the position of non-appropriators. Their position is not worsened by my privatization of a piece of desert when there is plenty of desert left, or they were not drawing any benefit from it in the first place. The condition can also be met by a privatization which worsens their position in one respect while improving it in another counterbalancing way. To counter-balance their loss of liberty the use to which the appropriated object is put must improve their position overall on what it would be had the object remained in common use.[33] If I privatize the only water-hole for hundreds of miles around, your loss of liberty to use it is a cause for serious grievance. But

---

[31] Ibid. 178.   [32] Ibid. 175.   [33] Ibid.

if I offer to let you draw water from it in return for some easily supplied good or service and in addition so improve the facility by, say, keeping it free of pollution, or installing a pump for easy access, or building a leisure complex in the vicinity, that you prefer the new arrangements to your previous freedom, then the use to which the appropriated water-hole is put improves your overall position in compensation for your loss of free access.

This is an attempt to tell a story about privatization which shows private property arising out of an unexceptionable process which does not violate any rights, or provides compensation which people have reason to accept. If the story washes, it shows how all the worldly resources which can be appropriated end up in private hands. Although that leaves some people propertyless—those who did not appropriate when the going was good—those who find themselves in that position have no grievance since their overall position is not worsened and may indeed be improved.

But what of subsequent generations? They do not enjoy the original rights in natural resources of their ancestors, which right ensured that privatizations compensated for lost liberty. Have they no cause for complaint? Nozick thinks not. Objecting to talk of rights to equality of opportunity or life he writes:

These 'rights' require a substructure of things and materials and actions, and *other* people may have rights and entitlements over these. No one has a right to something whose realization requires certain uses of things and activities that other people have rights and entitlements over. Other people's rights and entitlements to *particular things* . . . fix the external environment of any given individual and the means that will be available to him. . . . The particular rights over things fill the space of rights, leaving no room for general rights to be in a certain material condition.[34]

Evidently, intergenerational justice is settled on a first come, first served basis. And this is what undermines any claim to a general right to a certain welfare baseline. But how coherent is a theory of justice which generates bequeathable property rights but does not require first-comers to consider the impact of appropriation on later generations? The problem is that the

[34] Nozick, *Anarchy, State, and Utopia*, 238.

ancestors impose duties to respect private property rights on their successors, at the same time depriving the successors of both the rights they would have had under the persistence of common ownership and the compensation they would be due were such transgressions of their rights permissible. If the crucial point is whether appropriations worsen the position of others, then the theory does not hold together when latecomers are considered. If it is said that consideration of latecomers must be ruled out because it imposes a condition on appropriation which is impossible to meet (how can the impact of an appropriation on millions yet to be born be calculated?), the right response is to say: so much the worse for this way of validating titles in external resources. The response is motivated by the fact that the duties which the theory would have original appropriators thrust on succeeding generations are extremely burdensome. As Waldron puts it:

What we are being asked to accept . . . is this: that there are actions which individuals can perform whose moral effect is to place millions of others under obligations whose discharge may require them to put their own survival in jeopardy. Furthermore, it is not only survival that may be threatened, but also their ability to discharge whatever duties and obligations they have to see to the welfare of others. A parent may have a duty to see that his child is fed; but his ability to discharge this duty will be undermined if the resources which the child needs have been put 'off-limits' by the appropriation of somebody else.[35]

Waldron urges that a principle of just acquisition with so much power to affect the circumstances of people's lives should be tested against the actual or hypothetical consent of those who are to be bound by it. And he argues that such a principle could not be agreed by all, for at least some would be undertaking to starve rather than satisfy their needs from resources under the control of others.[36] However, this method of testing principles of justice cannot be invoked as long as the Nozickian theory of just appropriation remains sufficiently credible to motivate dismissal of the claims of the propertyless out of hand.

Now if misgivings about the fate of latecomers are to be laid aside, the case for the justice of initial privatizations must be irrefutable. But is it? One problem raised by G. A. Cohen is that

---

[35] Waldron, *Private Property*, 268.   [36] Ibid. 271–7.

Nozick restricts the range of comparison to conditions before and after a given appropriation, thus arbitrarily silencing the complaints of those who would have been better off under an alternative appropriation.[37] Why does the right not to be made worse off avail only against non-Pareto-superior privatizations, and not also against non-Pareto-optimal ones?[38] Or, if privatizations must be Pareto-optimal, since there are plenty of these each of which leaves someone worse off than they would have been under a different selection why does the right not to be made worse off not always avail against a would-be selection?[39]

There is also a fundamental problem with the whole idea of attempting to justify what on the face of it is a violation of original rights by reference to an improvement in the overall situation of those whose boundaries have been crossed. How can any putative improvement in the situation resulting from one person's privatization of an object in general use ever compensate others for their loss of liberty to use that object? The point is not that they are as well or better off than before but that it is not clear that unilateral privatization plus compensation is anything other than compulsory purchase of the rights of others. You may have cheap access to a plentiful supply of clean water after I privatize the waterhole, but you are dependent on my willingness to sell it to you, which in turn empowers me to make other demands on you. How can your loss of that liberty and the consequential risks to your independence in other areas be set against the benefit you enjoy? And if some transgressions of rights can be compensated why not all? And why bother with rights at all then? Once these questions are pressed, the impact of Nozickian appropriation on individual liberty becomes the crucial point. How can the principle of individual liberty which is the avowed concern of libertarianism be reconciled with the unagreed loss of liberty which occurs whenever an object is taken out of general use and put in private ownership?

The point is not so much that a particular liberty is lost: in

---

[37] See Cohen, 'Nozick on Appropriation', 95–8, 101.

[38] A Pareto-optimal or efficient privatization yields a configuration of holdings which it is impossible to change so as to make some person better off without at the same time making some other person worse off. A Pareto-superior privatization improves the situation of at least one person without making anyone else worse off.

[39] I am grateful to John Baker for helpful comments on this point.

conditions of plenty the loss of liberty occasioned by another's privatization would have virtually no impact on one's condition as a whole. It is rather, as Steiner has astutely observed, that privatization when resources are limited changes the situation of all others with respect to the distribution of *equal* liberties.[40] This matters, as Steiner says, because the right to equal liberty is the

(unstated) common progenitor of the right to punish, the right against enslavement (secularized self-ownership) and (one aspect) of the right to appropriate of . . . Locke's *Second Treatise*. And it is arguably this principle again that is implicitly motivating both Nozick's complaint against patterned distributions, that they require interference with people's lives, as well as his proviso on appropriation.[41]

Now if equal liberty is this important, the differential distribution of liberty which inevitably results from Nozickian appropriation is inconsistent with the motivation underlying the whole project of the historical entitlement theory. The theory cannot validate existing titles because it cannot get original titles off the ground. It cannot, therefore, validate capitalist private property. It cannot, therefore, provide any basis for the robust denial of welfare rights characteristic of right-wing libertarianism.

3.5. THE STEINER CONSTITUTION

Steiner has developed a package that promises to validate capitalist rights in private property while appeasing welfarist demands through development of an egalitarian economic constitution. His solution to the problem of just initial acquisition is to privatize virgin resources in an initial equal division.[42] Steiner's equalization of initial raw resources is the most natural interpretation of the equal right to liberty which, let us agree, is the foundational right of the system of capitalist property rights. For, before any resources have been acted upon it is reasonable to think that no one has more of a claim on them than anyone else. Hence the equal right to liberty is a right to the same

---

[40] Steiner, 'Capitalism, Justice and Equal Starts', 59. [41] Ibid. 58.
[42] See Steiner, 'The Natural Right to the Means of Production', 48–9; and also his 'Capitalism, Justice and Equal Starts', 64–9.

allocation as anyone else. Initial equal division has the great advantage of bypassing tricky questions about how labour or first possession give rise to title or how rights violations can ever be justified by the expedient of compensation without under- mining the role of rights in securing individual liberty. It may be endorsed as fully compatible with each individual exercising her self-ownership unthreatened by: (1) dependence on the say-so of others (as in joint ownership); or (2) reduction of the amount of liberty available to her as the result of the privatizations of others (as in Nozickian appropriation from initial common resources).

Of course, since Steiner wants to combine this economic constitution with self-ownership the initial equality of resources cannot be maintained. Those whose labour, thrift, and ingenuity lead to improvements in the value of their initial allocation may acquire extra resources through trading with others who are prepared to surrender raw resources for services or opportunities otherwise unavailable to them. And if that is passed on in gifts the starting points of the next generation will not be perfectly equal.[43]

Nevertheless, initial equality in allocations of raw resources and *laissez-faire* thereafter is a promising gesture towards egalitarianism. It gives everyone a right to a certain resources baseline, one consequence of which is that no one starts life dependent for subsistence on charity. And the *laissez-faire* component sustains self-ownership by allowing people to retain the benefit of their own labour and talents.

Equal division raises two computational problems, which need not detain us, but which we must note as calling for some method of commensurating and initially assigning natural resources. The first is how to effect equal division in a world where natural resources are heterogeneously composed and many of them are not readily divisible into the requisite number of equal parts. The second is how to estimate the total number of rightholders given that new ones are born every day. Assuming that some acceptable mechanism for resource valuation is to hand to solve the first problem, equal division can be effected, as Steiner points out, without impossible foreknowledge of the

[43] See Steiner, 'Capitalism', 70.

number of future claimants. The second problem disappears if, for example, we assume that what gets distributed is the pure rent of natural resources, for that is being constantly generated, and is therefore available for allocation to however many claimants there are.[44]

A further problem is how the value assigned to raw resources is to be extracted for redistribution under equal rights to resources (of equal value). But that is only a matter of determining the details of a tax aimed at recovering the revenue from natural resources. Such a tax, it should be noted, could not legitimately draw off any value added by the labour of the possessor of external resources. An exception to this is the labour-enhanced value of objects in the estates of dead people. Steiner proposes that these be treated as unowned (that is, as held in common) on the ground that the right of bequest included in the received view of ownership is unsustainable.[45] If there is no right of bequest, then as each generation dies the stock of common resources is renewed, often vastly improved in value. This stock is available for equal division among all rightful claimants either as an initial lump sum or periodic payments. At the least, the upshot of this economic constitution is considerable reductions in the social and economic inequalities of people at life's start. No one can be born into destitution in the midst of plenty.

Can Steiner buy off the welfarist? I think that the answer is negative. Note first that welfare figures only incidentally in the left-wing libertarian argument. The primary motivation for the right to equal resources is not concern with the material condition of people but with equal liberty. Now in circumstances of abundance Steiner's constitution can meet both equal liberty and, at the very least, basic needs. So although it is not aimed directly at securing basic welfare it seems churlish to condemn it for neglecting a concern that does not arise. But Steiner's constitution is vulnerable if either or both of the following holds: (1) scarcity threatens the survival of some or all under equal division when an alternative dispensation would assure it; (2) on a scale of points of well-being rising from basic

---

[44] Ibid. 65–9.
[45] See Steiner, 'Supernatural Powers: Can there be a Right of Bequest?'

survival the next point up (let us imagine it is a point marking
enjoyment of good nutrition, health care, and education) can be
reached by more people under an alternative to equal division,
and so on up the scale.

If scarcity is so severe that an equal division means that no
one can have basic survival needs met, then the choice under
Steiner is between satisfying the rights to equal resources of
some subset of the population, and satisfying none. But if that is
the choice, all must die, because there is no basis, under the case
for equal division, for preferring to satisfy the rights of some
over others. In severe scarcity unilateral acquisition of subsistence on a first come, first served basis, or distribution of
subsistence by lot, will strike some as preferable to equal
division. But then the foundational right is to self-preservation
which is allowed to trump equal liberty in the case of conflict.
This need not upset Steiner because the priority of a system of
equal liberties over other considerations requires reasonably
favourable conditions in any rights-based account of justice. The
trouble is that the differences in moral intuitions that open up
here about distributions in desperate circumstances persist
under the more usual circumstances of justice.[46]

Consider a more favourable situation of moderate scarcity,
one in which equal division provides allocations on which
people who are adept at managing resources can survive but
those with ailments or a deficiency in the relevant talents
cannot. Under equal division the strong let the weak die and
gain larger shares from the subsequent redistribution. This is
legitimate even if the strong could have kept the weak alive by
working the latter's resources as well as their own, for the weak
can claim no right to support from the self-owned labour of
others. This conflicts with the basic welfare belief that subsistence should be guaranteed whenever that is materially possible.
Note that this conflict does not betray any incoherence in
Steiner. What it shows is that equality of natural resources
cannot be guaranteed to put people in a material condition they

[46] I am grateful to Hillel Steiner for alerting me to the fact that our moral
intuitions may be very divided here, hence my suggestions reflect at most some
non-libertarian intuitions. Steiner has generously provided me with detailed
comments on much of this chapter, many of which I have not known how to
answer.

could enjoy were self-ownership not in force. Accordingly, the welfare consequences of Steiner must repel welfarists who should now see that their target must be the principle of self-ownership.

This conclusion seems too strong if the actual world has enough raw resources for equal division to guarantee survival for everyone. However, the welfarist objection is then redirected to the inequalities which are very likely to build up when Steiner's constitution is in force. One source of inequality is the fact that equal starts in life are upset by gifts. But these cannot be prohibited compatibly with the right to equal liberty.[47] How much inequality this would generate is hard to estimate. What is evident, however, is that the very great inequalities of capitalism are quite likely given unequal talents and/or luck and the exercise of self-ownership.[48] For, given one or both of these advantages, some people are able so to manage natural resources that it is worthwhile for them to buy the shares of less-productive people and employ those people at higher wages than they would otherwise get from labouring on their initial holdings.[49] Thus capitalism is generated out of equal division plus unequal talents plus the unfettered exercise of self-ownership.

Now the welfarist who finds cause for complaint about capitalist inequality (when survival is assured) is not merely envious of the more fortunate members of society, as is sometimes charged. Her complaint is that the less well-off are dependent for their livelihoods on the better-off. That dependence makes for vulnerability, especially under capitalism, where wages are forced down by maintaining a large pool of unemployed labour. Thus the less well-off do not enjoy the same chance of being in a particular welfare condition as the better-off. Although what counts as the relevant level or condition of welfare may be disputed, that does not affect the issue of dependence and its consequences which lies at the back of the

[47] See Steiner, 'Capitalism', 70.

[48] They are likely, not inevitable, because the moral culture may ensure rough equality of condition through voluntary redistribution. It is evident that we do not currently enjoy such a culture.

[49] I owe this point to Cohen, 'Self-Ownership, World Ownership, and Equality: Part II', 88–9.

welfarist complaint. From this perspective the the key institutional question is how comprehensive our egalitarianism should be in order to uphold people's equal membership of a political society which claims to respect people as free and equal citizens. Should we take an egalitarian approach to the distribution of personal powers as well as to natural resources? Or should the approach be confined, as in Steiner, to natural resources? The former comprehensive egalitarianism equalizes all resources.[50] The partial egalitarianism represented by Steiner's view does not. Now the complainant that I am representing here is a comprehensive egalitarian in the name of upholding equal citizenship.[51] What she wants would require vesting the less well-off with the right to attach the surplus resources of the better-off, a move prohibited under Steiner as inconsistent with self-ownership.

My conclusion is that if one starts with a commitment to welfare rights then Steiner's constitution cannot be thought to offer anything like enough (incidental) welfare. While the principle of self-ownership and the principle of welfare which clash here are both so fundamental to our moral thinking that it is hard to see which to abandon, it certainly seems to be the case that adoption of self-ownership precludes any accommodation of welfare sensibilities. But nothing in the libertarianisms we have examined shows why self-ownership must be retained at all costs. Certainly welfarists must reject the principle. Of course

[50] It might also be directed to equalizing welfare in the sense of a state of well-being. For this notion of welfare see Ronald Dworkin, 'What is Equality?: I: Equality of Welfare'. For the distinction between comprehensive and partial egalitarianism see Cohen, 'Self-Ownership, World Ownership, and Equality', 91.

[51] The claim that equal citizenship requires rough material equality is described in Rousseau's principle: 'In respect of riches, no citizen shall ever be wealthy enough to buy another, and none poor enough to be forced to sell himself.' (J.-J. Rousseau, *The Social Contract*, bk. II, ch. 11, p. 96.) A version of the claim phrased in terms of the requirement to sustain equal membership of the community is defended by Michael Walzer, *Spheres of Justice*, 78–83. This and other arguments from citizenship to welfare rights are discussed in Desmond King and Jeremy Waldron, 'Citizenship, Social Citizenship, and the Defence of Welfare Provision'. John Baker has argued that there are empirical grounds for comprehensive egalitarianism in 'Arguing for Economic Equality', 31–3. I defend the claim to rough material equality in Ch. 8 of this book. But I introduce it without defence here because it is a natural interpretation of the right to free and equal citizenship.

then they must face the question of what to say about people's rights in their persons and powers. Welfarism would be easier to sustain against libertarianism if there were an alternative to self-ownership as an account of these rights. The job of this book is to show that there is.

3.6. CONCLUSION

The libertarian dismissal of the claims of welfare is well-known. I have been suggesting that we should view that dismissal as drawing the principle of self-ownership under suspicion. I have shown, in Section 3.4 above, that a dismissal of welfare rights based on Nozick cannot be taken seriously because his theory of original titles in worldly resources is at best arbitrary and at worst incoherent. Steiner's account is neither arbitrary nor incoherent. His (raw) resource egalitarianism does not claim to be welfarist in impulse, but it might seem sufficient to spoil the appetite for welfare rights. I have argued that it is not so sufficient.

I have not shown that commitment to welfare rights is superior to commitment to self-ownership. I think that there is a clash of principles here which is too fundamental for any one-sided resolution to dispel qualms about what is denied when the other principle is dismissed. If we are to set self-ownership aside, as I believe we should, then we must find an alternative way of conceiving rights in personal powers. I pursue that project in later chapters. Can the project be justified on additional grounds, independent of the considerations raised in this chapter? I raise this question because it might appear that my argument is dominated by a welfarist perspective which inevitably thrusts duties on people and which is, therefore, inimical to a rights theory which aims to state the requirements of persons as moral sovereigns, that is, as having a right to determine for themselves what their duties are. The argument of the book as a whole should remove any disquiet on this score. Meanwhile, the next chapter shows that considerations of moral sovereignty, far from sustaining self-ownership, actually provide additional and decisive grounds for pursuing an alternative.

4

Proprietary Rights and Self-Command

4.1. INTRODUCTION

I turn now from arguments about what rights there are to some discussion of the idea that the right to be in charge of one's own life is adequately rendered by the idea of ownership. In this chapter I want to show the conceptual inadequacy of the whole proprietary approach to rights. Briefly, I give some general reasons for thinking that the idea that people need to be self-owners in order to be in charge of their own lives is unsustainable, at least, in the circumstances in which the question of justice and rights arises for us. Two related lines of criticism lead to this conclusion. The first is that by making the intelligibility of rights depend on the institution of private property as a basic social form, the proprietary conception favours capitalist rights as the only rights, or the only rights worth having. But the idea that rights are necessarily associated with capitalism and therefore incompatible with socialist society and common property is very difficult to defend.[1]

My second line of criticism concerns the idea that self-ownership is the most appropriate conception of the moral and legal barriers that free and equal human beings need in order to secure personal command over their own lives. Here the question is whether the liberty–constraint system which individuals need in order to defend their vital interests is proprietary in form and not, rather, something else. The development of these criticisms is preceded by a section which (re)introduces the conception of proprietary rights in the form of a brief conjectural history. The point here is to give some under-

[1] For the view that many important freedoms, of speech, assembly, worship, publication, movement, political participation, and so on, are not necessary concomitants of capitalism, see G. A. Cohen, 'Capitalism, Freedom, and the Proletariat', 15.

standing of the deep appeal of self-ownership and its concomitant institutions of capitalist private property by telling a story which shows how it might be seen as a politically relevant way of dealing with the dominant issues of a particular society given the conditions associated with political absolutism. When those conditions no longer obtain, when political absolutism is defeated, then an understanding of rights based on the association of power and unfettered ownership is no longer compelling. Proprietary rights are revealed as the terms of one historical political settlement, not the enduring basis of any settlement we might now fashion given our conditions, ideas, and problems. This theme, introduced in Section 4.2, recurs in Section 4.6, fortified by the conclusions of the intermediate sections. Sections 4.3 and 4.4 take up the conjectural history of proprietary rights by imagining the demise of private property as a basic social form and devising two possible sequels. In each case, I argue, we can intelligibly ascribe individual rights without implying the necessity of capitalism. Section 4.5 shows that the proprietary conception makes unintelligible the exercise of a right to self-determination to effect a transition from capitalism to socialism.

4.2. A CONJECTURAL HISTORY OF PROPRIETARY RIGHTS

Suppose that there is a population living under the rule of an absolute monarch who claims sovereignty over all the land and the people of the territory he controls. We need not suppose that the monarch is foolish enough to make all his subjects feel insecure in their lives and liberties for that would unite them against him. Nevertheless his *de jure* position is that he has power of life and death over his subjects and complete powers of sequestration over any possessions they enjoy. Consequently, a subject who falls out of favour has no recourse against the monarch exercising full ownership powers, including the powers to enslave or kill him. We can imagine that to combat such dangers the subjects of this absolute potentate develop a number of self-protective strategies. Some acquire military power and form alliances which make the monarch wary of exercising his power against them. Others relate themselves to

him by marriage or friendship. Or, they seek to make him
dependent on their advice. Or, they sanctify themselves
through allegation of an illustrious lineage leading back to
ancestors revered in a founding myth. Of course, many of the
subjects may be too humble for such strategies. And a few
(intellectuals?) may disagree with absolute power altogether.
Their part in the story comes later. For now, let us imagine that
we are at a period of internal peace and prosperity in the history
of this society under absolute monarchy. No one is overtly
challenging the rule of the absolute monarch. Indeed, if anyone
were asked (by a troublemaker from another society) about the
form of rule they lived under they would say that it was natural
and necessary, or that it was traditional, or useful, or accepted
by the people.

On this account of the situation some background legitimating
theory is accepted by nearly everyone in the population. Let us
suppose that the legitimating theory is the Filmerian story: the
monarch's powers have a pedigree which is established by
tracing them to an act of transfer by a previous absolute
monarch who, in turn, received his powers from a previous
absolute monarch, and so on back through successively antecedent transmissions of power to an original donation made by
God to the first absolute ruler.[2]

We should note that in this political situation the power to
rule is identified with the powers of ownership and these are
thought of as the unfettered powers associated with what is
now called capitalist or full liberal ownership. Clearly, the
situation described lacks detail about the beliefs, historical
origins, social roles, and economic conditions that mark real
historical societies and account for the basic social structures
they develop, renew, and destroy. Nevertheless the society
described displays the important marks of a politics of absolute
power, and it is plain that given the prevailing social understanding of the character of power relations any effective
challenge is going to have to exploit to its advantage the
available ideology.

Let us now suppose that a sense of frustration with the
existing order develops. The contributory causes of dissatisfac-

[2] Robert Filmer, *Patriarcha*.

tion might be religious, philosophical, political, or economic. The most powerful ideological challenge is bound to be one that harnesses existing ideas and shows that they are a shared social basis for transforming the political order. In the case we are considering the essence of the challenge to absolute power is to the idea that the monarch can own people. Plainly, this challenge can be mounted within the framework of the existing association of the ideas of property and power by claiming that each person is the moral owner of her own person and no one is the moral owner of any other person.[3] Of course, this move requires the public culture to share an additional idea—that of equality—if absolute power is to be redistributed to all citizens. The tactical brilliance of the move in the history of ideas of which Locke is now the best-known exponent is to connect in one theory a notion of divine creation as primary ownership, a notion of the equality of created souls as a divine purpose, and an account of that equality as a natural equal moral self-ownership, a position that no Christian monarch can attack without attacking both the divine basis of political power and ownership itself.[4] So the weapon it is natural to fashion out of the existing intellectual materials in a society such as the one I have sketched is an idea of self-propriety based on a common equal creation. Then the reason individuals cannot be the property of the monarch is the unimpeachable one: they are the property of God and created in his image as (dependent) self-owners.

So the principle of self-ownership is developed as the ground on which people in this society legitimate their claims to forms of consideration denied under absolute power. It is a contingent but powerful ideology because it merely extends an existing social practice of respect for property by bringing personal powers into that sphere. The primary social role of self-ownership in providing a moral defence, first, for resistance to absolutism, and then for creation of an alternative story of political authority, dominates the meaning of the concept so that any internal difficulties or incoherences are regarded as

---

[3] For an instructive discussion of one important example of this phenomenon in the thought of the English Levellers, see Michael B. Levy, 'Freedom, Property and the Levellers: The Case of John Lilburne'.

[4] Cf. Alan Ryan, *Property and Political Theory*, ch. 1 *passim* and esp. 31.2.

problems to be worked out rather than reasons for rejecting the concept.

Our imaginary political society which we will call *Respublica* develops over time into one that is very much like our own in that it has a well-developed practice of formulating moral and political issues as matters of rights together with an appropriate institutional setting for giving them effect. Now *Respublica* has private property as a basic social form and because of its particular historical development of the idea of property the notion has a wide sense that includes property in self. This simplifies the central political role of *Respublica* to the protection of property of every kind. This amounts to the securing of a system of individual rights whose principle is private owner-ship. What rights there are attach to the natural endowments, physical and mental, with which people come into the world. What they are rights for is to enable individuals to be in control of their own lives. What they may do with their natural assets is given by the social form of private property. Perhaps they can sell or give themselves into slavery. That depends on whether the social form confers unfettered rights of use, alienation, and bequest. If the society has a more constrained view of owner-ship then certain choices may be limited. Citizens may be excluded from damaging their persons with drugs, or from enslaving or prostituting themselves. *Respublica* may be imagined to have experimented over time with a variety of different rules of property and disputes about rights may be understood as having been about these rules. We need not suppose that the outcome of such disputes has always been consistent with the underlying commitment of the society to full liberal ownership. A theory need not be fully coherent in order to be socially powerful. What remains untroubled by any changes in the meaning of property is the idea that private ownership yields the form of all rights, both in personal powers and external resources.

On this account of the social practices of *Respublica* the institution of private property is intimately connected with the possibility of there being any personal rights. Wherever people speak of rights they are speaking of properties although the connection between rights and property is so familiar that it is rarely necessary to state it. Observe that all that is required to constitute the existence of rights is that people engage in a pattern of social relations in which they treat each other as having a private property in their own persons. This pattern of forbearances, composed within the rules of liberal ownership, is regarded by *Respublicans* as the essential ingredient of a society which respects persons in their roles as agents and authors of meaningful lives. Whenever it exists they speak of a society as respecting individual liberty to choose principles to live by. Where it is absent they cannot so speak, for the pattern of rights, responsibilities, powers, and immunities defined by ownership and applied to persons as well as external resources is, according to their theory, what respect for individual liberty consists in.

To claim equal rights in *Respublica* members of disadvantaged groups make two related claims: one is for extension of the principle of self-ownership to themselves; the other is for recognition of their equal personhood, for the denial of rights is typically made by excluding some people—women or aliens, for example—from full humanity. In *Respublica* the tendency of thought is to take as sufficient evidence of personhood the capacity for claiming revealed in demands for rights, for the first index of capacity for ownership is the ability to stake one's claim.[5] So the strategy of liberationists is to require implementation of the full implications of existing social ideology and this is more or less successful in winning equal treatment for members of groups who start out disadvantaged.

In early *Respublica* the most pressing problem which people face is how to remove absolute monarchy. They have to legitimate their assault on it as best they can with the ideological resources available to them. They are not in a position to think about the possibility of living under a system of rules which does not have property as its principle. Therefore, they have no

---

[5] I take it that one point of the words of Frederick Douglas, a Black leader in the Abolitionist movement of last century, is that the capacity for rights is shown in the demand for them. 'The man who has *suffered the wrong* is the man to demand redress . . . the man STRUCK is the man to CRY OUT—and he who has *endured the cruel pangs of slavery* is the man to advocate liberty. It is evident that we must be our own representatives and advocates, not exclusively but peculiarly—not distinct from but in connection with our white friends.' Cited by A. I. Melden, *Rights and Persons*, 23–4.

moral obligation to do so. But that does not show that their moral and political settlement is binding on subsequent generations who start out from a different political situation (and therefore have different problems), and who have a broader fund of ideas and traditions to draw on in forging their moral and political settlements. In so far as a society similar to *Respublica* is part of our history the question we face is whether our inherited habit of thinking of rights as proprietary—the residue of a political settlement for another time and its conditions—is appropriate now, given our moral capacities, our political conditions, our material resources, and our current moral/political problem of accommodating the triple demands of liberty, equality, and solidarity. In answering this question, the issue of the necessity of regarding rights as properties, of citing the rules of property in order to give the sense of rights, is central. In the next couple of sections, I want to show that there are good reasons for supposing that this connection is contingent.

4.3. THE WITHERING AWAY OF RIGHTS:
(i) TOTALITARIANISM

Let us now continue the story of *Respublica* by supposing that private ownership of the means of production and essential services comes to an end and is replaced by collective ownership. This could be the result of a revolution though it could plausibly happen also because the electorate repeatedly votes for governments with socialist policies. In whatever manner, the character of the state is changed from a private property-owning democracy to some form of socialist society with collective property. Call this *Respublica II*. Now under the conception of the state which takes as its sole aim the protection of private property, rights are identified and secured in terms of the social form of private property. Under the new dispensation private property is not a basic social form although people are allowed some personal property. But the latter is limited in amount and does not include absolute rights of disposal so individual accumulations of greatly unequal amounts of wealth are prevented.

By the argument of Chapter 2 above, the principle of self-ownership cannot be sustained in *Respublica II* for the limitations on personal property mean that people cannot use their talents and labour powers for their own exclusive aims. So if we have no alternative context in which to construct a meaning and basis for individual rights these must inevitably wither away, contrary to the increasingly common supposition that socialists can and should recognize rights.[6]

Now a withering away of rights is neither desirable nor necessary under collective ownership. I want to show this by considering a worst and a best possible case of society under collective ownership. These are different possible histories of *Respublica II*. They proceed from different responses to crucial issues for a system of collective property, namely, the basis of authority to determine the general interest and the appropriate form for the institutional mechanisms needed to apply that determination in concrete cases. Should there be a central planning committee, or a delegation of collective responsibility to expert managers, or some national democratic structure of decision-making, or local democratic decision-making? Or something else?[7]

The answer to the authority question which yields the worst-case history develops out of a victory over liberalism by some anti-liberal form of communitarianism. Imagine this as installing an élitist principle of political authority such as rule by the wise, or by the holy, which in turn sees to the institutionalization of political deference as the appropriate attitude of citizens.[8] This will be manifest in the absence or unimportance in the basic social structure of provisions for freedoms of thought, speech, association, and the other bases of moral independence. Under one or other version of an élitist principle of authority one possible history for *Respublica II* is that it becomes a totalitarian *Gemeinschaft* community focused on a single ideal of community identity and making total submission to that ideal the price of

---

[6] See Sect. 1.2.

[7] Cf. Jeremy Waldron, *The Right to Private Property*, 40.

[8] For an illuminating account of the connection between hierarchical authority and deference and the problem this outlook posed for theorists involved in creating the new American republic (and their solution) see Samuel H. Beer, 'The Rule of the Wise and the Holy: Hierarchy in the Thomistic System'.

inclusion in its network of civic care.[9] Of course, this is an
extreme on the *Gemeinschaft* spectrum and other points mark
more attractive polities.[10] What is common to the set of possible
histories that presuppose the élitist principle is belief in natural,
meritocratic, or divinely ordained hierarchies, and consequent
just inequalities in power, responsibilities, burdens, and opportunities. Contingent ethnic origins or gender differences, holdings of natural talent, social class, and the assets of privilege, are
the kind of features which determine who gets to decide for the
community. So, given collective ownership of resources and a
principle of rule by the wise or the holy what the withering
away of rights means in *Respublica II* is rejection of a certain
conception of individuals as having equal moral power to
contribute to determining the general interest. In this possible
history *Respublica II* departs from the democratic tradition of
politics. Lacking democratic accountability it will inevitably
degenerate into totalitarianism. Presumably, this condition will
give rise to demands for a return to 'traditional' *Respublican*
private property and the individual independence associated
with it or else for the continuation of collective property subject
to democratic control. Either demand affirms the desirability of
individual rights. But the second is the interesting one for the
development of our argument for it lends support to the claim
that collective ownership need not rule out the possibility of
rights despite the absence of private property as a significant
social form.

Suppose then that participatory democracy is the answer to
the question of how collective property is to be controlled. This
brings with it the idea that people have an equal right to a say in
decisions which affect their lives—a right of self-determination
or self-development. If we are asked why such a right should be
acknowledged the response is to take our questioner through a

[9] Ferdinand Tönnies has provided the classic formulation of *Gemeinschaft* as
an 'intimate, private and exclusive living together', *Community and Association*,
39. *Gemeinschaft* connotes social conformity with respect to an ideal of the good
society, and a social self which is constituted in its character and purposes by the
kind of community it inhabits. For a useful condensation of general features of
Gemeinschaft and its companion contrast-notion *Gesellschaft*, see Timothy
O'Hagan, *The End of Law?*, 87–9.
[10] For example, any Aristotelian polity, provided one is not a natural slave or
a woman.

set of considerations which argue for it to secure: (1) the good of individual autonomy conceived as the capacity to develop that enlarged sensibility which allows us to give justice to others and to identify and live a worthwhile life of our own; (2) the good of a society organized so that public decisions are justifiable to those who live under them thus promoting the likelihood of morally acceptable laws and policies. Now although the argument that participatory democracy presupposes a right to self-determination founded ultimately in the value of equal positive freedom or autonomy should be set out more fully than this, it is, I hope, unnecessary for me to do so here for it is very well known.[11] My point is simply that, on the most widely shared account, participatory democracy presupposes a right to self-determination. So we can tell a story involving collective property in which totalitarianism is blocked by participatory democracy and that is guaranteed by rights in the absence of self-ownership. If this story is intelligible it cannot be the case that having a right just is having a private property. Of course the intelligibility of talk of non-proprietary rights depends on the success of an alternative conceptualization of rights. But if we have a choice between giving up on the story and the proprietary model of rights, then the intuitive plausibility of the story adds its weight to the build-up of considerations against that model.

4.4. THE WITHERING AWAY OF RIGHTS: (ii) FULL COMPLIANCE

Consider also a best-case possibility. This is a possible history for *Respublica II* which yields a polity at the other end of the

[11] For an argument similar to the one sketched here grounding equal political participation in the respect due to persons on account of their capacity for moral agency see Keith Graham, *The Battle of Democracy*, 71–2. On the right to self-development as the foundation of participatory politics, see David Held, *Models of Democracy*, 262. The materials for the argument are also in William Nelson, *On Justifying Democracy*, chs. 3 and 6. Chs. 5–9 of this book may be seen as an extended argument of the same general form. The argument originates in Rousseau's defence of participation as enhancing the value of an individual's freedom by enabling him to be his own master. J.-J. Rousseau, *The Social Contract*, bk. II, ch. 12, p. 99. Carole Pateman, *Participation and Democratic Theory* is an important contribution to the discussion of the theory and practice of participatory democracy.

gemeinschaft spectrum from totalitarianism. There *Respublica II* also develops an economic system which allocates material resources by reference to the general interest defined in a holistic way. But, in this version, the general interest is thought of as what the members of the community have decided together. Let us envisage this as a Rousseauesque undertaking in which a common citizenship is forged out of everyone's interest in being free and equal.[12] The general interest is then defined by reference to the needs of free and equal citizens taken independently of the particular requirements of their different ideals of happiness, or the private interests of cabals and factions or any association that would offer its particular aims as in the interest of all.[13] Now this community develops as one in which rights wither away, in the sense that people rarely if ever have to stand on their rights, because the operation of just institutions has developed in them an acute sense of justice. They spontaneously cherish each other as capable of contributing to the identification of the common interest by the light of their individual rational moral powers.[14] What is due to people is encompassed by deeds of fraternal love so that issues about fair shares do not figure prominently among their concerns.[15] Now evidently, such a development presupposes acceptance of the concern for individual moral powers which rights protect, so while in this community there is no need for recourse to rights, that is not because rights have withered away but because there is full compliance with their requirements.[16]

As long as there is willing compliance in *Respublica II* with the principle of respect for personal moral powers to share in defining and implementing the general interest, we might think

[12] See Rousseau, *The Social Contract*, bk. I, ch. 6, pp. 59–62.
[13] Cf. John Rawls, 'The theory of primary goods is a generalization of the notion of needs, which are distinct from aspirations and desires. So we could say: as citizens the members of a well-ordered society take responsibility for dealing justly with one another on the basis of a public measure of (generalized) needs, while as individuals they and members of associations take responsibility for their preferences and devotions' (Rawls, 'Fairness to Goodness', 554).
[14] Cf. Beer, 'The Rule of the Wise and the Holy', 418.
[15] Cf. the appealing description of a more or less ideal family situation in Michael Sandel, *Liberalism and the Limits of Justice*, 33.
[16] Stanley Benn makes a similar case for rights in the foundations of a loving *Gemeinschaft* community which respects and cares for autonomy. See 'Human rights—for whom and for what?' 72–3.

that rights are redundant in theory as well as in practice. But this is not so, for there is no way of describing the community which does not presuppose certain rights connected with two related aspects of its existence: its voluntary character in virtue of which everyone has a right to participate in the design of its common life, and its civic character in virtue of which everyone is constrained from privatizing the political. So everyone in this possible republic has the right founded on citizenship to a political community devoted to the general interest. And they also have the liberty to engage in private pursuits and ways of life just as long as these do not subvert the character of their common citizenship. Correspondingly, no one has the right to alter the terms of citizenship so that the general interest is subverted into the strongest private interest (such as a particular economic, religious, or political interest). The fact that the complex of citizenship rights is observed goes to show that certain rules of conduct have been internalized, not that they do not exist. They exist as the constitutive rules of the community and they protect the citizen's individual interest in the community retaining its civic character. Any movement away from that character by the community as evidenced in the making of legislation to promote the aims of particular groups or in a practice of discrimination against certain members can be corrected by invoking the constitutive principles and rules of the community, and that possibility must exist even if members do not in fact experience the need to stand on their rights. So the background structure of rights cannot be detached even when we suppose full compliance with their requirements of respect and care for it has made the community's particular forms of forbearance and cherishing possible. Another way of putting the point: the social structure of its nature distributes rights even when full compliance with their requirements conceals their existence.

Since to have a right is to have a moral justification for using or threatening to use force, the constitution of the basic social structure as a scheme of rights seems at variance with the supposition of a developed sense of justice or civic virtue.[17] How can a coercive structure be required for a virtuous

---

[17] See Sect. 1.3 and H. L. A. Hart, 'Are there any Natural Rights?', 79–80.

citizenry? The answer is the hard truth that virtue is fragile in beings such as ourselves. While, in our imaginary community, people act as the general interest dictates we must not suppose that this is because they no longer have strong personal preferences. Were that the case we would be envisaging beings who lacked the strong emotional attachments to family, friends, and projects, the enthusiasms and the dedications, that mark real human capacities for commitment and agency. If this were the price of growth in civic virtue, no such virtue would be worth it or even motivationally possible for why should such passionless beings care about their community?

For us, and beings relevantly like us such as the members of *Respublica*, the development of civic virtue is a matter of people learning to set aside their particular private aims when they enter the public world. However successful this lesson is in the case of particular individuals, the practice of civic virtue is fragile for society as a whole. It is fragile for many reasons, but we shall note three salient ones. The first is that the institution of the family is a source of personal commitments that may be dearer than any others to individual citizens. In a situation of plentiful resources, these commitments do not clash with the overriding commitment to the general interest called for by civic virtue. However, should resources become scarce, people would naturally prefer to advance the interests of their close family members over those of less well-loved friends and neighbours. So, as long as the institution of the family exists and there is scarcity, the political is under constant threat from the priority of family affections. If we would rather live with that personal–political tension than abolish the family, civic friendship will remain fragile.

Even without the family as a forum of intimate ties more commanding than civic friendship the fragility might in any case exist if Aristotle is correct in observing that limits of time and the intensity of love preclude loving many persons.[18] He is surely right when he says that love among friends consumes emotional energy, requires an appreciation of the same things, and requires much time to engage in the common pursuits and to honour the responsibilities of friendship. So diversity of interests

---

[18] Aristotle, *Nicomachean Ethics*, bk. 9, ch. 10.

and natural limits on our emotional capacities and physical energies preclude a person's having many close friends. If love must exist within the bounds of our natural capacities, it seems psychologically difficult and even undesirable to put civic friendship ahead of personal friendship. Perhaps this is another tension we must live with, striking the best balance we can when an actual conflict occurs. But if this is right, civic virtue is very fragile indeed.

The third source of fragility is that philosophical, religious, and moral differences about the nature of human well-being seem bound to continue as long as human inspiration or creativity hold out. So civic virtue while favoured by just institutions would seem to be contingent on the absence of conflicts, a condition which cannot be fulfilled given human beings as they are and the size of modern political communities. That is why, finally, *Respublica II* and any real republic fashioned in its image, needs the assurance of institutions that underwrite citizens' mutual trust in one another's integrity. Individual citizens must have an internal guarantee that they themselves will be able to restore their community if it falls foul of private interests. Their guarantee takes the form of a system of rights against the state.

The point of developing these tales of *Respublica II* is to show that the general thought of rights can be detached from the familiar conception of rights as private properties. If the concept of rights can be intelligibly deployed in a context of collective ownership, the link with private property is contingent. And if that is so we need not suppose that in order to have rights, or be in command of one's own life, one must have private ownership of oneself and such external resources as come one's way through the legitimate exercise of proprietary powers.

4.5. A RIGHT TO CHANGE SOCIETY?

Our thought experiment with *Respublica* confirms the intuition that the concept of rights can be employed in a variety of political contexts, non-capitalist as well as capitalist. I want to emphasize now one of the points emerging from the experiment, namely, the fact that the exercise of a right of self-government to effect a transition from capitalist to non-capitalist society cannot be understood on the basis of the proprietary conception of rights. The conception holds that rights exist whenever people treat each other with the forbearance appropriate to recognizing each as the exclusive proprietor of her own person. A society in which such observances obtain inevitably recognizes unfettered rights in the property in external objects which individuals acquire through the rightful exercise of their self-owned powers. If this is correct, rights can never be fully established in the absence of a system of private property. While people may foolishly renounce their rights by installing a socialist or a communist society, that is akin to using one's moral self-ownership to sell oneself into slavery. Nothing in the new political arrangements make for the establishment of rights. Until such time as people have the wit to reinstall private property and a free market there will be a rights vacuum.

The dangers to individuals of life in a political society without rights are obvious and not usually freely embraced. Instead, modern political societies characteristically secure certain democratic powers and freedoms by constitutional arrangements which recognize a battery of individual rights. These confer on individuals the status, as citizens, to take part in their own government, to be party in various ways to the determination of the public interest, to be free in certain specified areas, to command equal respect for their own conceptions of the good, and so on. The foundational right which such civil and political arrangements specify is a right to self-government. Nothing about that right suggests that it is, or uniquely favours a conception of rights that is, proprietary. Indeed, as we saw in the previous sections, the right to self-determination may be employed to establish some form of non-capitalist society, and it is no more than blunt denial to see this as a renunciation of rights rather than as a possibility which shows the inadequacy of the proprietary conception. I turn now to some more extensive argument for this point.

In making the case for the possibility of rights in the foundations of a state with collective ownership and/or a high degree of political participation no less than in a minimal state, it is natural to introduce expressions that connote the active side of being in charge of one's own life—'participation', 'citizen', 'public interest', and 'self-government'. However, such notions introduce a new set of considerations of which no account can be given in terms of the practice of forbearance from trespass that is the social recognition of self-ownership. For there to be rights in a minimal state no more is needed than the institution of private property and extension of its cover to persons. But this is not enough to account for the self-determining powers people may assume to shape their political life as a state which expresses and secures an ideal of public interest that is not a mere aggregate of individual private interests.[19]

The most obvious reason for thinking that self-determination is not a case of proprietary power is that an exercise of proprietary rights to choose social institutions which deny prominence to private property or personal interests cannot but appear as irrational. But whatever our theory of self-government turns out to be it is plain that it cannot be reduced to what the proprietary conception permits, for the rights of persons to run their own lives must include the right to determine the principles that regulate the basic structure and institutions of their society and there must be alternative sets of choice-worthy principles if there is to be any choice in the matter at all.[20]

Secondly, the constitution of rights as proprietary yields a system of forbearances which cannot found any presumption that people would be able to develop the sense of collective interest and political efficacy necessary for them to exercise their self-governing capacities to redesign their social structure. If people are to be able to use the natural powers and talents on which a right to be in charge of their own lives is founded there must be, in their society, a general regard for the value of autonomy. There must be acceptance of a basic right of self-government under which individuals are allowed not merely the pursuits of private lives, but a proper part in the design and redesign of the social structure within which their lives are lived.

Talk of participation and citizenship does not figure promin-ently in the politics of the minimal state dedicated to the

---

[19] See n. 13 above.

[20] For the idea that individuals conceived as moral persons have a right to equal respect and consideration in determining the principles that are to regulate their social institutions, see Rawls, 'Fairness to Goodness', 548.

protection of proprietary rights and we may wonder why. In part the answer is that the function of the minimal state is to regulate private interests so that all may be satisfied in harmony. That is an administrative task which presupposes that the aims of individuals are established independently of political life. So there is no big role for citizens to play in the minimal state. Perhaps the most telling evidence of this is the fact that there is little space for them to debate about the character of justice because the principle of self-ownership is given as the baseline within which any debate must proceed. But if we are to take our practice of debating justice seriously, we cannot pre-empt the possibility of a theory of justice which develops a different scheme of rights. Nor can we limit citizen participation to periodic acts of selecting one package of economic, social, and defence policies for another. Citizens need more extensive political participation because their practice of politics includes perennial debate about justice and that cannot be left to the determination of a political executive or team of expert managers.

In fact, the assumption that self-ownership is a given, fixed, moral starting point is inconsistent with the most important reason we have for assigning rights to people, namely, their autonomy.[21] For it ignores a salient conceptual feature of autonomy, that is, its opposition to determining causes as heteronomous. From the point of view of autonomy no other antecedent values can constrain our moral choices or our deliberations about justice. No moral law is taken as pre-established.

So a theory which circumscribes in advance the debate about justice cannot be accepted as a defence of autonomy. That is why we can imagine without any logical strain autonomous beings choosing social arrangements and patterns of distribution other than those sanctioned by the minimal state. This is an intelligible engagement in so far as the arrangements and patterns selected are structured in accordance with principles which are acknowledged to express autonomy interests. There may be many such arrangements and which is best in particular circumstances is not decidable in the abstract. The upshot of all

---

[21] See Sect. 1.3.

this is that we should treat the principle of self-ownership and the proprietary rights which flow from it as a subject for consent rather than pre-established in some way. Then its position as the sole conception of the idea of being in charge of one's own life is open to challenge by competitor conceptions. In the next section, I want to show that the monopoly of the principle of rights as proprietary has indeed been broken and the way is open for an alternative articulation of the general form of rights.

4.6. FIXING THE SYSTEM OF FREEDOM AND CONSTRAINT

Rights theories are dedicated to the proposition that individuals have a moral right to certain spheres of freedom. We might regard the boundaries of these spheres as being set by social convention. And so in a sense they are. But our practice of debating and disputing these boundaries drives us to consider the moral basis of current and proposed conventional settings. A moral basis would settle the argument just as long as it was shared between competing proposals. If there was disagreement in moral assumptions and that extended to standards of selection for moral theories or outlooks, different proposals would be incommensurable and we would be unable to choose between them for purposes of a politics which requires political coercion to be morally justified.

Given a plurality of moral outlooks, each of which sets its own standards of morality, and none of which can establish its superiority over another without assuming the superiority of its own standards, justified political coercion is constrained to respect the moral integrity of citizens. Integrity requires that no one be forced to act contrary to her fundamental moral convictions. Then no one can be represented as having a duty to another except under the umbrella of a moral principle she shares with the rights-claimant and agrees as a source of rights and duties (that is, agrees as one that justifies coercion). Once moral integrity is regarded as important, coercion has to be under the authority of principles and rules which even the subjects of coercion can recognize as justified. This is to say, they must satisfy the criterion of being ones which all can agree.[22]

Two points follow from this line of thought. One is that we must reject any doctrine of natural or moral rights which gives no role to consent. The other is that the justification we give for any scheme of rights must employ premisses which our opponents actually accept. And the best source of those is in the moral and political culture we inhabit. These points add up to the need for a principle of endorsement.

The first point is addressed to classical natural rights theories which characteristically argue that some favoured feature of human nature is the basis of rights. Human interests in freedom, well-being, or rationality are typical candidates. Now the fact that humans have such interests is claimed to provide a standard for assessing conduct as good or bad. So we might articulate the standard as a set of social rules and these would determine what is owed to individuals as humans with such a nature. And we might then think of individuals as having rights corresponding to those duties which they all acknowledge under their shared theory of human nature. In this way of thinking the existence of a natural need is sufficient moral backing for anyone to stop another interfering with its fulfil-ment. Thus, as we saw in Chapter 3, Locke claims that the right to take what one needs from the state of nature is independent of the consent of others, for if we had to wait on their consent we would starve. This seems to be a muddle. If no one else is around it makes no sense to think that there is any question of rights involved. If someone else comes along and tries to stop me eating the berries from a bush then it makes sense to say that I may justifiably resist her. And the element of justification presupposes a background appeal to a principle of need that the attacker can also acknowledge, assuming that the attack is motivated by a similar need and not some view that berries are forbidden fruit or that people should hasten their entry to a better life by starving themselves to death.

If I and my attacker share a view of human needs then it may

---

[22] Obviously, this is the approach of the liberal conception of political philosophy, one of the functions of which is to reconcile the principle of individual autonomy with political and legal arrangements which are backed by force. This point is expanded in Waldron, *Private Property*, 271–8.

seem to us, when we start to reflect, that our rights not to be interfered with by each other are set independently of both of us by the exigencies of our needs. But it is because we share the background premiss of the importance of those needs that we can agree that a social rule of non-interference is right. Even then the rule we agree will not be independent of some judgement of how our competing needs are to be satisfied given the available supply of berry bushes. And we have to agree on that. It is not established for us by our abstract principle of need.

In the more complex case where we are in fundamental disagreement about how to live our lives, the need for the rules which establish our rights and duties to be consensual is even more obvious. In that case I can claim a right to stop another from imposing on me her own conception of the good. But her challenge is to the very legitimacy of my claim so she cannot be brought to acknowledge any moral duty to let me alone. I can oblige her by physical force to do so but I have no purchase on her internal moral allegiance. She cannot shape her conduct by my standard and we cannot agree a social rule or practice in which rights to mutual forbearance, never mind assistance, make sense.

The truth that rights presuppose the existence of socially established rules which have an internal aspect in that they are accepted as standards that inform our conduct, does not destroy the idea of moral rights.[23] As long as we understand these to be governed by moral principles, we do not have to think that the dependence of rights on an institutional setting means that there can only be legal rights. What it does mean is that moral rights have to be based on principles which, in fact, underlie the political culture we have, even if their detail has not been that well worked out in practice.

The second point—that justification must proceed from shared premisses—bears directly on the case for moral owner-ship of our persons. In keeping with the requirement that some shared premisses be available to found rights, libertarianism appeals to a background agreement on the importance of autonomy. Thus Nozick invokes autonomy as the justification for moral constraints on our conduct. The constraints, he says,

[23] For the internal aspect of rules see Hart, *The Concept of Law*, 55.

are 'connected with that elusive and difficult notion: the meaning of life. A person's shaping his life in accordance with some overall plan is his way of giving meaning to his life; only a being with a capacity to so shape his life can have or strive for meaningful life.'[24]

Autonomy may justify constraints. But it does not automatically justify the scheme of constraints set by self-ownership and the distributive outcomes it sanctions. To see this, consider the situation where we take as our baseline a system of natural liberty and we mean by liberty doing as we please without the interference of others. Then introduction of ownership rules of any sort sets constraints on natural liberty. We can no longer do as we please with respect to things which are in private or communal ownership. A system of ownership rules sets up a scheme of freedom and constraints and different systems draw up different distributions.[25] So it is wrong to think that an appeal to autonomy or natural liberty automatically settles which among various possible schemes is to be preferred. In particular, it is wrong to think in advance of relevant moral argument that the economic liberty which people have under private property rules just is liberty, or the only liberty worth having. From the point of view of an appeal to autonomy or natural liberty it is an open question where the constraints are to be set.

We might claim that a system of private property best protects natural liberty. But this is false because natural liberty encompasses every activity we wish whereas private property constitutes and protects some liberties by excluding others. For example, without private property rules we can take what we want from others in so far as we have the might to do it. So private property restricts natural liberty and the question is whether that restriction is more justified than any alternative scheme of constraints we could envisage. Only if we are in the grip of an identification of all constraints with rules of private property will we imagine that talk of constraints is only talk of private property, that it is our potential for ownership that is regulated and liberated by the minimal state.

[24] Robert Nozick, *Anarchy, State, and Utopia*, 50.
[25] For these points I am indebted to G. A. Cohen, 'Capitalism, Freedom, and the Proletariat', 12, 15.

So if we regard autonomy as an appropriate subject of defence by a system of rights what we have to establish is the general form of those rights. Are they to be rights that give us a kind of sovereignty over our persons comparable to the sovereignty an absolute ruler claims over subjects, one in which our liberties include powers of life and death and unfettered transfer over ourselves? And is the political culture so defined the one we want to have? Or is the kind of moral sovereignty in question better modelled on the constrained sovereignty of modern democratic governments (supposing that we can understand how to square limited moral sovereignty with freedom to run one's own life)? The answer, I think, cannot be given in the abstract. Different concrete historical circumstances provide different baselines which shape the way in which our initial concern about personal freedom and integrity can be met.

The point may be supported by considering conditions in which the libertarian contract may be rational. That contract is often rejected on the grounds that it perpetrates a fraud on the poor who are deemed to consent to a political culture which inevitably yields different life prospects for rich and poor.[26] But the circumstances in which the contract is made make a difference. If the baseline is a social condition in which the poor are in constant fear of sudden death or enslavement at the hands of the rich it is rational for them to renounce the use of force to take what they need from the rich in return for assured freedom from use of force by the rich to make them chattels. (The rich get relatively secure enjoyment of their possessions in return.) In the abstract that is a second-best contract for the poor. But the circumstances of any contract make a difference to what can be achieved. It is not a fair contract if that means that it is not the contract the poor would accept if all of the contractors were impartially situated *vis-à-vis* each other. But it is a rationally acceptable contract and one that has some claim to being just because the parties are situated impartially with respect to their own physical powers to enforce their wills on others. Furthermore, there are independent moral grounds for constraining arbitrary killing, slavery, and forced labour and

---

[26] Carole Pateman, *The Problem of Political Obligation*, 145–50, uncovers the fraudulent liberal social contract.

these provide everyone with reasons of a moral kind for adopting the system of constraints that suggests itself as a remedy for those evils and which is realizable in their society.

So the distribution of freedom and unfreedom that a private property system effects might indeed be the one that it is rational to endorse in some concrete historical conditions. But conditions in the society that libertarianism now addresses are not those just described. In a modern constitutional democracy the question of what the distribution of freedoms and constraints is to be starts from an established settlement on issues such as slavery and forced labour. No one wants to argue that they are legitimate. More or less established also are certain fundamental liberties, such as freedom of thought and expression, religious freedom, equality under the law, freedom from arbitrary arrest and detention, and personal inviolability, although the degree to which these are entrenched in different constitutional regimes may vary. Another important part of this settlement is welfare for the poor. Hardly anyone wants to argue that the poor should be left to starve to death. The level and comprehensiveness of public provision for welfare, not the principle, is what is at issue in most current debates about the state.

This is the political culture in which libertarianism wants to renegotiate the terms of social co-operation. But the baseline from which we now negotiate is one of formally equal citizenship and that at least means that no one has to bargain for their lives and certain entrenched liberties. So it is inconceivable that the poor could accept the distribution of freedom and unfreedom proposed by libertarianism. A better contract for them is the Rawlsian one which sustains all established civil and political liberties and permits economic inequality only in so far as it improves the position of the worst off over what it would be under equal division.[27] Of course, in the eyes of certain radicals, it is not necessarily better than social structures that might be gained by revolution, but if revolution is not feasible or has too many moral costs to set against an unpredictable outcome, the Rawlsian contract may be the best for now. It should be said also that the question of contract is not merely a matter between rich and poor. Other groups, religious fundamentalists and some

---

[27] Rawls, *A Theory of Justice*, sects. 11, 46.

varieties of communitarians, may want entirely different social structures which could not be accommodated by any contract-arian settlement. For them, better social structures can be envisaged and if revolutionary overthrow of the existing order is not possible, they may find it rational to subscribe to whichever proposal for distributing freedoms and constraints best serves their interests while working by peaceful persuasion for its replacement.

The upshot of the above is that the principle of self-ownership, considered as a subject for consent, cannot actually command it except in certain rather gruelling conditions. Later, I will show that the principle cannot command hypothetical consent either. For now, what has been shown so far suffices to suggest that the automatic identification of rights and private property cannot be sustained. In brief: (1) the concept of a right cannot be reduced to the conception of rights under capitalism, that is, the proprietary conception; (2) the proprietary conception cannot be the favoured interpretation of rights because it is unable to explain the possibility of a transition from capitalism to a form of socialism which embeds individual rights in its social structure, or can be intelligibly criticized for failing to do so; (3) a system of proprietary rights cannot be agreed by all in the circumstances of modern democracy.

PART II

Self-Government: The Political Conception of Rights

5

The Moral Basis of Rights

5.1. INTRODUCTION

The reigning conception of rights has been instructive in a
number of ways. First, it demystifies rights by showing them as
logically tied to certain normative descriptions of ourselves. In
the Lockian world what we must do to discover rights is to
recapitulate the conception of persons as self-owners. Once we
identify ourselves as self-owners, rights are given, for they
define the meaning of ownership. That rights are embedded in
normative theories is an important insight. It allows us to see
that talk of rights is one with talk of what is right and wrong
from the perspective of individual agents once these are
conceived in a certain way.

The fact that we challenge self-ownership as an appropriate
conception does not diminish the importance of the way of
looking at rights it suggests. By taking rights as ways of
expressing moral judgements made within a conception of
persons we avoid any metaphysical commitments of the sort
that makes sensible philosophers wary of rights. We avoid
supposing that rights, as Ronald Dworkin puts it, 'are spooky
sorts of things that men and women have in much the same way
as they have non-spooky things like tonsils'.[1] This is the sort of
supposition that Alasdair MacIntyre appears to have in mind
when he derides belief in rights as 'one with belief in witches
and in unicorns' and asserts that no good arguments for their
existence have ever been produced.[2] On the view taken by
Dworkin and followed here, it is a mistake to think of
demonstrating or doubting the existence of rights as if they were

---

[1] Ronald Dworkin, *Taking Rights Seriously*, 139.
[2] Alasdair MacIntyre, *After Virtue*, 67.

theory-independent ontological items.[3] Apparent ontological disputes turn out to be misleading ways of canvassing the merits and demerits of different conceptions of persons. So, for example, conceptions that favour certain traits such as separateness and independence may be regarded by some people as less revealing of human nature or less attractive morally, than ones which identify traits such as sociability and connectedness. If that is our position we will reject the claims, privileges, powers, and immunities that are associated with the rejected conception. But these rights claims cannot be treated as subject to assertion or denial independently of the theoretical context in which they are embedded. So we should see scepticism about individual rights as a misleading way of disputing theories that give priority to individual over communal interests. This dispute is muddied if we take the issue to be the existence of rights when it is really about selection of theoretical outlook.

Second, the notion that rights are given in a conception of ourselves such as self-ownership illuminates disagreements about the content of rights. Whether we acknowledge positive as well as negative rights can now be seen to depend on the importance to us of the liberties included and excluded in the different liberty–constraint schemes that specify different conceptions of the person. Thus the scheme of rights we endorse is inevitably connected with our judgements about the importance of certain liberties to our philosophically favoured conception of the person.

Consideration of the reigning conception has been instructive in another way also because its inadequacies help show us what is required of a better conception. For example, the root cause of the inadequacy of Robert Nozick's theory is that it fails the test of connecting his suggested basis for rights—the capacity to construct a meaningful life—with his liberty–constraint scheme.[4] This shows us that an alternative conception must make good its own claim to adequacy by tying itself more firmly to the interest(s) that rights are to protect.

---

[3] Dworkin, *Taking Rights Seriously*, 139.
[4] See Robert Nozick, *Anarchy, State, and Utopia*, 48–51, for recognition of the need for a moral foundation for rights.

5.2. A NEW BEGINNING

I argued in Section 6 of the previous chapter for a principle of endorsement with respect to rights. The case was that the right to impose a duty on another cannot be distinguished from brute coercion unless that right embodies a moral principle that can be endorsed by the duty-bearer. Yet moral rights are not conditional on particular voluntary acts of endorsement. Kate's moral right not to be harmed by Rosemary holds independently of any undertaking by Rosemary not to harm her. Moreover, moral rights can play their role in criticizing social institutions or practices only by belonging to persons generally under some moral description such as 'equal moral person' rather than as participants in particular social arrangements such as 'citizen of Florence'. So the principle of endorsement is not understood as the requirement that moral rights be derived from actual consent. Instead, the requirement is for rights to be derived from the consent of parties to certain principles in a suitably defined social situation.[5] This is a specially constructed point of view in which the acknowledgement that counts is of equal moral persons irrespective of their institutional relationships. Of course, the viewpoint must be one that has purchase on our actual thinking, otherwise its prescriptions could not be claimed as binding on us. Nevertheless, the construction has to abstract persons from their implication in existing institutional forms in order to arrive at principles with the moral force to bind people generally. Thus even though the derivation of principles of right employs some version of the contractarian idea it would be a mistake to think that the outcome is a scheme of conventional rights that we can alter at will rather than what we may be permitted to call 'natural' rights.[6]

Of course, rights are not 'natural' if by that is meant that they belong to individuals under any conception of human nature or

---

[5] I have drawn much of what I have to say in this and the next paragraph from John Rawls's discussion of natural duties in *A Theory of Justice*, 114–16. See also 505–6, n. 30 on 'natural' rights.

[6] By the 'contractarian idea' I mean the idea that the principles governing social and political arrangements are the subject of voluntary agreement by those who are bound by them.

none. Or if positing them favours one conception as better
revealing an independent moral essence. But dismissal of that
view need not deprive us of a usable idea of the 'natural'.
Borrowing from John Rawls's characterization of natural
duties, rights may be said to be natural if their application is
universal, unconditional on actual promises or consents, and
their content is not defined by the rules of actual institutions or
social practices.[7] These features of natural rights are not
damaged by the device of deriving the principles of rights from a
contractarian or similar point of view. Universality is honoured
once the viewpoint adopts a conception of the person that
ranges over all humans. Unconditional application is authorized
once the formulation of rights specifies no special acts of consent
as a condition of their application. The fact that the principles of
rights are thought of as agreed in a specially defined contract
situation means that they bind persons generally. It does not
mean that they must be agreed all over again in order to apply.
In the case of institutional independence I want to be more
circumspect than Rawls by distinguishing a boundary institution from one that exists within it. A boundary institution sets
the outer limits of our thought and activity. It may be described
as a 'cultural prejudice', a 'way of seeing' a 'horizon', a
'presupposition', or a 'framework'. It has a considerable degree
of stability, but it is nevertheless a social construct and not
immune to change. For us the thought that claims deriving from
the category of persons have priority over ones deriving from
particular social roles and relationships is a boundary institution. This institution is stable relative to the more variable social
institutions existing inside it, for example institutions of differential treatment based on gender, ethnic origin, class, or work
specification. Such institutions are the ones we want to refer to
when we talk of the institutional independence of natural rights.
We mean that rights belong to persons as moral agents
irrespective of their local social roles and relationships. Of
course, this leaves rights dependent on the boundary institution
but that does not imperil their traditional role in moral criticism
of local roles and relationships.

The important point to take from all this is that 'natural' moral

[7] Rawls, *A Theory of Justice*, 114–16.

rights can be regarded as binding on their correspondents only if they can be derived from a contractarian point of view as ones that would be endorsed by individuals under a conception of the person they have reason to hold. So the first task in working through a contractarian approach is to fix the appropriate conception of the person. This is the task for the remainder of this chapter.

5.3. LOCATING THE MORAL BASIS OF RIGHTS

The principle of endorsement requires that rights be derivable from background principles that would be acknowledged in a suitably defined social contract situation. While that situation will not be defined until the next chapter we can note in advance that its design must embody some assumption about the political context it aims to clarify. For us this is liberal democracy, a political culture that insists on the democratic equality of all citizens and recognizes the importance in their lives of certain fundamental liberties. Now in liberal democracies people subscribe to different, often incompatible conceptions of what makes life worthwhile. These may be religious, ethical, or philosophical views. Since such views are the subject of disagreement and are also sources of the deepest convictions people have about how to lay out their lives those facts must be represented as 'givens' in any model of the circumstances in which the question of rights arises for us. In other words, our thinking about rights takes place against certain background beliefs that are not in question within the liberal democratic perspective: (1) that citizens are to be treated as equals from the point of view of politics; (2) that certain liberties, such as the liberty to practice a religion, are of fundamental importance; (3) that disagreement about the fundamentals of human existence is to be tolerated (even regarded as a good thing) rather than stamped out by force. Together these beliefs direct us to find a moral basis for an acceptable scheme of rights, one that can be endorsed by all citizens, in some point of agreement which overarches differences in conceptions of what makes life worthwhile. Intuitively, the clearest point of agreement is that expressed in the third belief, that moral pluralism is to be tolerated. While this belief cannot stand in isolation from the other two (toleration would not be important to people who did not believe in democratic equality and fundamental liberties), it is a useful point of entry to the unifying moral basis of all three.

What justifies toleration of moral pluralism? I think that the best answer is one which relies on the idea of equal respect for persons. This may be expressed as the Kantian principle that persons should be treated as ends not solely as means. The thought is that treating a person as an end is respecting her distinctive capacity to set and pursue her own aims and projects. By contrast, treating her as a mere means ignores this aspect of her moral personality, usually by coercing her into conforming to the aims of another. Now in the context of moral pluralism the good a person identifies and pursues is not a good shared by all. So equal respect for persons cannot flow from the thought that others are due the respect we claim for ourselves because they are like us in sharing our judgements of what makes life worthwhile. Instead, equal respect must come from the thought that what matters is that people develop and exercise their capacities to form and implement their own plans and projects. This is the thought of people as capable of autonomous life and of autonomy itself as so deeply valuable an ideal that we shape our politics to secure it. In a similar way, democratic equality and the idea of fundamental liberties can be traced to commitment to the deeper value of autonomy. Thus the three beliefs I listed above are systematically connected via their common root in the value of autonomy.

Now autonomy is an ideal of the person that has to do with the way in which one holds a view of the good life. To be autonomous is to think of one's relation to one's goals and aspirations as contingent, to hold them now as the result of a deliberative choice and to entertain the possibility of abandoning them in the future. Thus people can be autonomous while differing in their substantive conceptions of the good. This is why autonomy can be the focus of the moral agreement that justifies the institutions of liberal democracy despite the fact that citizens disagree about what makes life worthwhile. Of course, the idea of autonomy needs a great deal more clarification as well as a fuller account of the reasons for making it the basis of our political morality. But what has been said so far suggests an outline of the argument for a scheme of rights appropriate for liberal democratic regimes. The best scheme of rights, this argument will go, is one that protects the autonomy interests of citizens. With this rough map of the route ahead let us turn to consideration of autonomy and the case for giving it a central political role.

5.4. AUTONOMY

The ideal of autonomy flows from the thought that individuals have a moral personality that enables them to discern good and evil for themselves. If we keep to a fairly literal reading of autonomy as 'self-rule', it is the vision of individuals themselves making the moral laws or principles they live under. As an initial reading of 'making moral laws' we might construe it as a matter of acting on one's own preferences rather than those of another. And this captures an intuitive idea of autonomy as having to do with choosing for oneself how one shall live, of progressively shaping one's own destiny by the deliberate choices one makes.[8] But the account of autonomy as acting on one's own preferences captures only the thought that autonomous action requires independence of the will of others. It does not cover the intuitive idea that a person lacks autonomy if she fails to exercise her capacity to choose her preferences and aspirations or if she is subject to the play of immediate stimuli.

A leading account of autonomy which deals with this element distinguishes between preferences which we happen to have (first order) and ones which on critical reflection we choose to have (second order). Autonomy is still the pursuit of one's own preferences but is displayed in their endorsement in critical reflection. Gerald Dworkin's characterization is exemplary:

Autonomy is conceived of as a second-order capacity of persons to reflect critically upon their first-order preferences, desires, wishes, and so forth and the capacity to accept or attempt to change these in light of higher-order preferences and values.[9]

---

[8] Cf. Joseph Raz, *The Morality of Freedom*, 369.

[9] Gerald Dworkin, *The Theory and Practice of Autonomy*, 20. The idea of autonomy as second-orderedness was introduced by Harry Frankfurt, 'Freedom of the Will and the Concept of the Person'. See also Richard Lindley, *Autonomy*, 66.

While this is not an adequate account of autonomy it fixes on a central feature, that is, the idea of autonomous action as the pursuit of reflectively endorsed preferences. Other accounts describe this feature in more intuitive language. Thus John Rawls expresses it as living one's life according to a plan: 'a person may be regarded as a human life lived according to a plan'.[10] The importance of a plan derives from the fact that 'a person's good is determined by what is for him the most rational long-term plan of life . . . This plan is designed to permit the harmonious satisfaction of his interests.'[11] Robert Nozick develops a similar view. He believes that what is important about the idea of a person is that it is the idea of

a being able to formulate long-term plans for its life, able to consider and decide on the basis of abstract principles or considerations it formulates to itself and hence not merely the plaything of immediate stimuli, a being that limits its own behaviour in accordance with some principles or picture it has of what an appropriate life is for itself and others.[12]

Joseph Raz formulates the idea as 'significant autonomy'. Significantly autonomous persons 'adopt personal projects, develop relationships, and accept commitment to causes, through which their personal integrity and sense of dignity and self-respect are made concrete.'[13] This formulation improves upon talk of plans of life which conjures up images of lives that are regimented, lacking in spontaneity, and governed as a whole by a single dominant pursuit. Raz recognizes that talk of plans of life can lead to confusion of autonomy with giving one's life a unity. He insists that the 'autonomous life may consist of diverse and heterogeneous pursuits. And a person who frequently changes his tastes can be as autonomous as one who never shakes off his adolescent preferences.'[14]

This is not to suggest that a person does not need a conception of the life she wishes to lead in order to be autonomous. The point is that we should not insist on the comprehensiveness of a single conception of the good either at a given moment in time or over a whole life. An autonomous life

[10] Rawls, *A Theory of Justice*, 408.   [11] Ibid. 92–3.
[12] Nozick, *Anarchy, State, and Utopia*, 49.
[13] Joseph Raz, *The Morality of Freedom*, 154.   [14] Ibid. 370–1.

may be characterized simultaneously as well as over time by a variety of pursuits which give it meaning and purpose, and these pursuits may well be ordered by values that are in some tension with each other.

A final point about this idea of second-order endorsement is that it is quite compatible with the fact that many of our pre-reflective pursuits are ones that we have been brought up to have. Autonomy is not prejudiced because we discover our-selves already loaded with projects and aims when we start to reflect. The crucial point is that we regard these commitments as open to question, that we continue with them or abandon them as a conscious choice and for reasons that have themselves been adopted on critical reflection.

This brings us to the question of the adoption of the reasons governing autonomous deliberation, the 'higher-order prefer-ences and values' mentioned in Dworkin's formulation. How does an autonomous person select these? A tempting answer based on the belief that all value derives from sheer choice is that they are simply chosen. Autonomous choice is depicted as free, that is, arbitrary. This answer must be rejected if autonomy is the root value of our political morality. For autonomy is not a plausible basis of political coercion if it is merely a matter of arbitrary self-determination. There is nothing very estimable about a person exercising her capacity for choice apart from any reasons to support the choices she makes as good ones. Autonomy is worthy of the respect that justifies its fundamental political role only if it proceeds in the light of reasons which can be acknowledged as independently sound. But these cannot be regarded as choice-independent reasons without prejudicing autonomy. So the problem is how to square the thought of the autonomous person ordering and reforming her desires and aspirations under the command of Dworkin's higher-order preferences and values with the thought of these as having independent normative force.

Kant is our historical source for the account of autonomy that combines choice and independent validity. Kant's most access-ible discussion of autonomy occurs in the third chapter of the *Groundwork*. There he clarifies the notion of autonomous choice in a discussion of freedom. First he defines freedom negatively as belonging to a rational will with the property of 'being able to work independently of *determination* by alien causes'.[15] From this, he claims, springs a more fruitful *positive* concept of freedom according to which free actions are neither dependent on alien causes nor lawless, that is arbitrary. Instead they exhibit a causality which conforms to laws of a special kind, namely, self-imposed laws. Thus he identifies positive freedom with autonomy, the condition of those who make their own laws. 'What else then can freedom of the will be but autonomy—that is, the property which will has of being a law to itself?'[16] Kant reiterates the identification when he writes, 'on the pre-supposition that the will . . . is free there follows necessarily its *autonomy* as the formal condition under which alone it can be determined'.[17]

This conception of autonomy as giving law to oneself meets the condition of independent validity for reasons in a particularly forceful way. For Kant's view is that the law we make is no mere subjective standard for assessing actions but one that we can will to be universal.[18] That is not a matter of prescribing our own standards for others, for they, as independent sources of value, will also have their judgements. So, if we follow the Kantian line here, we need to think of making moral laws that are intersubjectively valid because they express an agreement in moral judgements that is the *terminus* of many independent deliberations and judgements. How the many independent deliberators are to arrive at one and the same moral conclusion is the key problem here and the one that post-Kantian contract theory addresses. I shall not say anything more about that until the next chapter, because the characterization of autonomy we have been moving towards may be made independently of our theory of how to arrive at an intersubjectively valid moral principle. In brief, then, Kant holds that autonomy is a matter of acting on principles that all can adopt. By contrast with the common association of autonomy and independence to do as one pleases, Kant's view stresses a constrained autonomy bound by the requirement to identify principles that can be adopted by all.

This is also the view underlying Rawls's description of

---

[15] Immanuel Kant, *Groundwork of the Metaphysics of Morals*, 114.
[16] Ibid.   [17] Ibid. 129.   [18] Ibid. 88.

autonomous action: 'acting autonomously is acting from principles that we would consent to as free and equal rational beings.'[19] This is a useful formulation because it brings together the interplay of choice and independent validity characteristic of a Kantian account. Choice is represented by the role given to consent. The idea of independent validity is captured in the thought of principles that any free and equal rational being would endorse. Rawls's formulation is also useful in emphasizing that it is only for a certain conception of persons as free and equal moral beings that the question of identifying moral principles that can be adopted by all arises.

The account of autonomy as revealed in practical choices that are principled or law-like explains why autonomy is valuable. Thus Kant in a famous passage proclaims:

Our own will, provided it were to act only under the condition of being able to make universal law by means of its maxims—this ideal will which can be ours is the proper object of reverence; and the dignity of man consists precisely in his capacity to make universal law, although only on condition of being himself also subject to the law he makes.[20]

What is admirable about autonomy, Kant is saying, is that it discloses beings with the capacity to identify and live by principles that can be universally self-imposed. The really impressive point, he is insisting, is that individuals can devise principles that are not merely maxims for their own actions but ones with the character of moral law and thus appropriate for adoption by others also. This treatment of autonomy as revealed in the ability to identify and live under moral principles that all can accept calls for some caution in the reading of Dworkin's 'higher-order preferences and values'. These may not be understood as preferences and values which owe their 'higher-order' status to sheer arbitrary choice. Instead they must be ones which anyone capable of choice has reason to choose.

The ideal of autonomy that I have been putting together is the vision of people determining, to some extent, their own lives in the light of principles they would endorse as free and equal persons. I say 'to some extent' in recognition of certain facts of human existence: that each of us normally lives among others

[19] Rawls, *A Theory of Justice*, 516.   [20] Kant, *Groundwork*, 107.

who make choices, sustain institutions, and create possibilities that affect what any individual can do; that each of us has vital human needs which must be satisfied by the provision of nourishment, clothing, shelter, and so on, no matter what she wants to make of her life. I adopt Rawls's reference to 'free and equal persons' because that makes clear the indispensable condition under which principles that all would agree (Kantian moral law) can be identified.

Calling people autonomous may mean that they are in charge of their own lives or that they have the capacity for autonomy. Autonomy as an achievement is the ideal which endows the capacity with value.[21] In the achievement sense, autonomy is something each of us has to realize through her own choices. As Raz has observed others cannot make my autonomous choices for me.[22] Nevertheless autonomy as an achievement is dependent on the existence of those conditions necessary to secure it as a capacity. That is why those who make autonomy the basis of political morality tend to focus on the prerequisites of autonomy as a capacity. From within this view, though one cannot make another person autonomous, one can and must help to provide the conditions which enable her to make herself autonomous, as long as that does not prejudice one's own autonomy. To the extent that these conditions are met people think of themselves and of one other as free to determine the course of their own lives. They enjoy what we saw Kant referring to earlier in our discussion as positive freedom.

Now the conditions of autonomy are determinable by reference to various aspects of freedom to determine what is worthwhile in life. Freedom as autonomy in the capacity sense is the condition one is in when various component conditions for autonomous life are met. The account of these conditions that I follow has been provided by Raz. Among them some relate to certain mental and physical abilities of individuals and some to the social environment. The case for various individual attributes is fairly obvious.

If a person is to be maker or authoi of his own life then he must have the mental abilities to form intentions of a sufficiently complex kind,

[21] Cf. Raz, *The Morality of Freedom*, 372.
[22] Ibid. 407.

and plan their execution. These include minimum rationality, the ability to comprehend the means required to realize his goals, the mental faculties necessary to plan actions, etc.[23]

These attributes include 'the power to absorb, remember, and use information,' emotional and imaginative make-up', 'health', and 'physical abilities and skills', and character traits such as 'stability, loyalty, and the ability to form personal attachments and to maintain intimate relationships'.[24]

The social environment for autonomy must be one in which a person can actually use her mental faculties to pick what life to have. There must therefore be an adequate range of options from which to pick. And, finally, a person's choice must be free from coercion or manipulation by others. She must have independence. With this account of the conditions of autonomy to hand the determination of autonomy-based duties should be fairly straightforward. The duty of non-interference is un-contentious. But is there more one must do to contribute to the autonomy of others than leave them alone? Raz certainly thinks so. He believes that if autonomy is the basis for duties of non-interference then it yields other duties as well. These fall into two categories: duties to help create 'the inner capacities required for the conduct of an autonomous life'; and duties concerned with 'the creation of an adequate range of options' from which to choose what life to have.[25] But Raz's argument for this is somewhat understated. 'Every reason of autonomy which leads to the duties of non-interference would lead to other duties as well, unless, of course, it is counteracted by conflicting reasons.'[26]

But positive duties (and their correlative rights) are too controversial for such a brisk defence. After all, some subscribers to autonomy recognize only negative duties of non-interference. They say that so-called positive duties interfere with individual freedom or with libertarian self-ownership by coercing people to employ their talents and powers to provide services for others.

This long-running dispute concerning the scope and content of autonomy-based rights and duties should be settled by reference to principles that people would adopt as free and

---

[23] Ibid. 373.   [24] Ibid. 408.
[25] Ibid.   [26] Ibid.

equal persons. To work out those principles requires a more detailed account of how people think of themselves when they think of themselves as free to author their own lives. Before turning to that account in the next section it may be useful to signal the direction of my overall argument. For the purpose of constructing political theory the significance of attending to various aspects of freedom (that is to say, of autonomy as a capacity), as Rawls has shown us, is that these aspects can be given the key role in setting up a procedure to assess the merits of rival theories, of justice, for example, as in the case of Rawls's own argument, or of the liberties and constraints distributed by justice, as in the case of the argument I am developing. Of course, I am referring only to liberal political theory. Other theories have different strategies of argument.

5.5. AUTONOMY AS PERSONAL AND POLITICAL

The basic account of the ways in which citizens of an autonomy-based democracy view themselves as free is due to Rawls. I adapt his account to bring aspects of political as well as personal freedom into view. In Rawls's account citizens regard themselves as free in three ways: as self-originating sources of valid claims, as having moral independence, and as capable of taking responsibility for ends. I propose to treat these three aspects as referring to personal freedom though, of course, they are involved also in political freedom. I shall supplement Rawls's account by saying that citizens regard themselves as politically free in that they think of one another as equally entitled to participate in the choice of governments, as equally capable of giving justice, and as equally capable of taking responsibility for their own autonomy.[27]

(i) *Personal freedom*

If individuals are to be free to fashion their own lives they must regard one another as having a moral personality which is

---

[27] For the idea that autonomy is both personal and political I am indebted to the engaging discussion of autonomy in the context of Machiavelli's political thought in Hanna Fenichel Pitkin, *Fortune is a Woman*, chs. 1, 12.

entitled to consideration prior to any claims on them deriving from their social roles or self-assumed obligations. In the language developed by Rawls this is the thought of the person as 'a self-originating source of claims'.[28] The idea of moral personality as itself a source of claims is brought out by Rawls in a contrast with the case of slaves. Human beings who are slaves are not counted as sources of claims. 'Laws that prohibit the abuse and maltreatment of slaves are not founded on claims made by slaves on their own behalf, but on claims originating either from slaveholders, or from the general interests of society (which does not include the interests of slaves).'[29] Slaves are not recognized as rightful sources of claims because they are not recognized as moral personalities at all. Also under this aspect of freedom as self-origination fall claims that individuals regard as based on the requirements of their conception of the good, which may be founded in a religious, or a philosophical, or a moral doctrine.[30]

A second aspect of freedom picked out by Rawls is that individuals who are in charge of their own lives recognize one another as having the moral power to have a conception of the good. This means that they view themselves as free not only to espouse a particular conception of the good but to revise and change it with reason.[31] Thus as free persons individuals conceive of themselves as independent from and not identified with any particular conception of the good or doctrine of ends. They regard their moral power to form, to revise, and pursue a conception of the good as the basis of their entitlements. We can see why this is an aspect of freedom by contrast with the case of members of a society in which entitlements are based on religious affiliations, social class, and so forth.[32]

Rawls mentions responsibility for ends as the third aspect of freedom. This is the idea that, within a framework of just institutions and fair distribution of resources, people are capable of adjusting their aims and aspirations to what they can reasonably hope to provide for, and of restricting their claims in

---

[28] Cf. Rawls, 'Kantian Constructivism in Moral Theory', 543.
[29] Rawls, 'Justice and Fairness: Political not Metaphysical', 243.
[30] Ibid. 242.
[31] Rawls, 'Kantian Constructivism', 544, and 'Justice as Fairness', 240.
[32] Rawls, 'Justice as Fairness', 241.

subjects of justice to certain kinds of things.[33] Thus, given a fair distribution of resources, people are regarded as capable of taking responsibility for such things as whether they cultivate expensive tastes or ambitions bearing in mind the impact these have on their available resources. And the responsible pursuit of claims authorized by a conception of the good may also require them to be adjusted or restricted to accommodate conflicting claims. For example, the claims deriving from some religious conceptions of the good have to be moderated by a principle of toleration in contemporary democracies, even though that requires one tradition to acknowledge that beliefs and practices it thinks morally wrong, even reprehensible, are valid for another. Thus the doctrine of responsibility for ends applies to traditions as well as individuals for the purpose of constructing a free society.

(ii) *Political freedom*

Citizens who are free to make their own lives are free to participate in their own government. As free persons they think of themselves as having the capacity to rule themselves. Thus they are politically free as members of a polity that is internally self-governing. Such a polity recognizes rights of democratic participation in the political activity by which decisions for the whole community are made. This aspect of political freedom as self-government contrasts with alien rule as well as home rule by the wise and the holy, or by a dictator. In these cases subjects of political power are politically passive. There is no public recognition of them as persons with the capacity for citizenship—'to share in the civic life of ruling and being ruled in turn' as the classic Aristotelian definition has it.[34]

A second aspect of political freedom is that citizens regard themselves as able to give justice to each other. This means that they are able to form and live under collective principles that establish their civic identity as distinct from the 'non-civic' identity that their religious, philosophical, or moral convictions help to constitute. Citizens are politically free with respect to justice in that their civic status (and the rights and duties that go

[33] Rawls, 'Kantian Constructivism', 545.
[34] Aristotle, *The Politics*, bk. 3, ch. 1, pp. 95, 134.

with it) is regarded as independent of which conception of the good they hold, which religious affiliation, if any, which political convictions, and so on. The aspect of freedom as political independence is lacking in political systems in which claims founded on religious convictions about ends, or other conceptions of the good, are made part of the law. Legal enforcement of duties derived from a doctrine of ends destroys options available to those who do not adhere to that doctrine but to some alternative.

A third respect in which citizens view themselves as politically free is that they regard themselves as responsible for putting the value of autonomy into their own lives. The idea is this. Given background institutions designed to empower people to author their own lives citizens are treated as capable of deciding for themselves what degree of autonomy they want. They are free to base their lives on social forms such as parenthood or the way of life of a religious order, where autonomy is limited in various ways. They are also free to engage in activities thought to be depraved or a waste of their talents, to put their health at risk by smoking and drinking, to live lives of mindless inactivity, and so on. The fact that some people think those activities undermine autonomy is not a reason for governments to act to ban or discourage them. For, the merits of such activities are moral matters for each person to decide not for one group (the powerful) to decide for everyone. The point is that respect for autonomy is not consistent with governments deciding moral issues on behalf of citizens. Such decision-making affronts the dignity of citizens as moral persons. And it distorts political relationships by misconceiving political power as parental power.[35]

5.6. THE INTERPLAY OF PERSONAL AND POLITICAL AUTONOMY

I have analysed the capacity for autonomy understood as positive freedom into various aspects of personal and political freedom. In this section I want to indicate how reference to both

[35] Cf. John Locke, *Two Treatises*, ii., sect. 174, p. 431.

categories of freedom corrects certain misunderstandings of autonomy. These tend to arise when one set of aspects is exaggerated as the whole of positive freedom. I shall deal with just two cases.

Take first the aspects of personal freedom. These may be regarded as part of a conception of the person in which autonomous individuals have no ends or attachments outside themselves. Within this view individuals are theorized as rationally self-interested utility-maximizers whose political relationships are instrumental means of dealing with underlying competition and conflict and represent no deeper social ties than those required by calculated self-interest. I shall refer to this view as moral individualism.[36] If this view is correct then autonomy-based politics is inherently unstable, a factor that powerfully compromises liberal political theory. For if self-interest alone moves autonomous agents they cannot sustain any political obligation or loyalty to the polity more commanding than what is in the self-interest of each. Whenever there is a conflict between self-interest and political obligation the former cannot be rationally forsworn. This means that political agreements are hostage to shifts in individual interests and the distribution of power.

Now reference to political freedom helps to undermine the view of autonomy as moral individualism. It is constitutive of the autonomous life that it is lived in political conditions that are free. So political participation, just institutions, and independence of state paternalism are valuable to individuals not merely as a means to autonomy, but as an intrinsic part of what autonomy is. The ideal of autonomy entails, therefore, that citizens conceive themselves as capable of identifying with and valuing political freedom as an intrinsic good. That is to say, each person views herself as having the capacity to be moved by an autonomy interest of the self that transcends mere interest in self. Given that political freedoms are constituents of autonomy it follows that an autonomy-based politics is not inherently

---

[36] Raz uses 'moral individualism' to refer to the view that collective goods have only instrumental value and never any intrinsic value of their own. See Raz, *The Morality of Freedom*, 206. Others use the phrase to express the idea that the value of everything can be explained by its value in the lives of individuals (rather than requiring reference to collective entities such as states, nations, and the like).

unstable. On the contrary, since autonomy is an interest that is common to all citizens as moral persons there is the greatest assurance possible of political loyalty and stability.

Another familiar misunderstanding of the ideal of autonomy comes from focusing too much on the political freedoms. In keeping with the liberal instinct to limit the powers of government, the upholding of the political freedoms may be thought to exhaust the responsibilities of governments with respect to providing for individual autonomy. The argument is for state non-intervention in the cultural market-place of possible ways of life on the ground that intervention encourages some and discourages other ways of life in violation of people's autonomy.[37] If this argument is sound the social environment of acceptable options from which a person can choose her life is regarded as the product of a sort of cultural free-market outside of state control. Autonomy is viewed as an ideal that can be sustained outside of political society provided only that the state secures individuals from mutual interference. The difficulty here is that a cultural free-market is incapable of ensuring the existence of the cultural structure that provides a diversity of valuable ways of life.[38] Many cherished aspects of our culture currently depend for their viability on government action. If that public support were to be withdrawn there would be no assurance that the cultural market-place would sustain a rich diversity of valuable possibilities of choice. The non-interventionist liberal state is therefore unable to protect the cultural environment necessary for autonomy. Yet liberals seem bound by their commitment to autonomy to favour non-intervention. How is this impasse to be sorted out? Here the requirements of personal freedom must be brought into play to fix ideas.

Reference to personal freedom reminds us of the existence of duties to protect the cultural structure that supports pluralism. For, there can be no meaningful choice of a worthwhile life without an adequate range of worthwhile options and resources for their evaluation.[39] The autonomy-based state must therefore

[37] See W. Cragg, 'Two Concepts of Community or Moral Theory and Canadian Culture', 47.
[38] See Raz, *The Morality of Freedom*, 162.
[39] See Ronald Dworkin, *A Matter of Principle*, 229–32 on the importance of intellectual and artistic cultural activities for developing the capacity to imagine conceptions of the good life.

ensure an adequate range of options and protect the cultural activities by which they can be developed, renewed, and appreciated. So much must be said in favour of interventionism. But what exactly is required of the state acting to ensure an adequate range of options? One possibility is that the state should evaluate various options and promote those it thinks good. This conflicts with the anti-paternalist strand of personal freedom which insists that judgements of value are matters for individuals themselves and not for the state to make on their behalf. Another possibility is that the state acts to support an adequate range of options but not to promote particular options. The evaluation of these is treated as a matter for people in the cultural market-place of civil society and not a matter for politics. One mechanism for state support which exemplifies this approach is the provision of tax incentives to individuals who make cultural contributions in accordance with their own conceptions of the good.[40] The market-place of ideals is thus enriched without political endorsement of particular ideals. Whether these ideals are satisfying or not is left open for assessment by citizens themselves examining their merits and testing them practically in what J. S. Mill calls 'experiments in living'.[41]

5.7. THE GOOD OF AUTONOMY

While autonomy is a human good for a wide range of views about the elements of the good life, that fact alone does not show why it should be made the basis of that part of morality— political morality—where force or the threat of force is used to secure a moral value. Why is autonomy singled out from other human goods for special protection by a scheme of rights?

I think that the most compelling answer is that people's most vital human interest is in living meaningful lives.[42] This interest cannot be secured while they are at risk of slavery, social subordination, repression, persecution, and grinding poverty,

---

[40] A similar point is made in Will Kymlicka, *Liberalism, Community, and Culture*, 81. See also Dworkin, *A Matter of Principle*, ch. 11.
[41] J. S. Mill, *On Liberty*, 185.
[42] Cf. Nozick, *Anarchy, State, and Utopia*, 50.

conditions that history shows to be the lot of many in societies which do not recognize the value of individual freedom. So it is rational for people to want to develop the mental capacities and social environment necessary to living independent lives. Since what is at stake is the proper distribution of human freedom we have here matters of justice and rights, the province of political morality.

Autonomy is imperfectly realized in practice in the culture and political institutions of liberal democracies. Nevertheless, as Raz has pointed out, the value of autonomy is a fact of life.[43] People fare well in our society if they are autonomous and they fare badly if they are not. In these circumstances a government which fails to support autonomy fails to provide its citizens with the opportunity for meaningful life. Hence, governments in liberal democracies have special reason to acknowledge the principle of autonomy as the basis of political action.

I have been arguing that autonomy is the proper basis of political morality because of people's interests in living meaningful lives. Autonomy can also be defended because of its social role in helping to resolve the political impasse between the ideals of liberty and equality in Western democratic regimes. We have an ideal of democratic equality, yet the existence of poverty, the fact that the poor do not enjoy the kind of independent lives on which their equal citizenship is predicated, the unequal worth of democratic liberties to differently situated citizens, combine to create a general problem of instituting both liberty and equality. As Rawls points out, we disagree on the way basic institutions should be arranged if they are to implement the various liberties of citizens and meet the claims of equal citizenship.[44] And the context in which that disagreement takes place is one of more radical and politically intractable disagreements in philosophy, religion, and ethics.

If we are to deal with the fundamental problems of justice in our political culture we have to find some point of contact with each other on the basis of which we can agree common principles of right. This point of contact is a viewpoint on ourselves that is already part of our political tradition, namely, the view of ourselves as citizens who are morally autonomous.

[43] Raz, *The Morality of Freedom*, 304.
[44] Rawls, 'Justice as Fairness', 227.

It is one that has grown historically as the most comprehensive associative ideal that people of different ethical traditions can willingly implement in a common political life. If we can elaborate that ideal in a way that settles the internal problems of our political tradition we will have another powerful reason for singling out autonomy for special political concern.

In sum, autonomy is properly singled out for special protection by rights for three related reasons. It is the condition for meaningful life for beings liable to subjection. It is the condition for well-being for members of that kind of society where to prosper one must be autonomous. And it has a practical social role as uniting the members of a pluralist democracy on its fundamental institutions.

Of course, autonomy lends itself to playing a central role in a teleological theory as the good to be maximized no less than in a deontological theory as the boundary of all practical deliberation about the good. A theory of rights is the outcome of a decision against the primacy of teleological theory in political morality. For rights theory the notion of the right is set ahead of the notion of the good, in order to capture the separateness and plurality of persons. The idea is that there are certain deontological restrictions on how people may treat each other, certain forms of treatment that it is wrong even to consider. Your right to be free, for example, excludes from the outset any thought that you could be enslaved if that contributed to the cultivation of philosophical or artistic excellence in our society.

It is within this deontological outlook that autonomy is selected as the idea around which thought of rights is organized. So my remarks about autonomy being 'honoured', 'regarded', 'protected', and the like are made within an outlook that is already deontological. The argument between teleologists and deontologists is left aside for the purpose of working out various aspects of a (deontological) rights view.

It should be observed that the project of finding a moral basis for rights is part of a certain view about the structure of a rights theory. Roughly, this is the view that rights theory is not rights-based. In other words, rights are not basic theoretical items, but are instruments for the protection of basic values. According to this view our thinking about rights involves thought of (1) constraints on action in the service of (2) certain values held to

justify constraints, and (3) empirical beliefs about the fate of
those values with and without the constraints. Thus our
thinking about a particular right, say the right to freedom of
expression, involves the thought of: (1) constraints on actions
that would fetter freedom of expression; (2) freedom of
expression as being itself, or being necessary to, a basic value;
(3) the particular constraints proposed by the right—for example,
people may not be stopped from expressing political opinions,
but they may be stopped from slandering or libelling their
neighbours.[45]

5.8. OUR SENSE OF AUTONOMY

The principles or rules which give content to personal and
political autonomy are available to us in two ways. Our
historical attempts to define them are formulated in a variety of
global and regional declarations and conventions, such as the
Universal Declaration of Human Rights, the *Council of Europe
Convention for the Protection of Human Rights and Fundamental
Freedoms*, and the *African Charter on Human and People's Rights*.
The code of rights recognized in international law represents
our current though revisable judgements about the incidents of
autonomy. In them personal autonomy is characteristically
guaranteed in articles defending life, freedom from torture and
slavery, privacy, freedoms of expression, religion, and association. Political autonomy is guaranteed by rights of self-
determination, political participation, and the like.[46]
It is noteworthy that the systems of rights in the various
documents cannot be interpreted as self-ownership rights. A
list, such as A. M. Honoré's introduced in Chapter 2, of the
incidents of ownership, defines a system of economic freedoms
which is one specification of a right to private property, but it
does not correlate with the wide range of personal and political
claims, immunities and so on, which each document includes in
addition to any right to property.[47] These are more properly

[45] Here I follow T. M. Scanlon for the most part. See Scanlon, 'Rights,
Goals, and Fairness'.
[46] See Paul Sieghart, *The Lawful Rights of Mankind*, for a very useful analysis
and brief reproduction of basic documents of the international legal code.
[47] See A. M. Honoré, 'Ownership'.

interpreted as our current expressions of what the principle of autonomy requires of institutional practices. And they all specify political powers which are at the disposal of individuals against the state as well as of states against each other. So they are the political rights of citizens and the form they have is the form that citizenship takes for us. They outline the frameworks within which we may hammer out the details of the specific liberty–constraint systems of municipal law.

Of course, such frameworks may be flawed. They may be internally incoherent, or in debt to an underlying philosophy which is morally flawed or unsuited to the understanding of rights needed in pluralist democracies.[48] So while the historical documents that we acknowledge may be taken to express our sense of autonomy and justice we still feel the need for explanation and justification of the frameworks they provide. There is need of a way of sorting out better from worse ones, of critically assessing the detail of one or another formulation and of revising the formulations themselves. So we need a second way of arriving at the principles we take to define autonomy, one which follows their justificatory story. Although autonomy may be very imperfectly realized in the real world we can see what it would be like to meet it, and so what to aim for, by constructing an intellectual model which traces the connections between autonomy and its most evident general requirements. What happens in the model world helps explain the pull of much traditional rhetoric about rights and helps us to revise and redefine, where necessary, our various convictions and documentary formulations of rights. The next two chapters are devoted to the justificatory task.

5.9. CONCLUSION

Although little has been said yet about the detail of the principles or rules that give content to personal and political

---

[48] I take it that the objections of Nozick and Rawls to utilitarianism as incompatible with respect for the separateness of persons put that doctrine into the 'morally flawed' category while orthodox natural law theories fall into the 'unsuited to pluralist democracy' category. See Nozick, *Anarchy, State, and Utopia*, 33; Rawls, *A Theory of Justice*, 3–4; and my remarks on natural law and natural rights in Ch. 1.

freedom, if we take this complex capacity for autonomy to be what rights secure, we have a powerful alternative to self-ownership for understanding the general character of rights. Specific questions about the validity and source of particular rights claims, about the adjustment of rights to each other and the good of the community as a whole, about the connection between rights and a theory of human good, and the existential status of rights are now capable of elucidation in terms of the interests of citizens as morally autonomous beings.

The distortions and difficulties we encountered with self-ownership arise from the fact that it neglects to specify an ideal of the person under which a scheme of constraints is derived. The need for an ideal requires us to think in more detail about autonomy than is often done by theorists of rights. I have argued for a Kantian conception of autonomy which stresses the connection with self-imposed moral law. And I have suggested that autonomy is a complex ideal of positive freedom with personal and political aspects. The complexity suggests an interplay of personal and political aspects which operates to preclude their separate development in ways that undermine political allegiance or personal choice.

6

Constructing a Theory of Rights:
Ideal Conversations

The theory criticized in earlier chapters gives an account of
rights as properties of individuals. We have seen that the theory
fails to fit certain well-entrenched beliefs about what rights
people have. It denies welfare rights and is unsound on self-
determination. Its basic defect is that it fails to take seriously the
question of justifying its economic constitution to those who are
to live under it. So while paying lip-service to the value of
autonomy as the interest rights are to protect, the grounding of
self-ownership in autonomy is not sufficiently explained. No
satisfactory account is given of how various aspects of autonomy
are met by proprietary rights. Indeed the various aspects are not
brought into view. Chapter 5 sought to remedy the latter
omission by characterizing autonomy in a way that displays its
normative force and fits the central range of freedoms we
associate with democratic citizenship.

As I observed in the previous chapter the strategy of picking
on autonomy as the basis of rights is dictated by our political
interest in finding a shared starting point for constructing
political arrangements for citizens who have diverse moral
traditions and substantive ideals of human flourishing.
Autonomy as the basis of consensual rights in a pluralist
democracy is a locus of needs which we accept as good reasons
for making claims on each other. Its elaboration into the various
aspects of personal and political freedom should allow us to sort
out what kinds of claims it is appropriate to make and how
conflicting claims are to be adjudicated. With this in mind we
may say that to have a right is to have a justification founded in
autonomy for holding others to be under a duty to secure,

maintain, or respect the object of that right. And we may expect claims to rights to be determinable by reference to the background principles that express autonomy. The burden of theory construction is to find these principles. The next three chapters are devoted to that task.

6.2. DISCOURSE AND CONTRACT

How do we get from autonomy to an appropriate scheme of rights? The main task of this chapter and the one that follows is to develop a method for assessing proposed schemes. Justification of a particular scheme is then a matter of showing that it meets the standards of assessment laid down better than whatever rival is in the running. That is not to say that the most acceptable scheme at a particular time is final. Its current ranking is relative to available schemes, not to all the possible, but unknown, ones that might be devised. One further point about justification needs to be introduced. The most acceptable scheme is the one that we are driven to by rational deliberation. So we should see it as the outcome of a process of reflection that can be replicated by anyone who adopts the proposed standards of assessment. This must lead to an agreement in judgements that produces a definite solution to the problem of advancing autonomy interests, otherwise there is no meeting the wider aim of finding a scheme with normative political implications for all the members of a modern constitutional regime.

The method of assessment that I will be advancing in this chapter owes a great deal to the construction of conditions embodied in John Rawls's original position, a choice situation designed to model the set of acceptable restrictions we acknowledge as appropriate to the possibility of fair judgements about principles of justice.[1] However I think that the process of rational deliberation that leads to principles of right for self-governing beings is better represented as a social discourse than a social contract. That leads me to try for a definite outcome to deliberation through conditions adapted to the context of discourse. Debate and deliberation carried on within those

---

[1] John Rawls, *A Theory of Justice*, 17 ff.

conditions will be described as Ideal Discourse. And I shall require the conditions to be realizable so that none should disbar us, flesh and blood beings, from being able to engage in the discourse.[2] For reasons that will be given shortly deliberators observing the constraints of Ideal Discourse are not deprived of any information about their own conceptions of the good, social advantages, and the like. So if Ideal Discourse can produce a determinate conclusion on principles of right, it may meet a common criticism that Rawls's original position, in which the deliberators are denied such self-knowledge, is, for that reason, incoherent.[3]

While Rawls's original position seems to me to be one plausible system of conditions, considerations of kinship between the various ideas I am trying to bring together suggest that a more natural family results when autonomy is thought of as specified in principles concluded in an Ideal Discourse situation.

From the point of view of favouring a political over an economic understanding of rights, the language of discourse is superior to the language of contract for several reasons. The first is that contracts are, paradigmatically, exchange relationships in which goods and services are traded. In classical social contract theory people already own the resources they trade. This accounts for the traditional connection between contract theories and pre-existing rights and for the proprietary character of those 'natural' rights. Since we are not assuming that rights are underivable natural properties the notion of contract has associations that carry us in the wrong direction.

Discourse provides a more attractive and potentially applic-

---

[2] Cf. Joshua Cohen, 'Deliberation and Democratic Legitimacy' for an account of an ideal deliberative procedure which overlaps in part with mine although there are important differences in detail resulting from the way my account is formulated to reproduce a conception of autonomy.

[3] The most forceful statement of this objection is presented by Michael Sandel. He claims that the original position is one in which the person 'shorn of all contingently-given attributes, assumes a kind of supra-empirical status, essentially unencumbered, bounded in advance and given prior to its ends, a pure subject of agency and possession, ultimately thin'. This conception, Sandel argues 'cannot plausibly account for agency and self-reflection . . . we cannot coherently regard ourselves as the sort of beings the deontological ethic requires us to be'. See Sandel, *Liberalism and the Limits of Justice*, 94, 65. But see Rawls's reply 'Justice as Fairness: Political not Metaphysical', 239, n. 21.

able model than contract for arriving at agreements about non-economic matters including the foundations of political morality. As actual rather than hypothetical agents we have philosophical, moral, and religious beliefs which we do not regard as objects of barter or compromise. When we disagree about these, we resolve our disputes, if at all, only by tapping our deep Socratic conviction that through dialogue we may come to understand and correct each other, and thus arrive at reasonable agreements in judgements and, where necessary, agreements to differ.

The notion, implicit in contract, that we come to agreements by striking mutually advantageous bargains is inappropriate for the context of morality. While it is indeed true that our concern to secure our conception of the good has an important bearing on what we could reasonably accept as norms of political morality, it does not follow that political morality is to be constructed as the mere instrument of personal morality.[4] Reasonable agreement to a political morality incorporates a direct appeal to an ideal of the person in which the concern to give justice is as basic as the concern for our own good. In that ideal justice does not arise as a means to something else. It is an independent end of moral personality.

Second, discourse is a condition of autonomy. Autonomous authorship of one's life is, to some degree at least, the product of reflective deliberation. That is not a purely private affair. It necessarily takes into account, even though it is not made to depend on, the judgements of others on the substance of a worthwhile life. And while an autonomous person is under no duty to account to another for her chosen life, she nevertheless can provide reasons for holding her actions to be choice-worthy. Reasons are of critical importance for an individual whose judgement is the final authority in moral matters. When our judgement conflicts with that of others we are saved from mere pigheadedness by being able to hold on to it as adequately justified even though others fail to accept our reasons. Indeed the desire for rational justification of all moral judgements is at the root of the unwillingness to conform to received opinions

---

[4] For the view that the desire for reasonable agreement, not the pursuit of mutual advantage, is what morality is about see T. M. Scanlon, 'Contractualism and Utilitarianism'.

that characterizes autonomy. The context of reason-examining and reason-giving that is presupposed by autonomy is one of conversation or dialogue.

Finally, contracts cannot yield political consensus independently of discursive activities. The contractual model of agreement is, therefore, at least limited and perhaps wholly redundant. A contract, we may say, is a voluntary agreement made by people for mutual benefit. Assuming commonly accepted background conditions are met, such as absence of duress and deception, or an attempt to use contract to transform free relationships into bondage, the moral force of a contract comes from its being chosen or willed. On a fundamentalist interpretation of political voluntarism this means that people's choices are to be honoured, whatever they turn out to be. However, no abiding consensus can be expected from a multitude of acts of will unless they are constrained to follow very definite paths. So contract theory has typically insisted that individual acts of will be rational.[5] This transforms a merely volitional into a cognitive agreement and argues for a more discursive understanding of contract than a choice or will theory offers. If what is proposed for agreement is adopted for reasons that all understand and accept, the presupposition of contract is a dialogue in which terms are tested in the light of reasons. Agreeing a proposal then, is more a matter of assenting to it as the conclusion of a line of reasoning than of just choosing it.[6]

In so far as there is any work left for the notion of contract it is as giving effect to those discursively generated agreements in judgements that we describe as a rational consensus. That is, assuming that the question of what is right (in all the circumstances) is settled by dialogue, we may wish to represent discussants as agreeing to be bound by what is right in a final act that connects rational deliberation with implementation. We may suppose that they agree with each other to abide by the conclusions of their discussion.[7] This is a much more limited role for contract than the supposition that it generates norms. And it might be wholly redundant if the connection can be built

---

[5] See Michael Lessnoff, *Social Contract*, 7.
[6] See Sandel, *Liberalism and the Limits of Justice*, 129–30 for a useful discussion of different senses of 'agreement'.
[7] Ibid. 130 for much the same point.

into a dialogue situation by assuming that debate and the attempt to find shared norms is motivated directly by practical problems and is therefore a practical discourse, the outcome of which is relevant action.

One important consequence of this line of thought is that discourse can produce a more stable consensus than contract. That is because the primary aim of discourse is to justify beliefs or values, not to produce mutually advantageous agreements. Discourse taps a moral motivation other than the desire to advance one's own interest. That is the desire to be the sort of person who lives by beliefs that are sound and values that are worthwhile. That desire moves people to acknowledge the propriety of norms accepted on the best available reasons. As T. M. Scanlon has described this idea of moral motivation it is 'the desire to be able to justify one's actions to others on grounds they could not reasonably reject'.[8] So, while a discursively produced consensus is socially revisable in the light of greater experience, its stability is not internally threatened by changes in individual self-interest, or free-rider problems.

The concern for justifiable beliefs and values seems a much more controversial motivation than concern to advance one's own interests. So it may be objected that it is too strong to figure among the premises of a way of thinking that has the political purpose of producing a theory of moral rights for a pluralist regime. However, the desire to justify actions, principles, or institutional authority on grounds one takes to be acceptable in one's discourse community is in fact strong and widespread.[9] It is the cultural presupposition acknowledged by political authorities in their justifications of actions and arrangements ranging from shooting protesters in the streets to raising taxes for welfare. It is acknowledged by individuals in their refusal to simply conform to received moral opinion and their constant (if fallible) discriminations between bogus and sound justifications for their own and other's standards. So the basic idea of the approach I shall be using is that rights are founded in a process of deliberation that may be represented as a social discourse. The initial task of this approach is to develop ground rules

---

[8] Scanlon, 'Contractualism', 116.
[9] A similar point is made by Brian Barry, *Theories of Justice*, 284.

which regulate this communal dialogue so that it is free from distortion and produces determinate results.

The method I use develops the ground rules as implications of the ideal of autonomy as I have described it in the previous chapter. By way of clarifying the rationale for this methodology and acknowledging intellectual debts and disagreements I want first to sketch relevant parts of the work of a number of outstanding contributors to the development of a discursive model of political legitimacy. These are Jürgen Habermas, Charles Larmore, and Bruce Ackerman. My main aim is to show that the norms of rational political conversation that they construct incorporate the liberal ideal of persons as autonomous. It comes as no surprise then that the discursive constraints that I generate from autonomy in Chapter 7 are not dissimilar to those to be found in the work of these writers, particularly that of Habermas and Ackerman. The merit of my approach is that it is explicit about the implication of autonomy in political liberalism. It thus forces political liberals to face the question of whether to hold their ideal of the person as part of any ideal of a worthwhile life for human beings or in a more limited way as a political ideal for citizens of modern democracies.[10]

6.3. HABERMAS ON IDEAL SPEECH

One of Habermas's main aims has been to challenge the positivist claim that moral norms cannot be rationally defended and are properly interpreted as mere expressions of preference. He insists that a central element in the meaning of norms is the idea that they ought to be followed.[11] So whenever we put forward a normative claim we are setting up a standard to be followed. But something can be a standard only if those for whom it is to be one can assent to the reasons in its favour. When we make a normative claim we imply that our reasons for it are good enough to win the assent of others under ideal conditions of rational argument. This means that we envisage

---

[10] These alternatives are the positions of Joseph Raz and John Rawls respectively. See Raz, *The Morality of Freedom*; Rawls, 'Justice as Fairness'.

[11] Jürgen Habermas, *Legitimation Crisis*, 104.

the possibility of a 'discourse' in which claims are validated in rational argument.[12]

The idea that the vindication of norms requires a discourse is part of Habermas's general theory of the conditions required to fulfil the promise of rationality latent in speech in general. Habermas claims that the possibility of a discourse lies behind all speech which aims to be understood. Speech acts involve a number of validity claims which are normally taken for granted but are nevertheless open to challenge. Thus in any act of speaking a speaker claims: (1) that what is said is intelligible— that is to say, it makes sense in terms of the syntactical and other rules of the relevant natural language; (2) that the propositional content of what is said is true—in other words, whatever is said or presupposed to be the case is so; (3) that the speaker is truthful or sincere—that she does not intend to deceive the hearer; (4) that her speech act conforms to mutually recognized norms of what is appropriate in the situation—normative rightness (for example, congratulations rather than condolences at a wedding).[13]

A speaker may be challenged to make good on any of these four validity claims—intelligibility, truth, sincerity, and contextual propriety (normative rightness). Claims to intelligibility and sincerity are made good by appropriate action. A speaker may show that her utterance is intelligible by expressing it in a different way. She may show her trustworthiness in meeting commitments, keeping promises, and the like. And of course that may also be shown by how things turn out.[14] Claims to truth and contextual propriety require to be made good in a discourse. They are 'redeemed' according to Habermas, when a discursive consensus backs their supporting reasons as sound.

But the consensus projected as issuing from discourse is not any consensus however achieved. One forged by propaganda, deception, appeals to tradition, or the exercise of power could not be regarded as plausible tests of the soundness of beliefs or norms.[15] So the consensus implied in any claim we put forward with reasons must be one reached solely from consideration of

---

[12] Habermas, *Theory and Practice*, 17.
[13] Ibid. 18; and Habermas, *Communication and the Evolution of Society*, 3, 65–6, and ch. 1 *passim*.   [14] Ibid. 64.
[15] Habermas, *Theory and Practice*, 12, 17.

the strength of those reasons as assessed by their survival of criticism in substantial arguments.[16] This is a rational consensus and can issue from discursive argument if that can take place in circumstances in which disturbances to communication—ideological and socio-structural—are eliminated.[17] Such circumstances obtain in what Habermas calls an Ideal Speech Situation.[18] As Habermas characterizes this situation its features may be interpreted as flowing from the commitment to consensus involved in any claim proposed as rational. In effect, that commitment is to the idea that our best test of the soundness of reasons is that everyone standing in an Ideal Speech Situation would accept them.[19]

So the idea of a rational consensus is what structures the relationships of participants in Ideal Speech. These relationships are characterized by a number of features.

(1) equal freedom of expression: all participants have the same opportunity to make and criticize claims. This means that while there are no limits on the content of speech prejudices get addressed and criticized.[20]

(2) equal individuality: relations between participants are direct. Each represents her own view rather than having it mediated by another. Thus the separate existence or individuality of each is acknowledged.[21]

(3) equal power: all participants are related symmetrically with respect to power. This means that there is a complete absence of coercion or the threat of coercion. The only force is that of the better argument.[22] Consequently

(4) all motives except that of the co-operative search for truth are excluded.[23]

Although Habermas appears to think that there is only one notion of the conditions of Ideal Speech these conditions are, I think, better understood in a contextual way as norms of

[16] Habermas, *Legitimation Crisis*, 107–8.
[17] Habermas, 'Towards a Theory of Communicative Competence', 372.
[18] Ibid. See also Habermas, *Theory and Practice*, 18–19.
[19] For an instructive analysis and criticism of the Ideal Speech Situation idea see Philip Pettit, 'Habermas on Truth and Justice'.
[20] Habermas, *Theory and Practice*, 23; *Legitimation Crisis*, 108; 'Towards a Theory of Communicative Competence', 371.   [21] Ibid. 372.
[22] Habermas, *Legitimation Crisis*, 108.   [23] Ibid.

'modern consciousness' or 'our' way of thinking. There are two reasons for this suggestion. The first has to do with the nature of justification. The context of justification is disagreement over some claim or other. But for justification to begin it must proceed from a premiss that is shared by the parties to the disagreement. Now shared premisses and agreements on what counts as justification are a function of general views of the world and how to know it. These are given in historical traditions of thought and inquiry which are not universal and cannot furnish any transcendent notion of ideal conditions of justification. Ideal conditions are always connected with our historically conditioned beliefs about the way to justify claims. So it is implausible to suppose that there is only one set of ideal conditions.[24]

This point is reinforced by the second reason for suggesting a contextual understanding of ideal conditions of rational discourse. This is that Habermas's conditions describe a form of interaction that is possible and desirable if we conceive persons under the liberal ideal, that is, as capable of acting on principles they would adopt as free and equal human beings. The liberal ideal is embedded in the notion of a consensual justification of claims.[25] This notion requires the liberal motive introduced in the previous section in Scanlon's formulation, that is, the desire to live by principles that could not reasonably be rejected by people motivated by the 'desire to find principles which others similarly motivated could not reasonably reject'.[26] This motive is only intelligible given an interest in realizing the capacity for autonomy in the Kantian version, that is, the capacity to identify and live by principles that are self-imposable by a plurality. In the conditions of modern political societies—pluralism and the unacceptability of the autocratic use of state power—discourse aimed at reaching common political principles is unintelligible in the absence of the liberal motive. It therefore embeds a distinctive and controversial conception of the person as capable not merely of autonomy, but Kantian autonomy.

[24] See Charles Larmore, *Patterns of Moral Complexity*, 56–8 for a useful discussion of this point in relation to Habermas.
[25] I follow Pettit's interpretation here. See Pettit, 'Truth and Justice', 224; Habermas, *Legitimation Crisis*, 108.
[26] Scanlon, 'Contractualism and Utilitarianism', 116, n. 12.

6.4. LARMORE'S NEUTRAL JUSTIFICATION

The same point may be made about Charles Larmore's claim that his discursive justification of liberal political principles does not involve any commitment to the controversial liberal ideal of the person. Larmore proposes a 'neutral justification of political neutrality' which draws on Habermas for the idea of a 'universal norm of rational dialogue' on which, Larmore claims, political neutrality (prescinding in our politics from imposing controversial ideals of the good life) is based.[27] He argues that we have such a norm in the strategy of retreat to neutral ground that keeps a conversation going in the face of disagreement. He says that mutual respect calls us to try to solve problems on the basis of dialogue rather than the application of superior force. So when we are disagreed in certain beliefs we need to keep in contact through arguing on the basis of whatever beliefs are not in dispute. By bracketing the disputed beliefs and continuing to address each other out of shared beliefs we shift to neutral conversational ground in the hope of finding an angle that solves the problem at hand.[28] And, Larmore holds, retreat to neutral ground does not involve commitment to any liberal ideal of the person.[29] The defence of political neutrality is thus neutral with respect to all controversial ideals whether of the person or of the good life.

My disagreement with Larmore is over the possibility of neutral justification of political principles. I believe that his account of moral motivation is inadequate for establishing political principles and that a discursive justification of these requires the liberal motive identified by Scanlon. Larmore argues that the reason for favouring dialogue over violence or manipulation to establish political principles is 'the wish to show everyone *equal respect*'.[30] Equal respect is due to persons in virtue of their capacities to work out a coherent view of the world.[31] When another demands that we justify some action of

---

[27] Larmore, *Patterns of Moral Complexity*, 53.   [28] Ibid.
[29] Ibid. 55.   [30] Ibid. 61.
[31] Ibid. 64. John Baker has described this type of argument as the 'philosopher's idea of respect' and has raised important questions about the picture of moral reasoning it presupposes. See Baker, *Arguing for Equality*, 26–7, and 145–6.

ours which affects him he is recognizing that we have a perspective on the world in which the action presumably makes sense and is offering to discuss it rationally with us (of course, his perspective may differ from ours). The obligation of equal respect 'consists in our being obligated to treat another as he is treating us—to use his having a perspective on the world as a reason for discussing the merits of our action rationally with him'.[32] And equal respect is not dependent on whether people exercise their capacities 'autonomously . . . or through the uncritical acceptance of traditions and forms of life'.[33] Larmore thinks that equal respect is compatible with a wide variety of ideals of the good life including beliefs about hereditary rule. For, a hereditary ruling class could feel obligated to justify its fitness to rule to the other classes as some aristocrats have in the past.[34]

With these points I am in agreement given Larmore's notion of equal respect. But he appears to think that there is a single obligation of equal respect—to meet another's demand for a rational discussion of our beliefs or actions. This is because he usually focuses on conversational contexts in which the aim is to *understand* another's viewpoint, not necessarily to *agree* with it. I do not think that there is only one obligation of equal respect. This is because I do not think that all justification is a matter of reaching understanding. Understanding is sensitive to differences and to leaving things as they are. But with political principles one wants more than that others understand them (while, perhaps, rejecting those principles for themselves). One wants others to agree with them, at least, if one is a political liberal.

A conversation which has the aim of reaching agreement on political principles cannot reach a determinate conclusion if it is motivated solely by the desire for mutual understanding which Larmore's notion of equal respect captures. Assuming differences of viewpoints mutual understanding leaves things as they are. In a political conversation, therefore, agreement is possible only if the obligation of equal respect is taken to consist in each participant seeking principles which others can reasonably accept. Here we have the liberal motive and also, implicitly, the

---

[32] Larmore, *Patterns of Moral Complexity*, 64–5.
[33] Ibid. 65.   [34] Ibid. 66.

liberal capacity for autonomy from which the motive springs, namely, the capacity to identify and live by principles that anyone can consent to as a free and equal person.

I conclude that Larmore has not given us an account of motivation which will keep political conversation going between people who disagree about ideals of the good. But I do not regard the lack of a 'neutral' justification of liberal political principles as any great loss. For the purposes of my argument, the implication of the liberal ideal of the person in the institutions and legitimating discourse of modern democracies is sufficient reason for tracing out the discursive principles it generates. For the aim is to provide an account of the sense of a liberal theory of rights, not an all out vindication of liberal discourse.

6.5. ACKERMAN'S CONSTRAINED CONVERSATION

I turn now to that part of Bruce Ackerman's *Social Justice in the Liberal State* which deals with the norms of what he calls 'constrained conversation' or 'neutral dialogue'.[35] Ackerman claims that his theory does not incorporate the liberal ideal of the person, a claim I dispute.

Here is Ackerman's account of the basis and nature of neutral dialogue. (1) 'So long as we live, there can be no escape from the struggle for power.' (2) Power 'is never beyond challenge'.[36] When another challenges my existing holdings of resources it is tempting to suppress the challenger, especially if my power is extensive. But suppose instead that individuals were to justify distributions of scarce resources by reasoned argument. What would our social world look like? This is what a theory of distributive justice is supposed to tell us. Ackerman's argument is that the substantive principles of justice can be worked out once we develop the ground rules of a debate about power distributions in which all can participate. (3) The intent to defend holdings by meeting a question of legitimacy by reasoned argument instead of force leads to the first principle of debate which is termed *Rationality*.

[35] Bruce Ackerman, *Social Justice in the Liberal State*, 14.
[36] Ibid. 3.

> Whenever anybody questions the legitimacy of another's power, the power holder must respond not by suppressing the questioner but by giving a reason that explains why he is more entitled to the resource than the questioner is.[37]

(4) Rationality points to a social practice 'the dialogue engendered by the question of legitimacy' as 'the constituting matrix for any particular claim of right'.[38] (5) A second principle is *Consistency*.

> The reason advanced by a power-wielder on one occasion must not be inconsistent with the reasons he advanced to justify his other claims to power.[39]

Neither of the above principles places any substantive constraints on the claims that can be defended in a dialogue. The distinctive feature of Ackerman's method appears only with his third principle which is designed to capture the thesis (6): 'A power structure is illegitimate if it can be justified only through a conversation in which some person (or group) must assert that he is (or they are) the privileged moral authority.'[40] The principle is termed *Neutrality* and goes as follows:

> No reason is a good reason if it requires the power holder to assert:
> (a) that his conception of the good is better than that asserted by any of his fellow citizens, or
> (b) that, regardless of his conception of the good, he is intrinsically superior to one or more of his fellow citizens.[41]

These principles govern 'constrained conversation' or 'neutral dialogue'. At its simplest Ackerman's theory is that justice emerges from debate carried on under the rules of neutral dialogue. The details, which I leave aside, are a complex and ingenious defence of a liberal-democratic welfare state. Clearly then, much hangs on the strength of the reasons that back the crucial Neutrality principle.

For Ackerman any one of several paths can take us to Neutrality. One is a sceptical argument which denies that we can make out claims to moral knowledge. If that is our view we can never endorse one way of life as superior to another or make

---

[37] Ibid. 4.   [38] Ibid. 6.   [39] Ibid. 7.
[40] Ibid. 10–11.   [41] Ibid. 11.

distributions of resources that imply such endorsement. But Neutrality is not solely the province of moral sceptics. We might think that the discovery of moral truth requires that we be free to experiment in life without the interference of some moral authority. Or we might think that autonomous deliberation has a central place in human good and deny that people can be forced to be good. In either case Neutrality is 'made to order'. Finally, there is a pragmatic argument. Assuming that some of us know what the good is and think it can be enforced on others, there is the question of whether the right people will be the enforcers. 'People adept at gaining power are hardly known for their depth of moral insight; the very attempt to engross power corrupts.'[42]

There are clearly important correspondences between this account and the norms of Habermas's Ideal Speech Situation although Ackerman's argumentative route to the key principle of Neutrality is less grand than the argument from the exigencies of speech. But I shall not labour the correspondences or differences. The point I want to address is the self-interpretation Ackerman provides in a more recent defence of Neutrality when he writes: 'my method . . . does not commit me to any particular theory of "a moral person", Kantian or otherwise.'[43] Ackerman makes this claim to avoid the kind of criticism that Rawls attracted after his Dewey Lectures explanation that a particular conception of the person as free and equal grounds his scheme of primary goods and the priority of liberty over general welfare.[44] The criticism is that if one rests a proposed index and ranking of primary goods on such a controversial conception of the person then individuals who subscribe to other controversial conceptions of the person would have equivalent grounds for different schemes and rankings of primary goods. This defeats the aim of finding a determinate answer to the question of justice even in a liberal democratic society.

[42] Ackerman, *Social Justice*, 11–12.

[43] Ackerman, 'What is Neutral about Neutrality', 378.

[44] Primary goods are all-purpose means to living a life of one's own choosing (or developing and exercising one's moral powers to identify the good and the just). They comprise certain rights and liberties, opportunities, and powers, as well as income and wealth, and self-respect. See Rawls, *A Theory of Justice*, 90–5.

This criticism is a real problem for theories of justice and rights which defend their principles as requirements of autonomy. Why should someone who does not share that ideal of the person agree to live under the political principles it founds? Before addressing this problem I want to show that Ackerman's principle of Neutrality is no more free from commitment to the liberal ideal of the person than the principles of Habermas and Larmore set out in previous sections.

Consider how Ackerman proposes we deal with someone who disagrees with liberal judgements and demands to know why they are regarded as superior to his own.

The best way to counter this objection is to embrace it—for this may allow us to bring the questioner, through a dialectical process, to see that the concern for moral independence that motivates his initial question will . . . lead him to embrace Neutrality . . . Constrained conversations will come to seem the essential cultural foundation for each person's effort to make sense of the good in a way that does not impugn the like effort of his fellow communicants.[45]

This argument is too quick. First, it is not obvious that the demand for justification need be motivated by concern for moral independence (the claim each person makes to make sense of the good for herself) rather than, say, concern for truth. The questioner may simply want the liberal to demonstrate that the premisses of his judgements are true.[46] Second, even if the questioner is concerned with moral independence he may regard it as requiring a choice of ways of life from within a certain range. For example, he may think that moral independence may be adequately satisfied by tolerating a range of Christian ways of life, but not, say, Catholicism, and certainly not atheism. In this case his commitment will be to a limited pluralism rather than liberal neutrality. Third, the questioner may support moral independence but not as an overriding principle. He may regard moral independence as giving way before, for example, societal survival. Thus Patrick Devlin supported maximum individual freedom as long as it is consistent with the integrity of society.[47] On this basis he

---

[45] Ackerman, 'What is Neutral about Neutrality', 389.
[46] I am very indebted to John Baker for this point and clarification on other points in this paragraph.
[47] Patrick Devlin, 'Morals and the Criminal Law', 79.

defended the enforcement of a social morality which condemns homosexuality and prostitution. This illustrates how concern for moral independence is consistent with a substantive moral position contrary to the claim that moral independence must take us to liberal neutrality.

I suggest, therefore, that the move from moral independence to liberal neutrality that Ackerman wants to make requires a liberal understanding of the concern for moral independence or, at least, an acceptance that the concern will take liberal form in circumstances of moral pluralism. Given the arguments of the previous paragraph Neutrality is the 'essential cultural foundation' of moral independence only if two background conditions obtain. The first is that members of society have different, even incompatible conceptions of the good. The second is that their concern for moral independence is the concern that no one be constrained in her effort to make sense of the good by political principles she could not acknowledge from her own perspective. In the circumstances of the first condition the second requires an outlook that is already liberal. The condition requires toleration of opposing views and respect for them as embodying the normative judgement and choice (or moral personality) of their advocates. Most tellingly, it is premissed on a controversial liberal ideal of the moral person as concerned to act (politically) only on principles that no one could reasonably reject. I shall have more to say about the problems this raises in the next section. For now it suffices to sum up by saying that Ackerman's move to liberal neutrality presupposes a certain background setting which has a liberal ideal of the person latent within it.

This issue aside, I share Ackerman's discursive model of rights claims. Rights, he insists, are founded in communal dialogue brought about when we choose to settle competing power-claims by examining their justifying reasons rather than by force.

The Rationality principle supposes that rights have a reality only *after* people confront the fact of scarcity and begin to argue its normative implications. If you were completely confident that no one would ever question your control over X, you would never think of claiming a 'right' over it: you'd simply use it without a second thought. . . . Rights are not the kinds of things that grow on trees—to be plucked, when ripe, by an invisible hand. The only context in which a claim of right has a point is one where you anticipate the possibility of conversation with some potential competitor. Not that this conversation always in fact arises—brute force also remains a potent way of resolving disputes. Rights talk presupposes only the *conceptual* possibility of an alternative way of regulating the struggle for power—one where claims to scarce resources are established through a patterned cultural activity in which the question of legitimacy is countered by an effort at justification.[48]

Ackerman's approach makes rights non-mysterious. They are simply claims to power that have had their legitimacy established through a process of social dialogue. Moreover, it leads away from proclamations of rights as self-evident or intuitive, a common focus for charges of the obscurantism of rights-talk. Most important of all, it provides a way of understanding rights as social constructs rather than individual pre-social assets. This promises a possibility of affirming each person's autonomy without denying her dependence on others.[49] Following this approach, I shall argue that rights are developed to secure the undominated interdependence of autonomous beings.

6.6. POLITICAL LIBERALISM

In the Kantian interpretation which I favour, autonomy as a moral ideal requires that people should act in accordance with self-legislated principles they would adopt as members of a 'kingdom of ends', that is, a society where everyone is of equal worth and no one is a means to the ends of another. This is a thesis about the nature of morality and as such cannot enter into the foundations of a political liberalism dedicated to avoiding controversial philosophical, ethical, and religious doctrines. So how can autonomy be made the basis of a liberal theory of moral rights?

To answer this question I draw on Rawls's distinction between a 'comprehensive' religious, philosophical, or moral doctrine and a 'political' conception. A comprehensive doctrine involves an account of what is worthwhile in life and ideals of personal virtue and character which are to govern one's life overall.[50] A political conception has three elements. First it is a

---

[48] Ackerman, *Social Justice*, 5.   [49] Ibid. 345–7.
[50] Rawls, 'The Priority of Right and Ideas of the Good', 252.

moral conception worked out for a specific subject in response to a practical problem. In our case the subject is the basic structure of a constitutional democratic regime and the problem is that there is no shared conception of the good that can provide a publicly accepted basis for a theory of justice (or of rights).[51] The aim of a political conception of justice or of rights, therefore, is to serve as a basis for 'informed and willing political agreement between citizens viewed as free and equal persons'.[52] To secure this agreement we need the second element of a political conception. It has to be independent of controversial philosophical and religious and moral doctrines.[53] So it is presented as a reasonable conception for the basic structure alone, not for the whole of life.[54] Third, it is formulated not in terms of any comprehensive doctrine but in terms of certain fundamental intuitive ideas viewed as latent in the public political culture of a democratic society.[55] In terms of this distinction the ideal of autonomy may be viewed in two ways. As part of a comprehensive moral doctrine it is a substantive moral ideal which governs all parts of one's life. As a political conception autonomy is presented as a principle governing the basic institutions of a constitutional democracy. The idea is to provide a basis for civil peace and co-operation among people who differ in their views of what makes life worthwhile but who are also prepared to respect each other as normatively engaged in making sense of the good. In this political role autonomy is presented as a basis of informed and willing political agreement between citizens, not as a moral ideal of the person. Thus, while the state is obliged to provide the conditions of autonomous life, this is so people can live the lives they choose, this being the condition under which they will voluntarily submit to a common political authority.

So the political conception meets the liberal concern for political neutrality by prescinding from imposing autonomy as a perfectionist ideal of the person. That is to say, no reasons drawn from the thought that autonomy provides the best ideal of the person can form any part of the justification for political arrangements or legislation. The state cannot attempt to

51 Rawls, 'Justice as Fairness', 224–5. 52 Ibid. 230. 53 Ibid.
54 Rawls, 'The Priority of Right', 252. 55 Ibid.

maximize autonomy, or to channel autonomous choice between only those options that are worthwhile. Accordingly, the reasons a state or legislature offers for its arrangements and policies must be drawn only from autonomy as developed for the purpose of a political conception. This is a conception developed for, and confined to, the political aspect of people's lives. So although autonomy is a moral ideal of the person it functions in the political realm to generate and systematize a set of conditions which enable but do not prescribe autonomy in all the degrees which citizens may wish to enjoy it in their private lives.

A political conception stands or falls with the claim that it provides a basis of agreement between citizens. The political conception of autonomy is widely accepted in the public political culture of liberal democracies but it is certainly not universally so. Why should those who dispute the value of autonomy support a liberal public political order on that basis? There is a Hobbesian answer to this question but it is unsatisfactory. This answer commends the liberal political order as a *modus vivendi* which allows individuals to pursue their own good subject to certain limits which each takes to be in her interest given existing circumstances. The main problem with this is instability. Political arrangements become hostage to shifts in power distribution among citizens whose conditional allegiance allows them to withdraw their support when that is to their rational advantage.

Many liberals look to a moral ideal such as autonomy to provide a more enduring basis of agreement than prudent self-interest. But our anti-liberal disputant does not support autonomy as a perfectionist ideal of the person. Why then should she support it as a political ideal? The key to the answer to this question is that the political ideal allows for, and is indeed developed to make possible, a certain practice of political justification. This is a practice of justifying political claims to each other engaged in by citizens in recognition of their common equal membership of a political society. The practice is an aspect of democratic accountability in modern political cultures. And it is the context for the anti-liberal's demand for an explanation of the moral grounds for requiring her support for a liberal political order. The crucial point here is that the demand occurs against a background of common membership which requires the disputant no less than the liberal to think of justification as acceptability to the other. This was the missing context in Ackerman's argument for Neutrality which left it open to the criticisms made above. Of course, it is possible for the anti-liberal to dispute the claims of others (those with the wrong views) to common equal membership. When someone puts up a good case for that kind of anti-liberalism it will be time to deal with it.

The demand for justification and the practice it occurs within is premissed on a conception of persons as having the moral powers necessary to engage in a scheme of political co-operation justifiable to all who live under it. Rawls has identified these moral powers as a capacity for a sense of justice and a capacity for a conception of the good. Of course, Rawls has connected the development and exercise of moral personality to being free and equal in what may be called a liberal sense. But the concept of moral personality itself is not identifiable with any one conception of it. This is what allows it to function as a point of contact between the liberal and the anti-liberal members of liberal democracies. The anti-liberal who questions liberal judgements thinks of herself as having the moral powers for a view of the good and of the just. Doubtless, she also thinks that these are best exercised and developed in the light of some alternative to the liberal conception of freedom and equality. Nevertheless, once she accepts the practice of justificatory political conversation she is committed to defending the moral powers (her own and others') which underlie it.

Such defence requires political arrangements developed to suit particular political memberships. In the case of liberal democracies these particular political memberships are characterized by a condition of moral pluralism. So justificatory political conversation is between citizens who must recognize and accept each other as adherents of different views of the good. In these circumstances the defence of moral powers leads to the liberal constitution. This provides the conditions of autonomy for those who take autonomy as their personal ideal at the same time as defending the moral powers and conversational partnership of those with conflicting ideals.

Clearly a political conception of justice or of rights cannot form the basis of voluntary political arrangements unless citizens are already somewhat liberal in their outlook. I have been arguing that such an outlook is embedded in the political culture of liberal democratic regimes as evidenced in the practice of mutual political justification that citizens sustain. I do not deny that some citizens are outside the democratic consensus— neo-Nazis, white supremacists, male-supremacists, certain religious fundamentalists, some rich people, terrorists. They do not acknowledge common equal membership of political society, equal respect, or conversational partnership. So they cannot be brought to agreement on the political conception. I do not believe that this poses a serious problem for the idea of a political conception. There is an uncontroversial moral basis for imposing the liberal political order on those who would disestablish it. This is simply individual self-preservation. If the disestablishers devise the political institutions individuals who disagree with them will not fare well. Such individuals will be persecuted, killed, imprisoned, subject to degradation, serf-dom, impoverishment, and discrimination. By contrast the liberal order preserves the lives and liberties of its enemies as well as its friends. And it does not have to be regarded in a perfectionist way to be clearly better for individual self-preservation than the anti-democratic orders of its enemies.

6.7. SUMMARY

In this chapter I have argued for four main conclusions. First, the way to think about how to get from some value or interest to rights to secure it is in terms of a process of social dialogue rather than social contract. Whether a claim can be made good as a right or not depends on the soundness of the reasons in its favour and that is a matter for discursive argument not contractual compromise or accommodation. Second, discursive argument, if it is to be a fair procedure for assessing claims must observe certain ground rules of discussion. They must be norms of rational discussion for people capable of thinking, judging, and giving precedence to the search for agreement over their more particular concerns. Third, the norms proposed by leading advocates of a discursive model of legitimation are not neutral norms of rational discussion. They embody a conception of persons as morally free and equal conversational partners. Indeed, it is hard to see how any scheme of norms could be developed in abstraction from a view of persons whose norms they are proposed to be. Fourth, I have argued that the liberal conception of the person which underlies what is variously called Ideal Discourse, Ideal Conversation, or Constrained Conversation may be held in a non-perfectionist way by a political conception of it as a basis for voluntary political agreement in pluralist democracies.

7

Constructing a Theory of Rights: Building in Conversational Constraints

Brian Barry has shown that the structure of original position theories is a function of the answers they give to two questions—the first about the information available to the parties, the second about their motivation. The first question is: 'Is the choice of principles to be made by people who are aware of their personal identities, or is it to be made from behind a veil of ignorance that denies the parties knowledge of at least that?' The second question is about the motivation of the parties who are choosing principles. 'We are to ask whether they are to pursue their own self-interest . . . or whether they are to seek agreement by trying to find principles that represent a reasonable accommodation of their conflicting interests.'[1]

My original position is an Ideal Discourse. Its structure is defined in relation to the first question by permitting the parties to know who they are as well as much else about the state of their society. There is no veil of ignorance as in Rawls's theory. I can do without the veil of ignorance because of my answer to the second question of structure. This is that the parties are assigned what has been referred to in Chapter 6 as the liberal motive. They are moved to seek agreement by trying to find principles that they could all reasonably accept. Given this answer, the veil of ignorance is not needed to get a determinate outcome from the deliberations in an original position. The liberal motive overcomes the stalemate that self-interest under full knowledge produces by steering the parties to principles that aim to accommodate each other's interests. The liberal motive also permits the contract idea to be interpreted as a

[1] Brian Barry, *Theories of Justice*, 320.

matter of reasonable discussion rather than as a bargaining game under conditions of uncertainty.

I do not think that one can borrow the liberal motive without also taking the deeper basis of respect which it presupposes. This is the capacity for autonomy. Parties in an original position try to accommodate each other out of respect for each other's capacity to shape their own life. A discourse may be concerned with the proper distribution of rights, liberties, and other resources. Then it is a discourse about justice. Other normative claims may also be the subjects of a discourse. Thus any claim to a right may precipitate a discourse. The question of what rights we have presupposes an answer to the question of what it is to have a right. Is it to have a property of some kind? Or is some other sense of dominion more appropriate? And the answer to this question invokes a conception of autonomy. The agenda for a discourse about rights, therefore, is to agree an understanding of the sense of claims of rights appropriate to the favoured conception of autonomy. Conclusions meet the following condition:

> A rights-claim is vindicated if and only if its justification is in terms of principles which anyone would accept as the result of following a process of reasoning constrained by autonomy-regarding norms of rational social discourse.

This abstract condition is given content by the norms, to be developed in this chapter, of autonomy-regarding discourse. The idea that conclusions must be such that 'anyone would accept' them is meant to guarantee the general agreement required if those conclusions are to have normative force for citizens generally. The idea may be expressed as a consensus test that principles establishing rights must pass if they are to be regarded as generally binding.

The idea of constraining reasoning by norms of 'rational' social discourse is meant to rule out acceptance of principles based on the dictates of those in power, or claims to privileged moral insight that are in principle unavailable to everyone. Also excluded are principles accepted on the basis of faith or belief in magic. These exclusions are built into the presumption of rational discussion as our relevant tradition of enquiry and discovery. That tradition holds to the idea of truth and goodness as rationality and so enquires into the best available reasons for beliefs. So rational discussion abstracts from all considerations of force and claims to advantage except the force of the better argument. And since the operative motive of participants is the desire to find principles that can serve as their shared specification of autonomy, the social and natural advantages which might incline people to make proposals favourable to their personal situations are corrected for.

Clearly, rational discussion of the kind projected is not even a possibility outside a tradition which values autonomy and democratic reason. Even then such discussion is threatened by self-deception, domination of one by another, and fraud. So there is reason to regard rational social discourse as an ideal, only imperfectly realized in the actual world. We have, therefore, to try to work out what such discourse would conclude as principles for the general political framework, if the distorting effects of existing power arrangements and partialities were eliminated.

7.2. CAN IDEAL DISCOURSE BIND?

We might be asked: 'How can what *would* be agreed under hypothetical conditions have the smallest relevance to us?' The problem is familiar from hypothetical contract theory where it is readily agreed that hypothetical contracts cannot bind. Neither can the conclusions of hypothetical discussions. So the question remains: what is the significance of Ideal Discourse? I take the right answer to this question to be the one Rawls gives when the same difficulty is raised about his original position and the agreement reached there. Rawls describes the original position as a 'device of representation' which draws together our fundamental convictions about the conditions under which free and equal persons can make binding agreements with each other. For example, we think that among such conditions is absence of threats of force, coercion, deception, and factors which give one party an unfair advantage over the other.

This position models what we regard as fair conditions under which the representatives of free and equal persons are to specify the terms of social cooperation in the case of the basic structure of society; and since it also models what, for this case, we regard as acceptable restrictions on reasons available to the parties for favouring one agreement rather than another, the conception of justice the parties would adopt identifies the conception we regard—*here and now*—as fair and supported by the best reasons.[2]

Rawls's answer is of a piece with his general claim that his theory of justice articulates in one comprehensive conception ideals which are latent in the public culture of a democracy, ideals which on reflection we accept as underlying many of our intuitive ideas about persons and what is due to them. So the original position is 'a means of public reflection and self-clarification' which helps us to work out what 'we now think'.[3] Thus we are to see the hypothetical agreement of the original position as a way of talking about the most appropriate principles for organizing all the elements of our fundamental intuitive idea of society as a fair system of co-operation between free and equal persons. In sum, talk of hypothetical contracts or agreements is to be understood as a metaphorical way of talking about ideals excavated from the deep thought of our public culture and given systematic expression.

Following Rawls's answer, I shall say that Ideal Discourse models what we regard as appropriate ground rules for discussions between autonomous persons about the character of their basic political framework. Ideal Discourse is to be understood as the more articulate form of the already available thought of ourselves as citizens. It is a deliberative viewpoint which anyone can enter and by reasoning within its restrictions clarify what they think about principles of justice and of rights. Restrictions are imposed by the twin aims of the discourse: the particular aim of finding principles that secure and advance moral autonomy, and the general aim of reaching rational agreement. We deliberate as citizens concerned to solve our political problems in ways that respect the autonomy that is the very basis of our citizenship. So the discourse is particular rather than universal. It is shaped both by the description of the participants and by the character that circumstances lend to their problems and possible solutions. Self-description and

---

[2] John Rawls, 'Justice as Fairness', 237 f.   [3] Ibid. 238.

circumstance combine to identify a system of needs that people have as citizens of particular regimes and which are specified by the list of goods they claim as of right.

Since the concept of citizenship is itself historical the needs of citizens cannot be interpreted in a timeless discourse that fixes them once and for all. Whether we think of citizenship rights as having an evolutionary history from civil through political to social rights, or, as associated with more comprehensive conceptions of human society (those which fill a spectrum with libertarianism at one end and communism at the other, let us say) citizens of a given regime cannot but interpret their good in line with the available conception of citizenship and the potential of their society to support the relevant institutions— courts, parliaments, and welfare bureaucracies.[4] If this is right, the standpoint of the citizen incorporates the best available information on the concepts and other resources of her society. So instead of eliminating information by placing discussants behind a Rawlsian veil of ignorance we give them full information. The hazards to impartiality are avoided by the motivational assumption I have so frequently mentioned, namely that discussants are motivated by the desire to find principles they all accept.

The deliberative viewpoint represents that of the citizen by meeting a number of constraints. Since we are supposing that our final aim is to find a conception of rights that has normative force for the citizens of a modern democracy, the viewpoint cannot be thought of as the province of a single thinker. So room must be made for the assumption that the viewpoint is accessible to a plurality of separate persons. The separateness and plurality of persons must be represented by the thought that many distinct viewpoints are brought to the dialogue situation. Each participant must therefore take an attitude to the variety of viewpoints that distinguish other participants. Since what is common to the participants is a concept of themselves as free and equal for the purpose of politics, the question of how to situate their separateness and plurality can be considered as the question of how to represent various aspects of positive freedom

---

[4] The aspect of rights which creates new duties is called by Raz 'the dynamic aspect of rights'. See Joseph Raz, 'On the Nature of Rights'.

identified in Chapter 5. These aspects, I suggest, are represented in six primary conversational constraints.

7.3. AUTONOMY-REGARDING CONSTRAINTS: PERSONAL

(i) *Equal Respect*

First, there are the aspects collected in the previous chapter
under the heading of personal freedom. The first of these is the
thought of ourselves as authoritative initiators of moral claims.
That enters the situation of political dialogue as the requirement
of *Equal Respect* for all conceptions of the good. This is shown by
not requiring the participants to justify the claims they wish to
make on foot of their conceptions of the good. The role of the
condition of Equal Respect is to establish mutual recognition
between persons of diverse outlooks. It blocks claims which
hinge on assertions of the superiority of some persons or
conceptions of the good over others.

Equal Respect for all conceptions of the good derives from
recognition of the equal worth of persons as bearers of the
powers of moral personality to determine the good and the just.
To acknowledge those powers is to acknowledge that each
person has her own perspective on the world adopted for
reasons that seem to her valid. Of course she may share her
perspective with many others. It may be the perspective of a
moral tradition with many adherents. The crucial point is that
the members of a tradition do not have to account for their view
in the political discourse. This is not to deny that some
conceptions may be better than others, or that anyone can know
that to be the case. It is to say that such matters cannot be
decided politically without thwarting an aspect of personal
autonomy.

(ii) *Reasonableness*

The second feature of personal autonomy noted in Chapter 5
was independence in the sense of reflective freedom from
absorption in a system of ends. Autonomous persons must be
able to distance themselves from and assess their final ends. So
they cannot be bound for life to one conception rather than

another. Accordingly the aims in which their conception of the good implicates them must be subordinated to their autonomy interest in being able to stand apart from and survey such aims. That interest is represented in the political dialogue by requiring participants to give priority to securing agreement on the social conditions of moral independence over their concern for the good. A condition of such agreement is that they frame their discussion by a condition of *Reasonableness*. Rawls incorporates this condition, which he calls the 'Reasonable' into the background set-up of his version of an original position. He describes the 'Reasonable' as an element of the conception of fair terms of co-operation, that is, terms that each participant may reasonably be expected to accept on condition that they all accept them.

Fair terms of cooperation articulate an idea of reciprocity and mutuality: all who cooperate must benefit, or share in common burdens in some appropriate fashion as judged by a suitable benchmark of comparison.[5]

The role of Reasonableness is to focus argument on to the background conditions of being free to revise one's allegiance to a conception of the good. To secure those conditions people must be prepared to take the attitude of Reasonableness in political dialogue. They must refrain from pressing proposals reflecting their personal ideals in favour of proposals which each could reasonably accept on condition they all do.

(iii) *Generality*

Now the condition of Reasonableness requires arguments to be framed so as to appeal to shared considerations of positive freedom rather than those given by a particular conception of the good. It forces participants in the dialogue to confine claims on the basic social structure to ones that are generalizable. Given the circumstances of disagreement about how to allocate resources of various kinds, people cannot expect others to meet claims they do not share reasons for acknowledging. This means that claims to advantages that are purely sectional must be adjusted in the light of what can be reasonably expected. So Reasonableness embeds a condition I call *Generality*. It is useful

[5] Rawls, 'Kantian Constructivism in Moral Theory', 528.

to pull this out for separate consideration for the light it throws on the limits to the claims that can be engrossed by political dialogue. The role of Generality is to lock the discussion on to claims that articulate considerations of shared interest rather than ones drawn from particular conceptions of the good. Thus it gives direction to the condition of Reasonableness. It requires people to frame proposals with the interests of others in mind. As well as flowing indirectly from personal freedom as independence, Generality flows directly out of the third aspect of personal freedom, namely, responsibility for ends. Under this aspect persons regard their autonomy as shown in the ability to rise above the demands of even their most cherished personal ideals and to work for a common good which they identify in concert with others. This capacity of persons to be moved by considerations of general interest as well as by their particular conceptions of the good is represented in Ideal Discourse by restricting proposals to ones which satisfy Generality.

7.4. AUTONOMY-REGARDING CONSTRAINTS: POLITICAL

(iv) *Symmetry*

Political freedom is embodied in the Ideal Discourse situation by conditions which overlap with, or are implied in, those listed above. But their development to meet the representation of political freedom is worth making to improve understanding of the character of the constraints. The first aspect of political freedom was the conception of persons as equal in their potential for citizenship, that is, as equally capable of self-government. This aspect is represented by situating all participants in the dialogue uniformly with respect to power. Call this the situation of *Symmetry*. This situation is marked by a complete absence of external domination and internal hierarchy or patriarchy. Everyone has the same powers, freedoms, and opportunities in the discussion.[6] Thus no one is in a position to suppress the views of another. So the discussion is swayed by no power considerations other than the Habermasian power of the better argument. The deliberation progresses through the

[6] Cf. Rawls, 'Kantian Constructivism in Moral Theory', 530.

examination of proposals in the light of reasons and adoption of the most powerfully backed ones.

It might be objected that Symmetry is unfair to those with special natural talents and acquired skills because it precludes them from influencing the choice of principles. The reply is that the question of how special natural talents and acquired skills are to be rewarded is a question about the character of the social structure. And that character is what the discourse has to establish. Symmetry shapes the relationships in the discourse because people have an interest, as moral persons, in just social relationships, no less than in pursuit of their conceptions of the good.

(v) *Secularity*

Political freedom as civic independence of an established doctrine of ends is represented in the dialogue situation by a condition I call, with some misgivings, *Secularity*.[7] I intend this to capture the idea that the justifications for proposals must be in terms of reasons of a certain class, namely, reasons which appeal to the value of each person's autonomous organization of her own life. Understood in this way Secularity is the doctrine that political conversation should be motivated by the concern for conditions which enable individuals to make their own evaluations and choices. Thus it gives some content to the conditions of Reasonableness and Generality introduced earlier by requiring political justification to invoke reasons of autonomy (the general interest). It is also connected with the principle of neutrality espoused in various versions by leading contemporary liberals. In the version which follows from Secularity the principle of neutrality prohibits political justification from appealing to reasons given by conceptions of the good. The point is to avoid political arrangements which interfere with each person's effort to make sense of her own life by imposing on her someone else's ideal of the good.

Secularity drives a wedge between considerations given by the idea of political arrangements justifiable to all and considerations given by sectarian doctrines of the good life. One familiar

---

[7] My misgiving is that this will encourage misunderstanding of political liberalism as a secular humanist 'civic religion'.

echo of this feature occurs in the doctrine of separation of state and church. But Secularity as a constraint of political conversation is logically prior to that doctrine as well as to the more comprehensive doctrine of neutrality with respect to conceptions of the good. Secularity forms part of the foundation of such doctrines and is independently motivated by the supreme value attached to individual reflective evaluation of desires and projects and the effort to make one's own sense of the meaning of life. I labour this point to dissociate the kind of political neutrality implied by Secularity from any general doctrine of value-neutral politics. The liberal state is not value-neutral. It is founded in a moral ideal of the person according to which the best that can be wished for an individual is the autonomous creation of her own life. This normative position entails neutrality itself as a normative view: it is wrong for certain considerations to enter political dialogue.

It might be thought that Secularity requires an impossible split identity among people of the well-ordered society represented in Ideal Discourse—a civic or public identity in virtue of which their primary motivation is to facilitate each other to pursue self-chosen conceptions of the good, and a private identity in which they pursue their own conceptions as perfectionist ideals. The response to this worry is that people are able to acknowledge and act on principles and rules in one sphere which they do not consider appropriate in another. As the capacity for autonomy has been characterized (in the idea of freedom as self-origination, for example) it is a feature which enables people to rise above their own perspectives and respect the different perspectives of others. Autonomous persons are able to see that from the point of view of others their own perspective is but one more sectarian doctrine of final ends. And they are able to allow the outsider's view to affect the outcome of the discourse for the sake of social co-operation provided everyone else does likewise. Of course, they also have an insider's view of their own conception of the good. Their special talent as autonomous agents is that they can separate the sphere of the good from the sphere of justice and act within the norms of each sphere without experiencing any strain either of principle or of psychology. The explanation of this possibility is that they are attributed with a moral personality characterized in Rawls's way as comprising twin moral powers—the moral power to determine the first principles of justice as well as the moral power to discern the good. For this reason persons are able to form political relationships which are independent of their convictions of the good and reflective of the notion that reasonable people may disagree about the ends of life but nevertheless give justice to each other.[8]

(vi) *Universality*

The third aspect of political freedom is that citizens think of themselves as responsible for putting the value of autonomy into their own lives. They think that they are equally able to decide moral issues for themselves and that governments should not interfere with the process of individual moral evaluation even if such intervention would prevent people from choosing morally bad actions and goals. This aspect of freedom is represented in the political discourse by not requiring participants to justify their moral competence to each other. Thus no one can be excluded from the discourse on grounds of bad character or bad judgement. This opens the discourse to everyone, a feature I call *Universality*. Universality points up the connection between democratic participation and recognition of the value of individuals deciding moral issues for themselves. If this value shapes the political discourse then one person, or a select band of persons, cannot decide for others, and, if that is so, all who are to be affected by the outcome must have a voice in the discussion. To be a member of the forum that determines political principles the only relevant feature is that one has an adequate capacity for moral personality. (Moral personality is a range property, like intelligence. The minimum point on the range is sufficient to qualify for membership in the discourse.)

The restrictions which have been elaborated may be thought of as representing what is due to citizens who regard themselves as morally autonomous persons. Thus a fair dialogue situation for persons so defined is one that observes these conditions. It should be observed that such a dialogue is not value-free. It

---

[8] Cf. Rawls, 'The Domain of the Political and Overlapping Consensus', 238, 'When we are reasonable we are prepared to find substantive and even intractable disagreements on basic questions.'

embodies an ideal of the person and its companion ideal of an autonomy-regarding political society.

Clearly the restrictions that I have introduced are not an exhaustive list of the ground rules of discursive argument. A full account would make space for others, including Habermas's fair distribution of chances to speak and freedom to seek and offer help, strategies for relieving dialogic impasses such as Larmore's retreat to neutral ground, and Ackerman's consistency and rationality principles.[9] But, I believe that the principles listed are adequate for understanding how autonomy-regarding conversation is regulated. Even if we do not accept Habermas's claim that it is the mode of conversation indicated for any inquiry into the truth, it is clearly the appropriate mode for political conversations that aim to clarify the implications of valuing autonomy for the basic structure of a modern democracy.

In the remainder of this chapter I argue that when we envisage political conversationalists regulating their discussions by autonomy-regarding restrictions it becomes quite clear that they could not find consensus on a model of themselves as sites of self-owning rights. That is because they are already embedded in an alternative and incompatible model of social connection. In the first part of my argument I want to establish that the exercise of autonomy requires recognition of a kind of interdependence that is fundamentally at odds with the self-containedness of self-ownership. The second part connects that general idea with interpretations of the restrictions on political conversation so that we see in more detail how self-ownership offends against autonomy.

7.5. THE INTERDEPENDENCE OF AUTONOMOUS HUMAN BEINGS

In this section I argue that autonomy requires the existence of a discursive community and its supports contrary to the common association of autonomy with independence and separateness.[10]

---

[9] See Ch. 6, nn. 20, 27, 37, and 39.

[10] A typical example is Michael Sandel's claim that on the liberal conception of the self 'we are essentially separate, independent selves'. See his introduction to Sandel (ed.), *Liberalism and its Critics*, 5.

This prepares the way for our final encounter with the doctrine of self-ownership in the following section. First, a brief recap. The thought that lies behind my version of autonomy is the Kantian one that a person becomes a moral agent when, instead of remaining in the grip of her found appetites, she orders her conduct by a law, and instead of conforming to a law given by others, she gives the law to herself. I understand the giving of a law to oneself to imply that the moral world must comply with principles which we as rational beings can freely acknowledge. Kant regards this as a matter of principles arising from self-legislation. But such principles are not the maxims of private acts of moral law-making, but principles that command the assent of a plurality of agents.[11] In the absence of empirical conditions favouring impartiality we must envisage the relevant assent as hypothetical. It is the assent that we would give were our motives and rationality unwarped by all those traits of personal and social character that we ordinarily regard as prejudicing the pursuit of goodness or justice. I have taken the working out of hypothetical assent to be a matter of using Ideal Discourse to model appropriate conditions in which subjectively originated claims can be assessed for objective plausibility in reasoned debate, the survivors being those that all acknowledge as having the better of the argument. This means that moral law-making is essentially a social construction in which the finality of individual judgement is preserved by the requirement of consensus.

Now the content of subjectively originated claims has to be assessed in a relevant universe of discourse. We can distinguish between discourses about justice and rights and discourses about the good. Discourses about justice and rights range over all citizens. The aim is to find principles for the basic social framework within which citizens share a political life. There must be rational consensus on the content of these principles else political life can be no more than a succession of tyrannies. But since the framework is autonomy-regarding it is designed to permit a plurality of goods. For, autonomy would be pointless if it did not issue in different conceptions of the good. If we were

[11] I have borrowed Onora O'Neill's phrase 'plurality of agents' in order to have the possibility of non-universal discourses. See O'Neill, *Constructions of Reason*, 44, 213, and *passim*.

all so constituted that on reflection we came up with the same view of the good the deliberation of any one of us could conclude for the rest. Recognition of the possibility of autonomy is thus one with recognition of the possibility of difference. This is a conceptual point which bears on the exercise of autonomy. Where there are no options there can be no choice and where there is no choice there is no room for the exercise of autonomy. So a plurality of goods is a condition as well as outcome of autonomy.[12]

Discourses about the good, therefore, are made within a context of general acknowledgement of a plurality of forms of human good. These discourses range over different moral communities according to the doctrine of ends that is under scrutiny. The main point of discourses about the good is to establish the worthwhileness of schemes of final ends. But since no overarching consensus on adoption of a single form of life is possible or desirable the agreement anticipated in a discourse about the good must be sought within narrower moral traditions than the broad tradition of autonomy-regarding justice. (Since not all traditions embody the values of rational enquiry or autonomy my remarks below are confined to those that do.)

By a moral tradition I mean a way of life regarded as fulfilling and of some historical endurance such as we normally find ourselves enjoying as a result of particular circumstances of birth, education, and general upbringing. We learn its goods, its methods of rational justification, its successes and failures. Within that context we may take a belief or action to be rational when we suppose that a discursive argument would lead, under ideal conditions, any challenger to agree with us. This does not mean that we cannot take a belief or action to be rational in the actual world until we have got the agreement of a relevant conversational community. That would mean that we could rarely have confidence in the rationality of our beliefs or actions. When there is no consensus on a belief in the actual world, it is rational to assume that our disputed belief would be vindicated in ideal conditions just as long as we are satisfied that our deliberation meets those conditions and we have an explanation

---

[12] For an extremely valuable discussion of autonomy and pluralism to which I am much indebted, see Raz, *The Morality of Freedom*, ch. 14.

of why our antagonists cannot see things our way.[13] Thus women who believe in the ordination of women to religious priesthoods defend their belief as rational within the same tradition of belief, authority, and mode of enquiry as the men who oppose them. They explain the failure of agreement in terms of the moral blindness of men to the distorting effects on judgement of patriarchal, hierarchical, and misogynist religious culture. This is an example of a general strategy whereby we justifiably hold on to contested beliefs by explaining why our opponents' judgements are defective and accounts for the importance of the study of ideology.

Traditions are historical and rarely develop in isolation from each other. So the kind of discursive argument that goes on in the ideal speech of a tradition may embody beliefs borrowed from another and, perhaps, given a different meaning. (A striking example is how the notion of subjective or individual right which is developed in one way by liberal theory is treated by natural law theory as derivable from its own version of objective right.)[14] That may lead to disagreements that cannot be resolved even in ideal speech until the history of a concept traces it to its language of origin. That may enable us to account for and resolve a discursive impasse. It also suggests that we are often, at least partial, inhabitants of several traditions which overlap and diverge. That is why we typically find our deliberations enriched by forms of thought that allow us to revise our tradition of primary identification, or, to reject it for another with which we have partial familiarity.[15]

[13] We need not assume that the ideal conditions under which the good can be identified are the same as those for justice. As Charles Larmore has observed, when individuals' conceptions of the good conflict, they often also have rather different notions of ideal conditions under which they can justify their beliefs to others. See Larmore, *Patterns of Moral Complexity*, 58. This is a good part of the reason why moral debate does not resolve certain sorts of moral disagreement. It is also why I locate moral traditions as the relevant discourse communities for evaluating the worthwhileness of conceptions of the good.

[14] See e.g. Jacques Maritain, *The Rights of Man*; John Finnis, *Natural Law and Natural Rights*; Michael. B. Crowe, *The Changing Profile of the Natural Law*, 234–5 traces recognition of human rights in ancient and medieval sources.

[15] John Baker has pointed out to me that the point about shifting, overlapping, changing traditions shows that the notion of agreement cannot be adequately defined. My answer is that a discourse fixes in advance the boundaries of the tradition it addresses. For the purpose of a given discourse a tradition is defined by its core positions on certain issues. These are not written

How does this account treat novel ideas and beliefs? Many of these may be accommodated within a given tradition as compatible with its standards of rationality and human fulfilment. But what of those that break with authoritative standards of rational justification? Our problem is to explain how novel ideas may be held worthwhile against the current of our discursive community and in the absence of relevant standards of rationality. The first thing that should be said here is that novelty is itself a good in an autonomy-regarding culture, so the absence of shared reasons for a new belief or course of action does not undermine the presumption of worthwhileness in the way it does for ideas that have been around long enough to prove their infertility. We can have inductive grounds for confidence in the ultimate, if remote, justification of at least some new ideas. We know that Galileo was not vindicated for several hundred years. But he was vindicated. We know that new ideas have generated their own standards of rational acceptability, their own discursive communities and traditions of enquiry, their own problems, and solutions to problems that defeated older traditions. So we have plenty of inductive support for holding that new ideas including ones about human fulfilment may turn out worthwhile. What we need to do to make good on that claim is set up the new standards of assessment a new idea requires. One of the largest cultural projects of this sort in this century has been the feminist project to establish new perspectives and standards of appraisal in the arts, the humanities, indeed a whole fabric of new ways of thinking, living, and relating to others.

The significant feature of the idea of discursive redemption of claims is that it reveals the interdependence of agents who would be autonomous. If, as Kant writes, 'the dignity of man consists precisely in his capacity to make universal law, although only on condition of being himself also subject to the law he makes' then autonomy cannot be achieved in isolation.[16] The Kantian interpretation directs us to engage in dialogue to

in stone but they are relatively stable when they express matters of deep principle rather than policy. Of course, a matter of principle may become the subject of a discourse also. Then the relevant tradition has to be defined in terms of the remaining core positions not affected by that principle.

[16] Immanuel Kant, *Groundwork of the Metaphysics of Morals*, 107.

come to a reasoned view of what counts as a worthwhile life or fair terms of social co-operation. One such dialogue may be with our moral tradition of origin in which we test the accuracy of our knowledge of that tradition, or our grounds for redefining or resisting it. Whatever our final judgement we cannot come to it independently of the conversational partners, living and dead, whose arguments provide the testing ground for the strength of our own.

Another such dialogue may be with our political tradition or origin. In modern democracies we enter political dialogue knowing that there are irreconcilable oppositions between traditions, which must nevertheless find a common political life. Again, we depend on each other to provide the medium of critical assessment for any claim we put forward about how to arrange our common life. Lest this interdependence appear merely cerebral we should note its social ramifications. The condition on which autonomous beings can form and pursue a conception of the good is that they co-author and sustain a kind of society in which autonomy is seen as morally valuable and, as such, a reason for promoting it in everyone.[17]. Such a society is one in which the free reflection and social supports necessary to autonomous choice and pursuit of a worthwhile life are permitted and resourced. It is a society in which as rich as possible a fund of cultural resources and forms of life are made available for individuals to draw on and not merely as abstract opportunities but as ones they are economically able to take.

7.6. AUTONOMY AGAINST SELF-OWNERSHIP

If autonomy is better understood as relational, a human self-command that lies not in radical independence of others but in recognizing our mutual dependencies, then the moral and political task of autonomous agents is to structure their interdependencies in ways that prevent domination of some by others. The task arises because domination is an inherent risk of interdependence. So the social structure must be devised in a way that inhibits two related forms of domination, one

---

[17] Raz, *The Morality of Freedom*, 407.

structural, the other personal. The first occurs when the social structure itself appears to individuals as an alien constraining power through failing to embody institutions that keep people alive to their own powers in (re)producing its conditions. The second occurs when specific institutions put some people in positions of economic and social power over the lives of others. The social structure to be aimed at is one that makes for what I shall call undominated interdependence.

If the concern of autonomy is for undominated interdependence we are able to read the constraints on political conversation introduced earlier in a fresh light, one that shows them translating that general concern into heads of reasons for rejecting the liberty–constraint scheme of liberal self-ownership.[18] We are able to see how the case for self-ownership then, far from deriving from considerations to do with autonomy, is finally broken by those considerations.[19]

Under the head of Equal Respect we have seen earlier that political conversationalists are committed to accepting a plurality of conceptions of the good. Our subsequent discussion has shown that the existence of a plurality of options is a condition of autonomy so the commitment is not just a pragmatic response to the fact of pluralism in modern democracies. Autonomous beings have a shared interest in advancing plurality. It follows that they have a shared reason for creating a social structure that enables many different forms of human good to flourish. They must, therefore, provide everyone with the conditions that allow as wide a range of options as possible to be developed and pursued. After Rawls, we now describe these conditions as primary goods—liberties, rights and opportunities, income and wealth, self-respect, and leisure—goods a person needs whatever her final aims.[20] Whatever the detailed specification of primary goods turns out to be, their rationale in autonomy gives reason to secure them as substantial resources rather than mere absences of restraints. Autonomous agents

[18] Cf. Jeremy Waldron's suggestion that we might use a contractarian hypothesis to rule out some possible conceptions of justice. Waldron, *The Right to Private Property*, 273. Waldron shows how this idea works in the case of parties in a Rawlsian 'original position' at 274–80.

[19] Robert Nozick makes, although he does not elaborate, the connection between autonomy and rights in *Anarchy, State, and Utopia*, 48–51.

[20] Rawls, *A Theory of Justice*, sect. 15.

must be empowered by material means to author their own lives as well as being free to do so. So they must regard themselves as collectively responsible for securing to each a sufficiency of material means. And the system of allocation for these must be designed to exclude the growth in time of patterns of wealth and poverty which abridge the development and exercise of the autonomy powers of those who end up poor, or put some in positions to control the lives of others.

On this account to treat someone with Equal Respect requires acknowledging her as a rightful claimant to a fair share of social assets. This is a substantive notion of Equal Respect but one that springs from the principle of autonomy coupled with the condition of interdependence. By contrast, the understanding of Equal Respect required by self-ownership springs from the central place given to the principle of liberty—the idea that what people value most is freedom from restraint. Coupled with the radical moral independence of self-owners (they are moral sovereigns who do not depend on social discourse to establish their own conceptions of the good) this leads to a social structure designed to secure to everyone transactional justice and freedom from interference. Political membership involves no other debts of mutuality. It follows that Equal Respect is understood as no more than a principle of impartial treatment under rules of negative liberty.[21]

These different understandings of Equal Respect flow from systemic differences in the associated conceptions of persons. Conceived as autonomous, persons give substance to their moral independence by mutual support of forms of undominated interdependence whereby they secure the plurality of forms of good that makes choice and moral assessment of choice possible. Conceived as moral absolute sovereigns, persons are moral individualists. They have no need from society of anything more than the assurance of non-interference. From within the standpoint of autonomy the demands of Equal Respect cannot be met by the scheme of negative rights that fulfils Equal Respect for self-owners. In autonomy-regarding discourse, therefore, the constraint of Equal Respect operates to bring about rational rejection of that scheme.

[21] For an instructive discussion of different senses of equal respect see Larmore, *Patterns of Moral Complexity*, 61–3.

It may be recalled that the condition of Reasonableness is intended to move people to give priority to securing the social conditions of their moral independence. It incorporates the idea that benefits and burdens are to be distributed on a basis that the members of society can justify to each other as fair. Now interpretation of what they could reasonably expect others to agree in Ideal Discourse depends on how their moral independence is affected by a proposed distribution of burdens and benefits. A distribution acceptable to those who do worst under it must at least afford them fair equality of opportunity to withdraw from existing social roles and ends into ones of their own choosing. It must not be one that condemns them to servitude, or to the bare right to refuse their labour to another. This rather minimal conception of Reasonableness rules out a libertarian constitution for that cannot secure the worth of independence to those who inevitably end up poor under its operation.

The constraint of Generality, I noted above is implied in the condition of Reasonableness. Here I observe that Generality derives its meaning from its place in autonomy. Without shared belief in the value of autonomy there can be no agreement to the priority of moral independence over particular conceptions of the good. So concern for autonomy is a social, or general, as well as an individual interest. This means that people identify with each other's interest in autonomy and recognize a duty to promote it as a good for all. By contrast, the doctrine of self-ownership locates Generality in a shared interest in negative freedom rather than autonomy. The radical moral independence of self-owners confines their generalizable interests to securing the conditions of freedom from interference. Self-owners understand by taking responsibility for ends the necessity of limiting actions for the sake of formal equal self-ownership. They do not take responsibility to imply any positive duties to secure the conditions of others realizing their ends. Once again, we find that the concern of autonomy cannot find expression in political arrangements that presuppose self-ownership. For that reason proposals embodying the principle of self-ownership cannot command the support of participants in Ideal Discourse.

The remaining constraints—Symmetry, Secularity, and Universality—emphasize the same conclusions. Ideal Discourse situates discussants symmetrically to represent the intuitive idea of civic equality. While all of the conditions are mutually supportive some are more immediately related than others. For example, Symmetry supports Reasonableness by ensuring that the justification of burdens and benefits is not skewed in favour of the powerful. Secularity gives content to the scheme of conditions as a whole while Universality supports Symmetry by expressing the unrestricted scope of membership in the civil society. While the doctrine of self-ownership need not deny any of the intuitive ideas that these restrictions represent it cannot provide the conditions for their realization.

To see this, imagine the participants in Ideal Discourse examining the doctrine of self-ownership with the question of how to give force to these restrictions uppermost in their minds. They would know that under the minimal state required by self-ownership there would be uneven distribution of resources. And that would translate the equality of citizens that Symmetry expresses into a merely formal status for those who would end up bound to passive citizenship by the effort to meet their pressing survival needs. They would be aware of the affinities of power and wealth and the consequent risks of domination run by the less well off. They would also be conscious that the superiority of reason and dialogue over force as a means of allocating resources is not obvious if the result of adopting the principle of self-ownership puts the survival of some of them at risk. So they would realize the impossibility of justifying to all a distribution of burdens and benefits that leaves some worse off than if they took their chances on meeting their needs using their own force. In sum, the parties to Ideal Discourse could not, from their situation of symmetry, adopt the principle of self-ownership.

The condition of Secularity may be best seen as disestablishing any sectarian doctrine of the good in the name of moral independence. In developing their varying conceptions of the good people recognize the need for moral pluralism and are therefore motivated to endorse whatever principle secures it. The relevant principle is political neutrality. This can be understood as a response to the problem of devising a political framework that can claim the allegiance of citizens who pursue a multiplicity of, often incompatible, ideals of the good life. The doctrine of political neutrality asserts that a modern democracy should not seek to promote one over another of its contained ideals. Robert Nozick writes: 'a state or government that claims . . . allegiance . . . must be *neutral* between its citizens.'[22] Nozick takes this to mean that a government is restrained from political actions undertaken to promote or hinder any ideal of the good.

Political neutrality in this sense of neither helping nor hindering is of a piece with the doctrine of self-ownership. Since the self-owner is an independent moral sovereign she is entitled to choose what life she will as long as she does not harm others. A government, which is merely a bunch of other citizens, is in no better position to determine what a valid form of good is than she is. So if the state intervenes in the cultural market-place to help or hinder ideals of the good, it inevitably imposes controversial judgements, in effect, giving the judgements of the people in power superior weight to those of everyone else.

But does this interpretation of political neutrality ensure the social conditions of moral independence? It seems evident that without state support there are very diminished chances of survival and flourishing for certain of the arts, for certain minority languages, for an itinerant way of life, to name but a few aspects of our culture. If political neutrality is a matter of neither helping nor hindering it cannot ensure the survival of the rich and diverse culture people need when forming their aims and aspirations.

The interpretation of political neutrality that naturally couples with self-ownership is not the only one. Given that state support for a rich cultural structure is necessary, it does not follow that there need be any controversial ranking of ideals of the good. It may be recalled that I adopted in Chapter 6 Ronald Dworkin's idea that the state could ensure an adequate range of options by providing tax incentives to private citizens to develop aspects of the cultural structure. Of course, the question is: 'which citizens?' But the answer to this question does not have to involve governments in controversial evaluations of the worth of proposals. Governments can support proposals in the

[22] Nozick, *Anarchy, State, and Utopia*, 33.

name of providing an adequate cultural stock of meanings and opportunities while leaving the evaluation of those to citizens themselves in civil society outside the organs of the state. Naturally, procedures would have to be developed for distributing resources fairly between the various claims that could be legitimately made on behalf of the culture of autonomy. But that does not seem impossible. The really vital point is that the reasons for government intervention should be to do with promoting an adequate range of options, not with the promotion of particular options.

Political neutrality here is neutrality of reasons relative to conceptions of the good. It is joined with promotion of autonomy as a political ideal. For that reason, the state is concerned to promote a variety of forms of human flourishing including ones that call on more resources than equal treatment would sanction. The cost of maintaining and enhancing an island way of life off the west coasts of Ireland or Scotland may be much greater than what an equal division of resources would sanction, but the value to an autonomy-regarding society of there being such a way of life is a sound reason for calling on special support from the state. The same general point applies to minority cultures. It is not enough for the state to tolerate them. To whatever extent necessary and possible, it is enjoined to resource them by the principle of autonomy.

The appropriate way of reading the condition of Secularity is as supporting a doctrine of political neutrality understood in this second way, in which the context of autonomy is crucial. Secularity asks us to give precedence to securing the social conditions of freedom for individuals to find for themselves the good they wish to pursue. What that means, on the present outlook, is that political conversationalists place themselves under a condition of reasoning that selects a framework designed to advance moral pluralism. I conclude that observance of Secularity would preclude us, or our counterparts in Ideal Conversation, from selecting the form of political neutrality associated with the doctrine of self-ownership.

Finally, let us consider how things appear with Universality in mind. This condition recognizes equal moral personality by securing open access to the dialogue situation. Participants in the dialogue have to consider how the operation of the principle

of self-ownership preserves the claims of equal moral personalities. Again the problem is that equal citizenship for all
becomes a merely formal status for those who end up poor
under the libertarian constitution. Discussants would be aware
that if a minimal state were to operate some, perhaps a good
many, citizens would be unable to provide themselves severally
with the material and cultural means that go into being able to
stake one's claims on the design and interpretation of the social
structure. While they would enjoy the formal civil and political
liberties of a free society they could not be sure of adequate
education, the material supports of health and well-being,
access to culture, and to the means of cultural reproduction and
development—philosophy, the arts, and sciences.

   It has always been fairly clear that a libertarian state could not
be derived within a contractual approach to politics. The
considerations I have been adducing above are aimed at
showing why that is so. Given a specification of autonomy we
can see that a libertarian state would fail to satisfy the autonomy
interests of all those who were to be bound by it. Of course, the
libertarian may dispute the specification of autonomy offered
here. But that would require a much more extensive debate
about conceptions of autonomy than currently engaged in by
libertarians.

7.7. FROM *MODUS VIVENDI* POLITICS TO EXPRESSIVISM

I have been arguing that fundamental political principles should
be ones whose justification depends on autonomy rather than
on the merits of one or another of the substantive ideals of
goodness that autonomous persons espouse. Though the
pursuit of our own ideal of human flourishing is of the highest
importance in our personal lives that ideal cannot be made the
overriding value of the political realm. There are many conceptions of happiness. Their relative merits are disputed. From the
point of view of autonomy they function as so many resources
from which we can choose our conception of the good, provided
only that they fall within the range of autonomy-regarding
moralities. But none of them may be appealed to as the source of

political principles. That is what the principle of Secularity amounts to.

What is the consequence of this outlook for our understanding of the character of the political realm? There are two sorts of answer to this question.[23] The first holds that the political realm is the site of a *modus vivendi* between individuals or sub-communities who differ in their views about the ends of life. For the purpose of devising their common political life they have to reach an accommodation on its governing principles which leaves aside their differences while permitting them to co-exist. The *modus vivendi* view is most persuasive if we are imagining a state being formed between people whose central values differ. Circumstances of common location and the potential for strife might combine to motivate people to make common cause for peaceful co-existence within a framework of power limited to such matters as internal and external security and economic development. Such a state would have to enshrine a strong form of political neutrality. All its principles and policies would have to be justified on grounds neutral between its internal opponents. Unfortunately, it is a notable fact of political life that divided societies do not see a neutral state as the answer to their problems of co-existence. Most of them contain elements with separatist aspirations.

The *modus vivendi* view seems most cogent on the assumption of moral individualism. For self-interested beings politics is a contingent response to problems that may arise in the attempt to live without public rules and impartial arbiters of disputes. Confined to resolving those sorts of problems politics has no claim or duty to fulfil the lives of citizens. It provides the means of living peacefully together for citizens whose different routes to self-fulfilment may cross and result in strife. The trouble with this view is that it cannot secure stability. As I noted in the previous chapter political arrangements premissed on moral individualism are hostage to shifts in power between different groups and political allegiance is always highly volatile.

There is a second view we could take of the character of the political realm. This is an expressivist view which holds that the political realm must enable human beings to express their

---

[23] Cf. Larmore, *Patterns of Moral Complexity*, 70–7.

nature. It can be specified in different ways by different ideas of human nature. In its Aristotelian specification the idea that humans are essentially social or political animals leads to a view of the *polis* as the site of natural fulfilment. Human good is best realized in political activity which is second only to the life of theoretical contemplation. This idea that political life is a natural human end and not a mere means to other ends is taken up in civic humanism to encourage active participation in democratic politics. All that has changed is the view of human nature which differs from Aristotle's in making the bare capacity for rationality a sufficient qualification for citizenship.

A different version of political expressivism is suggested by the autonomy-based moral pluralism I have been advancing. An expressivist view is wanted because autonomy is most fully achieved in conditions of undominated interdependence. Since the exercise of autonomy leads to incompatible personal ideals there is no option but to regulate their claims collectively in politics. So if we value autonomy then we are committed to a political realm that expresses that value. To connect with the general form of expressivism we may say that the role of the state is to enable human beings to express their autonomous nature. Where this differs from the traditional idea of expressivism is in denying that the life of the citizen must be given over to political activity as her primary good. Autonomy yields heterogeneous goods and does not rank them. Each is of paramount importance to those who take it as their deepest commitment and of equal importance from the point of view of the whole society which values the variety as composing a complex ideal of the good life which all can enjoy even though not all of it can be enjoyed by anyone. A part of what that good life assures is that people need not be dominated by the good of political participation. While some will undoubtedly find their own flourishing in vigorous political participation, others can dedicate their energies to the pursuit of sport, or caring for others, or scholarship, or marketing, or art, or whatever. For politics to be one form of human flourishing, albeit one that is significant for all the others, the institutions that express the common interest in autonomy must be strong and their guardians virtuous. When they are not, politics should dominate the lives of all citizens, for the time it takes to resolve a political crisis or undo corruption. But normal politics may be conducted within the framework of institutions that represent the general interest. Citizens do not have to shout for their interests all the time when those interests are represented in an appropriate liberty–constraint system embedded in their political framework. Thus room is made for active engagement in the diversity of ends that is the hallmark of autonomy-regarding politics.

Liberals often shun political expressivism for its association with anti-liberal doctrines which call on the state to promote some substantive account of human good insensitive to individual liberty and moral pluralism. But liberals whose basis is autonomy and who agree that it is conditioned by interdependence are bound to end up with some such version of expressivism as I have described.

7.8. SUMMARY

In this chapter I have argued for three main conclusions. First, the conception of autonomy described in the previous chapter yields interconnected norms of Equal Respect, Reasonableness, Generality, Symmetry, Secularity, and Universality. Second, interpretation of these norms is led by an understanding of autonomy which precludes the possibility of any conversation constrained by them concluding in favour of self-ownership and its proprietary rights. Finally, if autonomy is our moral and political ideal we are committed to an expressivist rather than a *modus vivendi* view of politics.

8

Principles of Self-Government

8.1. INTRODUCTION

Rights derive their sense from their role in defining a conception of persons for shared political use. They are intended to settle in an intelligible, public, and authoritative way, the details of our image of the citizen. Thus, the libertarian scheme of rights gives concrete expression to an image of the citizen as self-owner and that in turn is drawn from an abstract image of the person as, to some extent at least, the author of her own life. I have argued that self-ownership is not a plausible conception of that more abstract image of the person. So I must now find principles that give us a better rendering of autonomy and justify embedding particular rights in the constitutional scheme of a modern democracy.

In the previous chapter I identified various norms of autonomy-regarding conversation and applied them to turn down the doctrine that proclaims self-ownership as the basis of the state. I would like that argument to be viewed as part of an exercise in *comparison* of rival theories which continues here. The principles I propose do not carry any claim to be the unique solution to the problem of meeting the requirements of autonomy. They are chosen in a field that is confined to them and the liberty–constraint principles of self-ownership.[1] And with self-ownership down I suggest that the proposed principles stand until it can be shown that autonomy is better defended and developed by some other principles.

Here, it may be useful to review the strategy we are following in the argument as a whole. Our aim is to replace the unsatisfactory principle of self-ownership with the principle of

---

[1] The field is confined by the resources available in our tradition of rights-based moral and political philosophy.

self-government. We want to say that each individual is the morally rightful governor of her own person and powers and that she is therefore free to make her own life as long as she does not engage in acts that hinder others pursuing their independent lives. And she may be rightly called on to help others in view of the fact that autonomy is a social as well as an individual ideal. To give substance to this general aim we need to find principles of liberty and constraint appropriate to the needs of citizens as self-governing beings. The principles are to establish a background which defines the rights, liberties, and opportunities one rightfully enjoys as a self-governor. The background draws the parameters of what one can and cannot do as a self-governor, much as the principle of private property is spelled out in systems of rules that establish what one can and cannot do with resources in one's proprietary control. Now the principles we seek are to be identified by reference to the requirements of an ideal of the person as autonomous. That ideal carries the demand that persons are to be governed solely by principles or laws they have made themselves. Clearly, that demand can be met for a plurality of persons living under common laws only if the laws are the product of consensual agreement. Such agreement cannot arise out of a common understanding of the content of a worthwhile life, for moral pluralism is both a presupposition of autonomy and a fact of modern life. Nor can agreements which do take place be regarded as rational if they are forged by propaganda, deception, or economic coercion. So to discover the principles that specify self-government we envisage a model conversation designed to show what the content of a rational consensus is for autonomous persons under the assumption of moral pluralism but with the sources of fraudulent consensus removed. This is the construct called Ideal Discourse. In it various elements of autonomy are reproduced as norms of autonomy-regarding conversation. Then the argument is that conversationalists whose discourse is constrained by those norms have reason to agree on the social supports necessary to sustain the norms or the competencies and interests they presuppose. The norms identified—Equal Respect, Reasonableness, Generality, Symmetry, Secularity, Universality—function as bridges between the abstract ideal of being in control of one's own life and the constitutional liberty–constraint scheme that aims to make the ideal effective for every citizen.[2]

Rawls has argued that the selection of principles of justice by the parties in his original position is grounded in their need for primary goods, a list of rights, liberties, and opportunities that are essential social supports for a wide range of ways of life.[3] In Rawls's list the primary goods are: freedom of thought and liberty of conscience; the political liberties; freedom of movement and free choice of occupation; equal opportunities to take political, social, and economic offices; income and wealth; and the social bases of self-respect.[4] We might take these as illustrative of the notion of democratic citizenship much as the incidents of ownership listed by Honoré illustrate liberal ownership. A list of such primary goods carries no claim to be unique or exhaustive. All the grand proclamations, from the declaration by the people of Virginia to the *European Convention on Human Rights* provide lists of what ought to be, or are, the rights of democratic citizenship. But there are different routes to such lists and these can make a difference to the content of rights or other primary goods as well as to whether socio-economic rights are added to the better-accepted civil and political rights. The argumentative route that I take is designed to develop a system of liberty and constraint which gives political substance to the conception of autonomy developed in previous chapters and a coherent underpinning to our intuitive notions of self-determination. While my point of origin and destination are similar to those of Rawls, the route that I travel is more scenic. There is no veil of ignorance and the journey is made by people more blessed with the skills of conversation than of calculation.[5]

A final preliminary point is that I do not discuss in detail the particular constitutional rights that might be justified by the principles I introduce although I mention several. This level of

---

[2] This strategy is broadly similar to John Rawls's method of arguing for justice as fairness. See 'Kantian Constructivism in Moral Theory', 520, and 'The Basic Liberties and their Priority', esp. 21–2, and 24–39.

[3] Cf. Rawls, 'Social Unity and Primary Goods'. Rawls no longer sees primary goods as all-purpose means *tout court* but as 'social conditions and all-purpose means to enable human beings to realize and exercise their moral powers' ('Kantian Constructivism', 526).   [4] Ibid. 526.

[5] See Sect. 6.2 for my preferred version of an 'original position'.

abstraction is useful in allowing for the possibility of a family of democratic constitutions devised for political cultures with different histories and traditions. Particular rights and liberties that make sense in one political culture—the notorious 'periodic holidays with pay' of the *Universal Declaration* of 1948, or special protection for the press for its role in presenting political issues to a mass audience—may make very little sense in a poor or illiterate culture.[6] But it seems reasonable to suppose that the abstract principles can be met in ways other than by the particular rights we currently think of as part of democratic citizenship.

8.2. PRINCIPLES OF SELF-GOVERNMENT

(i) *Rule of Democratic Law*

Our situation may be described as follows. Our discussions in the previous three chapters have given us an image of the person as autonomous in virtue of being the bearer of certain moral powers although these cannot be exercised and developed in isolation. That gives us an outline of the image of the citizen we need to offer and defend in order to meet the autonomy and other needs of persons. The outline encompasses four main features:

(1) that each citizen has an equal right to the liberties, opportunities, and powers of citizenship;
(2) that the citizen is incomplete outside relations to others, so citizenship cannot be defined through the provision of rights of non-interference by a minimal state;
(3) that their interdependence means that citizens must stand to each other in relations of mutual concern and respect expressed in their co-operation in a just state;
(4) that their necessary mutuality and reciprocity is shown in citizens' acceptance of dialogue rather than force or deception to settle their political arrangements and resolve the conflicts that arise from time to time.

[6] Art. 24 of the *Universal Declaration of Human Rights* enshrines 'the right to rest and leisure, including reasonable limitation of working hours and periodic holidays with pay'. The point of the provision is to protect individuals from lives of unremitting toil. Its effect is to force up the wages of workers from wage-slavery levels.

Our problem is to identify principles which establish the rights and relationships posited in this abstract scheme. It should be noticed that the dependence of this notion of citizenship on a notion of the person as autonomous precludes any thought that the construction of citizenship is a matter of recognizing prior natural rights. Autonomous beings must be governed by self-imposed constraints. So being a right-holder is a political status in that it must be established by agreement rather than recognized as a 'natural' in the sense of a 'given' standing. (This does not mean that people have only those rights that a particular legal system assigns them. In the version I am articulating, the existence of moral rights is not dependent on actual law but on whether they can be represented as founded on reasons that command the assent of all as autonomous human beings.)

I shall propose various principles of liberty and constraint that I believe a constitutional base devised to respect autonomy would assign to everyone. These may be viewed as translating the abstract requirements of autonomy into a concrete form appropriate to their being given effect in political life. It is worth reminding ourselves here that politics is distinguished from other social practices by the fact that its principles are coercively enforced. This is because politics as we know it is a response to the Humean circumstances of justice: scarcity of material resources and limited affections. We now add to these the circumstance that the ideal of autonomy generates conflicting claims on the choice of political principles as an inevitable consequence of the conflict between conceptions of the good.[7] So the norms of autonomy-regarding political conversation have to be given legal force to ensure that they are in fact met. This means that they have to be developed into a form in which they can be given effect. And so the principles we seek have to specify what counts, from the point of view of politics, as being given equal respect, being reasonable, and so on. It should be observed here also that the principles can be justifiably enforced only because they sustain autonomy. The same holds for the policies a government pursues within the framework of such principles.

[7] See Charles Larmore, *Patterns of Moral Complexity*, 72.

The Ideal Discourse has been defined so that the selection of political principles is governed by the maxim that each seeks to adopt only those principles that all could agree. The reason for following this maxim is that it expresses the requirement of autonomy to live by self-imposable principles that are law-like, with law-likeness being established through the idea of a possible consensus. The reasoning for constitutional principles, therefore, must show that they provide an adequate conception of self-government in a situation where the maxim applies. The principles which I discuss are all available to us from our existing political tradition. We might think of them as ones (among many) we find ourselves having to live with or contest and so we decide to pull them out for reflective scrutiny.

To give effect to autonomy in the extended Humean circumstances partners in Ideal Discourse would, I believe, recognize the rule of democratic law as a first principle of their political association. I shall describe this principle in a general way before giving the grounds for its adoption.

The principle of the rule of democratic law shapes the constitutional schemes prevalent in our political tradition by requiring the democratic development of systems of standing, known, law. Besides providing for the regulation of the conduct of citizens this principle has an important role in responding to the fear of arbitrary rule. Hence it grounds the demand that political authority respect the rule of law. Thus it forbids dictatorship, subversion of the ideals of the state by the holders of state power, military coups, the declaration of emergency powers (except in very clearly defined democracy-threatening conditions), hereditary rule, arbitrary arrest and detention, and control or undue influence over the state by unelected religious, economic, or other powers. In short, it sanctions constraints on the taking and use of power of the sort common in the basic law of modern constitutional democracies.

The principle imposes familiar constraints on executive and legislative branches of the state acting extra-legally. The requirement here is for the officials to act in accordance with law, for legislators to be elected and for them to produce law within familiar constraints, for example, in public, supported by reasons, and as the outcome of a vote, rather than by edict or diktat. Of course, many questions arise here about the details of an appropriate procedure for making law. I shall ignore most of these as outside our present remit and simply assume that normal procedural democratic constraints on legislature and executive are part of the full description of the principle of the rule of democratic law. These may be summarized as matters of procedural fairness and accountability.

Procedural fairness is shaped by the now accepted political commitment to treating all citizens as political equals. The processes which we devise to satisfy political equality are interesting and important. The issues are of methods of election, of procedures for introducing, amending, passing, and defeating proposed new legislation, of offices and institutions for interpreting and implementing the law. Their proper consideration is a matter for another sort of work and I set them aside here.

One aspect that deserves special note however is the idea of equality before the law. In our political culture subjection to the rule of law depends on continuous voluntary recognitions of law by citizens rather than on use of massive force. One reason this can be the case is that citizens have at least some access to the machinery of legislation through having equal political rights. A related reason is that the law is perceived to conform to standards of civility and justice worthy of our allegiance. These grounds of recognition preclude, in principle at least, laws that are partial to the interests of one class of people or that discriminate in one way or another. Precluded also are forms of representation of interests or assumptions of overlordship in families or communities which deny members of those social groups independent civil status. Civil independence is established by distributing the burdens and rights of citizenship equally. The great practical importance of equality before the law is that it argues for the presumption of citizenship and thus contributes to the case for just law. Equality before the law is sustained through mechanisms for fairness in application. As Locke observed, men are not impartial judges in their own cases or those of their friends.[8]

So an adequate assurance of fairness in applying the law

---

[8] John Locke, *Two Treatises of Government*, ii., sect. 13, p. 316.

requires an institutional instrument—an independent judiciary—which understands itself as an arm of the civil association not of the government. Whatever other institutions figure in the constitutional base, and I do not discuss those here, this one has a central place wherever limits on government power are enforced and citizens are given maximum assurance of fair and impartial treatment before the law.

Political accountability also deserves special note as a principle that must have a controlling influence on the construction of the base. Here the questions are of regular submission to electoral processes and conformity to whatever constitutional constraints exist. The reality of accountability depends on publicity, through the operation of a free press; on there being a choice of potential governments as enabled by a right to form political parties, and cultivation of the idea of a constitutionally loyal opposition; and, once more, on the existence of an independent judiciary capable of upholding a constitution in the face of a government's attempts to stay in power beyond its term or to enact laws that override the constitution.

The mechanisms of procedural fairness and political account-ability are designed so that legislation remains faithful to the overall aim of pursuing policies within a self-governing frame-work. This overall aim is best satisfied when the constitutional base allows people to fine-tune their representatives' version of their interests by regular electoral checks and there is an institution of judicial review which is independent of both of them.

The argument for the principle of the rule of democratic law starts from the fact that people need to be able to pursue their plans and projects confident of their own physical security and the long-term forbearance of others. Unless people have such assurances they know that the multiplicity of independent judgements of what is good will threaten each with violence from another. Now the partners in Ideal Discourse recognize their need for the rule of law (a state) because of their Humean circumstances of justice. But not any rule will do. They cannot all agree to a form of rule which risks a loss of power for some to play an effective part in the determination of political affairs. Thus they are drawn to democratic law because it offers not only basic security but insurance against a loss of control of political power. This latter aspect comes out in the main ground for democratic law.

This ground invokes the constraints of Equal Respect, Symmetry, and Universality. These conditions forbid acceptance of principles which would have the effect of undermining belief in the normative equality of each human being. Thus rule by the wise and the holy is forbidden by the conditions, not because the wise and the holy are not virtuous rulers—they may well be so—but because it undermines a sense of the worth of everyone's effort to find for herself the good she is to pursue. The principle of the rule of democratic law has a clear advantage over a principle of rule by the holy and the wise because democratic law subverts possible claims to political authority by social aristocracies, or economic, religious, or moral élites posing as expert planners, advisers, or discriminators of the common good. It thus helps to ensure mutual respect among citizens as bearers of equally valuable moral personalities, the interest represented by the constraints.

Furthermore the principle has a positive role in fostering the development and exercise of peoples' capacities for choice. It values as the best state of affairs one in which decisions are arrived at in ways that honour individuals' own judgemental dignity even if those decisions cost more, leaving less time and resources for other goods, or are not optimal in making the political community wealthy. Thus it gives positive support to the capacities (e.g. for self-origination) which the conditions on Ideal Discourse express.

Another attractive feature of the rule of democratic law is that it is self-sustaining in some measure. I mean that its institutional structure embodies features such as the separation of legislative and executive powers and constitutional barriers to the pooling of power in the hands of the few. This means that citizens do not find that the cost of defending their liberties is a commitment to politics so full that they must set aside other ambitions and projects. Disengagement from concern with public life is related to possibilities of engagement which are culturally as well as personally crucial—artistic and creative and intellectual projects of various kinds. These are often absorbing activities which consume such quantities of time and energy that individuals cannot both dedicate themselves to them and represent their interests in a public forum. So while self-rule must be taken to require that every citizen has rights and opportunities for political participation it would be quite at odds with the idea of multifaceted autonomy to suppose that politics must be at the active centre of every citizen's life.

Thus there are good reasons for partners in Ideal Discourse to adopt the principle of the rule of democratic law. It is clearly in their interests as free and equal persons to select a principle which helps to insure them against despotic and paternalist rule, which fosters mutual respect and capacities for choice, and which releases them from constant political engagement. However, it should not be thought that the principle can be adopted in isolation from the rest of the principles to be considered. For each principle is interpreted and applied in the light of the others so partners can know that all the constraints on valid agreements are satisfied only when they have the package as a whole before them.

(ii) *Limited Moral Establishment*

The constitutional base for respecting autonomy would also respect a principle that Neil MacCormick has called Limited Moral Establishment.[9] MacCormick states the principle as follows:

> State powers may be and ought to be exercised so as to enforce moral requirements, but only those which are other-regarding duties of respect for persons, and only to the smallest extent necessary to securing for all the conditions of self-respect as autonomous beings.[10]

This principle faces squarely the issue of the enforcement of morals by allowing, while setting a clear limit to, legislation of morality. Its rhetorical advantage over the formulation of the same idea in the more familiar terms of political neutrality is that it offers no basis for hostile misinterpretation of it as an impossible doctrine of the value-neutral state.

The principle of limited moral establishment is proposed in the Ideal Discourse as translating the constraint of Secularity into a

---

[9] Neil MacCormick, *Legal Right and Social Democracy*, 35.
[10] Ibid. 37.

politically intelligible form. It prescribes what the state must and must not do in the name of autonomy. This feature may be brought out by observing the way the principle situates liberty, toleration, and harm in relation to autonomy.

Clearly, people capable of forming and reforming their lives in the light of circumstances, experience, and moral growth require others to refrain from imposing on their plans of life or final ends. Now the principle limits moral establishment to securing the conditions of self-respect for autonomous beings. So it restricts the state from enforcing any conception of substantive morality whether it be that of the majority, or a dominant moral élite. Thus it secures maximum liberty for citizens to order their lives as they see fit.

The principle also situates toleration in relation to autonomy. Autonomy generates a plurality of distinctive moralities, each with its own practices, aims, and character virtues. The attitudes and emotional responses associated with any one of these may well lead adherents to experience feelings of impatience with others who display the virtues and concerns of rival moralities. More seriously, they may develop a moral distaste for other views or their protagonists, or a sensitivity to moral offence that readily translates into intolerance. So, in addition to developing the virtues internal to a substantive morality, people need to develop a second-order virtue of toleration if they are to address the problem posed by the conflicting claims on the form of a common life that different moralities make.

To be accepted as a virtue toleration must appeal to a mutual recognition by members of different moral outlooks of each other as pursuing a good, each in her own way. That requires an attitude to moral commitments that may not be imaginable within certain moral views, ones which enjoin imposition of their conception of the good on everyone else.[11] So toleration implies an attitude of regard for others as sources of valid interpretations of the good that is of a piece with taking autonomy as an ideal. Thus toleration has its place within the ideal of autonomy and is not a morally neutral principle. We see toleration operating as a defence of the autonomy interest in moral pluralism when it is invoked to argue against limiting

[11] Jeremy Waldron, 'Theoretical Foundations of Liberalism', 145.

styles of life, or ethnic, sexual, or religious practices even in the face of any moral distress that some of these might cause to people of different beliefs and backgrounds.

The place and nature of the harm principle may be understood as follows. The stated aim of the principle of limited moral establishment is to secure to all the satisfaction of their needs as autonomous beings. If all that such beings need from each other is freedom from interference this aim will be met by introducing a harm principle which excludes interfering with a person except to stop her harming others. If, on the other hand, as the argument of Chapter 7 suggests, autonomy is better seen as a condition of undominated interdependence, considerations of autonomy will undoubtedly sanction enforcement of positive as well as negative duties towards each other. Thus what constitutes harm is broadened to include harming others by neglecting to provide them with a fair share of the resources necessary to develop their autonomy. It follows that a state whose responsibility is to provide the conditions of autonomy for its citizens undertakes to secure to them a sufficiency of worldly resources, services, and cultural conditions for the exercise and development of their autonomy even though that involves re-distribution of resources and provision of public goods and services.

Of course, such a generously interpreted harm principle derives from the principle of autonomy, and does not therefore permit favouritism for forms of life that are widely seen as desirable, for that would upset the condition of moral pluralism. Deference to the latter condition is also why practices and cultural forms that are seen in civil society as especially worthwhile but vulnerable, or ones that are special to a people's identity—a minority language, or particular cultural tradition, for example—might be privileged by a more favourable distribution of special rights and resources than equal distribution would sanction. Such treatment is enjoined by the desirability of including in the range of conceptions of the good life ones that have particular cultural significance or that people have special reason to want as an option.

Now for the parties in Ideal Discourse a very great attraction of limited moral establishment is that it presents the parties with an overall view of the place in autonomy of the freedom, toleration, and harm principles. Thus they see themselves being able to have a constitutional base which has a high degree of integrity, especially as more principles manifesting a family resemblance come into view. This is bound to help the integrity of law-making and future constitutional interpretation thus ensuring a great deal of stability in the basic social structure. This in turn will help to make people feel secure in their knowledge and possession of their rights further reinforcing stability. It will also release people from the need for constant vigilance over their liberties. For these reasons, in addition to its obvious suitability for manifesting Secularity in the basic social structure, the principle of limited moral establishment is adopted by the parties in Ideal Discourse.

(iii) *Publicity*

Respect for individual capacities for identifying and pursuing a worthwhile life generates a requirement that political authority should be intelligible and acceptable to those who live under it. The point and workings of the political order should be open to view, in the sense of being available for public examination and assessment. As Jeremy Waldron puts it, the social order should be 'transparent'.

People should know and understand the reasons for the basic distribution of wealth, power, authority and freedom. Society should not be shrouded in mystery, and its workings should not have to depend, on mythology, mystification, or a 'noble lie'.[12]

A written constitution is, I believe, the most powerful expression of this publicity condition. As the public text of the terms of political association, it signifies that the aims and mechanisms of the state are accessible to all, thus reinforcing the value of political equality. As symbol of transparent political relations it helps to undermine any general case for state secrecy, or for political aims which are opaque and justified by claims to superior political expertise.

Even where there is a written constitution, publicity cannot be assured apart from the operation of free media of communication. In democratic politics freedom of the media has a claim to special protection that may be stronger or wider in scope than

---

[12] Waldron, 'Theoretical Foundations', 146.

that offered under the general principle of freedom of speech. The basis of that claim is the *political* content of the press and other media. While much editorializing and reporting is politically partisan or ideological, a free media that is not under monopoly ownership, has potentialities for political exposure and for open criticism of public officials and policies, that mass democracies need in order to keep control over officials and check the aggrandizing tendencies of governmental power. Just as important, is the potential of a free media for promoting the widespread public deliberation of political issues that is the ideal of a democracy.[13]

The argument for the various rights and liberties that the principle of publicity sanctions is primarily an argument from respect for individual self-governing powers. The presumption of shareable knowledge built into that idea argues for political justifications that employ public and intelligible methods of reasoning, accepted tests of truth or falsity, and common-sense knowledge. Thus the principle of publicity requires the use of less controversial arguments in politics than elsewhere in life. The reason is that political allegiance cannot be commanded unless arguments are *seen* to be sound as well as being so.

The principle of publicity is a way of confirming Equal Respect and Symmetry in the basic structure. It also has a powerful claim on the parties in Ideal Discourse as installing Universality in the basic structure. If no one is rightly ruled by others then no one is to be excluded from knowledge of the aims and workings of the political system. Partners in Ideal Discourse recognize that the discursive partnership of all could not survive a situation where political knowledge becomes opaque to ordinary citizens or ends up as the province of experts or so-called moral leaders. They cannot risk the development of a situation where there is no check on the employment of political principles which are grounded in the moral intuitions or claims to moral superiority of certain people, or which rely on controversial empirical claims about human nature. They cannot risk the development of political practices, the workings of which are a mystery to all but the dedicated specialist. So to insure against political inequality,

---

[13] For this point I am indebted to Frederick Schauer, *Free Speech: A Philosophical Enquiry*, 107.

frustration, and apathy, the partners would adopt the idea of designing their social arrangements on a principle of publicity. Of course, publicity can fulfil this role only in conjunction with other principles. We need not suppose that every form of rule by the holy and the wise, or even by a dictator, is clandestine in its aims and workings. But within a democracy there is special reason for publicity because of the inbuilt presumption of democratic accountability.

(iv) *Integrity*

We must consider what principle Ideal Discourse establishes to protect the link between a person's beliefs and commitments and her actions, for moral personality is set at nought if people's agency cannot express both their conceptions of the good and the contingent way they hold those conceptions. An adequate account of self-government must therefore include a principle to protect moral agency in line with considered convictions. Accordingly, the constitutional base should include a principle I call integrity. This operates by protecting various freedoms of expression and access.[14] Freedom to speak and practise one's convictions preserves the link between belief and expression necessary to moral agency. Furthermore it provides a person with the opportunity to persuade others to share, or at least understand, her convictions, a crucially important factor in her sense of their significance for life. For, our deepest convictions are never purely private. They call for public acknowledgement and witness. Freedom of address is also crucial to preserving those convictions in the face of attack by others. We find in this principle therefore justification for orthodox civil liberties, ranging from freedom of conscience and freedom of thought to freedom from censorship, surveillance, and brainwashing.

The principle of integrity also secures people's freedom to examine, and change their conceptions of the good, for moral agency is constrained if people are forbidden opportunities to form and test their convictions in the light of information, imagined alternatives, fantasies, and the like. Thus the principle

---

[14] Cf. Ronald Dworkin's principle of authenticity which has several correspondences with the principle of integrity. Dworkin, 'What is Equality? Part III: The Place of Liberty', 34–6.

enjoins free access to information, imaginative and other literature, drama, and film. (Of course these freedoms have other supports besides integrity. We should expect the several principles in the system to co-operate in their construction of the base. They also have to be adjusted to each other.) Access includes support for the common human conditions in which moral agency is nurtured and informed. So assaults on the communal and familial bases for introducing individuals to traditions of thought and feeling are condemned. And assault is understood broadly to include lack of appropriate positive support as well as repression.

A constitutional base which takes integrity as a controlling principle also supports the protection of privacy in the base for there can be no more direct attack on the unity of our physical, mental, or moral selves than the intrusions of observers. Intrusion is a form of disrespect that violates both our need to escape from the public gaze and our attempt to form and sustain a view of the world which is independent of the opinion or coercion of others.

Integrity also confirms constitutional arrangements which allow considerations of rights in Dworkin's image to 'trump' considerations of general welfare.[15] This is because integrity respects individuality, our substantive separate moral personalities. Individuality is constituted and continuously affirmed in activities and expressions that reflect our self-understandings and the standards of conduct we have elected as our own. Understood in this way individuality is the product of autonomous self-creation and grounds the claim to personal inviolability that rights protect in repudiation of any involuntary sacrifice of vital individual interests for the sake of the social whole.

The principle of integrity is most centrally connected with Equal Respect. The liberties that integrity collects are necessary for development and exercise of capacities to follow a conception of the good. The free social conditions that these make also encourage development of the capacity to give justice to others and to identify with one's society as a good society. The general character of the principle in relation to moral agency, its

---

[15] Dworkin, 'Rights as Trumps'.

grounds, and effects, are therefore reasons for its adoption by partners in Ideal Discourse. Indeed it would be irrational for them to reject it given their knowledge of the way religious bigotry and moral zealotry affect the moral agency of their victims.

(v) *Moral Rights against the State*

A political constitution is the public expression of a covenant which creates and limits that concentration and monopoly of coercive power which is the state. As covenant it signals background assumptions of autonomous agency. These are given political effect through principles of political, civil, and social rights of the kind I have been canvassing.

But nothing in the principles introduced so far ensures that individuals' security in their rights does not fluctuate with what the general welfare, or majority interest, requires at a given moment as would be the case under some kinds of socialization of the idea of rights.[16] T. H. Green's statement of the reasoning is representative of what I have in mind: 'A right is a power of acting for his own ends—for what he conceives to be his good—secured to the individual by the community, on the supposition that its exercise contributes to the good of the community.'[17] On this kind of account, as Green observes, rights *against* the state are 'an impossibility'.[18]

Now if it is the case that rights are instituted in order to serve the good of the community as determined by a maximizing principle of happiness or preference satisfaction, then it is indeed true that the idea of rights against the community is incoherent. When rights conflict with maximum community good or happiness they are simply invalid. But if rights are instituted in order to secure aspects of well-being without which no individual human can thrive, such as the distinctively human powers for autonomy, then what the society or state must secure to each individual just *is* a right to insist that her vital interests are not overridden by the state claiming to act for the

[16] This is one of the points Hart makes against utilitarian entitlements in his *Essays on Bentham*, 86.
[17] T. H. Green, *Lectures on the Principles of Political Obligation*, lect. M, p. 207.
[18] Ibid., lect. H, p. 145.

good of the whole. To make sure that considerations of rights 'trump' considerations of general welfare, the discourse partners design their constitutional base to include a principle that makes this explicit. This is the principle of moral rights against the state.

The principle constrains the principle of the rule of democratic law by insisting that majority rule be adopted only as checked by an institution of individual rights. The case for this appeals to the Equal Respect ground for democracy. When we defend democracy on grounds of Equal Respect our defence rests on a more fundamental case for respecting persons, namely their equal worth as moral personalities. An autonomy-based doctrine of democracy draws its support from that normative conception, so too does a doctrine of constitutional rights, for these are the political face of the individual moral rights that allow for the exercise and development of moral powers. So individual rights belong on the same root-stock as the principle of democracy. This is why democracy at the deepest level of justification rests on the case for individual rights. These constrain governments and majorities, for democratic power if it rests on individual rights is not the power of numbers, but the power of a constitution to support citizens to have a hand in devising the standards and objectives of their civic life.

When we think of individual moral rights against the state we should remember that the object is not merely to protect citizens from those in positions of official power, but also to protect citizens from one another. A variety of forms of discrimination happens in economic and social spheres without any help from political institutions. The principle of individual rights against the state asserts a common civil status in the name of which unacceptable discrimination is outlawed. So it protects members of ethnic minorities from forms of treatment that betray judgements of superiority and inferiority. It protects women from social limitations on their education, opportunities, and chances in life. This is especially relevant for estimating the force to be attributed to the requirements of an ethnic or religious community that women play traditional roles in the home. Arguments for support of traditional women's roles, in so far as they succeed under the principle of integrity, are not threatened by the principle of individual rights for that principle supports the choices women make for family and community values. But the latter principle does outlaw arranged marriages and educational, social, and civil impedimentss to equal access to the means and enjoyment of autonomous life.

The basis for the principle of individual rights against the state is autonomy in all its aspects. So this principle is well-grounded for partners in Ideal Discourse. They have no reason to prefer a principle which secures individual rights for the good of the community. Indeed such a principle not only makes rights hostage to considerations of general welfare but also treats persons and their interests as of instrumental, not intrinsic importance. This makes for a society which is no respecter of persons and where people find it difficult to be confident of their own value.[19] This is a grave disadvantage for people concerned to develop institutions empowering them to author their own lives. It would therefore be unwise, not to say irrational, for discourse partners to reject the principle of autonomy-based rights against the state in favour of a community-good-based principle.

(vi) *Strong Social Provision*

The idea underlying political association is social provision. That is the thought that the society as a whole makes provision for certain goods for all on the basis of need and regardless of individual contribution. Social provision is basically redistributive. This is why, as Michael Walzer, observes, every state 'is in principle a "welfare state" '.[20] Social provision is given separate expression as a principle to ensure that the provisions of the basic social structure are regarded in a certain light, that is, as making a community in which the range of political authority is co-extensive with enjoyment of the rights and responsibilities of membership. The principle calls for the fulfilment of those needs of members on which the claim to political authority rests. Thus the principles considered so far are proposed as terms of political association under which autonomous beings can work together to provide for their own needs. The terms themselves are objects of social provision for all members.

---

[19] Cf. Rawls, *A Theory of Justice*, 181.
[20] Michael Walzer, *Spheres of Justice*, 68.

The principle of social provision is not inherently controversial. The idea that the state must redistribute from the well-off to provide security for all and basic subsistence for the very poor is not seriously challenged even by advocates of the minimal state. The question is whether the constitutional base must include social provision for needs of members, other than security from interference or bare subsistence. This is the question of strong social provision.

The conception of autonomy that I have advocated does provide reasons for adopting a principle of strong social provision to cover a more comprehensive range of needs. Many of these are the subject of ongoing political determination, as circumstances, resources, and self-interpretations change. The base cannot anticipate, though it must facilitate, ongoing assessments of needs and policies for meeting them. But it can provide for distributions of income and wealth to join the other primary goods—the basic liberties, rights, and opportunities that come under our various principles as the all-purpose means of autonomous life. Now the undertaking to regard autonomy needs as a matter for social provision implies creation of common assets, though not, I think, a determinate view about whether those assets are to be provided through collective or private control of resources.

The principle of strong social provision is neutral as between various property regimes under which income and wealth can be held. The purpose of property is to allow maximum scope to autonomy as specified in the several principles that constitute the base. Since no system of property rights is natural, in the sense of antecedent to these principles, but is to be devised in social deliberation constrained by the demands of autonomy for all, different systems of property may suggest themselves in different historical and social circumstances. The regime chosen must be able to serve the interests of autonomy. The very minimum requirement here is Rousseau's principle: 'In respect of riches, no citizen shall ever be wealthy enough to buy another, and none poor enough to be forced to sell himself.'[21] So if private property in capital resources is selected, the appropriate conception is unlikely to be specified by the rules of full

---

[21] J.-J. Rousseau, *The Social Contract* bk. II, ch. 11, p. 96.

liberal ownership. In circumstances of scarcity relative to
demand on resources, the principle of autonomy provides the
basis for a system of limited property rights fettered by
restrictions on transfer and total accumulation and sometimes
on use and control also. Similarly, if collective ownership of
capital resources is selected, the experience of the limits on
personal independence that arise under familiar collectivist
regimes will argue for effective restrictions on the massing of
power in a one-party state.

In reality, a mixed regime of property is coming to be
regarded as appropriate to the needs of modern constitutional
democracies. But the particular mix is everywhere disputed on
economic and ideological grounds. The base should not attempt
to adjudicate the outcome of these disputes which are the stuff
of ongoing political debate. Instead it recognizes a right to the
means of autonomous life and leaves the determination of how
that abstract right is to be met to the ongoing political debates a
political society has, in the context of concrete knowledge of
resources, moral and economic traditions, and historical experience.

In Chapter 7, I showed that self-ownership would be rejected
by Ideal Discourse partners invoking all the constraints on
conversational agreements. This means that the libertarian
doctrine confining social provision to the protection of antecedent property rights is not acceptable. The case for strong
social provision is that it is a condition of autonomy as positive
freedom. To be autonomous in this sense is to be in a position to
exercise one's moral powers. A person is not in this position if
she is struggling for survival. The satisfaction of basic needs is a
precondition of being able to form and pursue a view of a
worthwhile life, and to change one's view for another. But more
than the fulfilment of basic needs is required if there is to be
more than the possibility of formal autonomy. A substantive
autonomy requires a social environment which sustains individual access not only to the material means of life but to a
sufficiency of means to participate in the cultural pursuits and
practices to which she may reasonably aspire. The necessity to
provide the conditions of autonomy is a basic ground for our
discourse partners to choose the principle of strong social
provision. The case might be made by invoking several of the

constraints on discourse. But it can be made most expeditiously relying on the condition of Reasonableness. It may be recalled that Reasonableness is an element of the conception of fair terms of co-operation, terms that each accepts on condition they all do. Now Reasonableness blocks universal acceptance of any principle of social provision which foreseeably leaves some people with little more than formal autonomy. A principle acceptable to all must offer prospects of substantive autonomy for all. Now strong social provision meets this condition. Being grounded in the idea that the point of social co-operation is to sustain the autonomy of all, it provides the necessary background guidance to distribution and redistribution. Discourse partners will see in the principle a case for providing everyone with something like equal starts in life, at least as the baseline from which deviations have to be justified. So, given that they want autonomy for all, they have every reason to choose the principle of strong social provision.

8.3. SUMMARY

The principles I have adduced provide a constitutional base in which familiar civil and political rights are to be found. Our general understanding of what it is to have such rights is framed by a complex notion of autonomy in which separation and attachment interests both have a role. While the interest in separation from others is traditionally given such prominence that liberty rights are treated as requiring non-interference only, the interest in attachment is no less crucial since autonomous life has no meaning apart from socially founded deliberation and choice. What is required, therefore, is a political society in which the attachment interest of autonomy is honoured in social provision of the means of autonomous life for all members. That means that economic and social rights flow from our understanding of autonomy no less than rights to liberty.

In introducing the principles of self-government I have appealed to the various elements of autonomy as brought together in the construction of the Ideal Discourse situation which we may regard as the mediating link between the abstract ideal of the person as autonomous and an autonomy-regarding

190

political society.[22] The Ideal Discourse situation allows us to test proposed political principles for autonomy-regardingness. A principle that can be consensually agreed in conditions of Ideal Discourse passes the test. Now such consensus is not to be thought of as a happy coincidence of outcomes of deliberations pursued by individuals in independence of each other and each other's interests. Each participant is represented as rationally wanting only what all can want, if she wants a whole society of autonomous individuals. I take it that she does for two reasons. One is that if autonomy is her ideal she must acknowledge that it is a good for all. Second, since autonomy requires inter-dependence just as much as independence, it must be shared in order to be enjoyed. To keep this element of reference to others in play we have to envisage putative political principles being assessed as a system from the point of view of autonomy as elaborated in the norms of Ideal Discourse. Thus a system including principles that fail to preserve, say, the equality of power represented in the condition of Symmetry, or the suppression of purely private or sectional interests represented in the condition of Generality, is rejected even if it sustains other important autonomy interests, for it could not possibly win the assent of those who stand to lose under its operation.

This said, the political principles taken severally are not equally central to each autonomy principle. However, each political principle has a place in the system only in so far as it has work to do for one or more elements of autonomy. So I would like to point up the connections each principle has with such elements in a summary fashion.

The principle of the rule of democratic law distributes political authority to citizens along with the powers to maintain a pattern of limited political powers. Thus it provides conditions which are of the highest significance for empowering citizens to stand before each other in political relations that manifest their equality. So this principle finds a place in the system because of its special role in instituting political arrangements designed to sustain norms of dialogic partnership, especially Equal Respect, Symmetry, Reasonableness, and Generality. We might repres-

---

[22] The original for this is Rawls's account of the original position as the mediating link between the moral person and that of the well-ordered society. See 'Kantian Constructivism', p. 520.

ent the inclusion of the principle as the result of an ideal agreement by all dialogic partners because they are all committed to the norms that it implements. In similar fashion the other political principles are construed as outcomes of agreement in reasoning from inevitably shared norms of Ideal Discourse to conditions of their enjoyment and development in the actual world.

The principle of limited moral establishment is prominent in providing for Equal Respect and Symmetry also, but its most central role is to translate Secularity into a politically intelligible form. Thus, in the circumstances of moral pluralism, what subordinating one's conception of the good to the demands of what is right *means* in political terms just is being prepared to accept a constitution that is blind to substantive moral goals. The significance of publicity lies most clearly in its connection with Symmetry, but of course that harks back to respect for powers of moral determination so reasons drawn under the heading of Equal Respect and Universality also figure prominently as grounds for its acceptance. This is typical of the mutual support of principles in the system. Integrity is most centrally concerned with Equal Respect. Like the other principles that give voice to Equal Respect, it passes through that condition to the underlying moral powers, the valuing of which gives rise to respect. Thus it connects with all the other principles of the system. The central significance of the principle of social provision lies in its intent to make an autonomy-regarding political society. It is a principle that Ideal Discourse partners have reasons to adopt under all the terms of their conversational partnership. The principle of individual rights is also implicated in this central way in all the terms of autonomy-regarding political conversation. Its significance lies in its distribution to each individual of all the rights and powers that come under the other principles in defiance of demands of individual sacrifice made under the aegis of utilitarian or perfectionist ideals of the good.

At the beginning of this chapter, I outlined the image of the citizen that we construct when we espouse the ideal of autonomy. We may now see how that image is given definition by the political principles. It will be evident that they criss-cross and overlap to establish and maintain substantive equality of citizenship by distributing rights equally and assuring their equal worth. The principles assure the co-operation required of beings who are interdependent for enjoyment of autonomy. And they are designed to make intelligible the possibility of resolving conflicts by discussion rather than force. So they meet at once the autonomy interest in discursive community and the practical political interest of modern democracies in resolving conflicts by agreements reached through dialogue rather than force. Of course I make no claim for the completeness of this scheme of principles. Others may cry out for inclusion. And a constitution has to settle many other matters besides questions of fundamental rights so there are many more principles governing the base than the ones I have identified.

I have indicated what sort of rights we have under each principle. These are mainly rights on which there is a consensus in the various documents of the international code of human rights. Many more might be cited but my overall aim here is not to debate the merits of particular rights but to provide a framework into which the central range of rights in the international code may be fitted in an intelligible and defensible way. Thus the task of making sense of what it is to have a right ends here.

I have argued that the meaning of a rights claim is to be found not in ideas of ownership but in ideas of government as specified by principles of democratic citizenship built on the complex ideal of autonomy. The difference between the proprietary and the political understandings of right-holders may now be elucidated in the following way. Under the proprietary conception of rights people are ascribed *alienable* rights in personal endowments. Thus self-ownership is the idea that each person is assigned alienable rights in her person and personal powers within a system of property rules—the rules of full liberal ownership. By contrast, the political conception places persons outside the instrumental realm of property altogether by assigning them *inalienable* personal rights in recognition of their moral status as ends in themselves. Thus self-government is the idea that each person is assigned inalienable rights in her person and personal powers within a political system—the principles and rules of a liberal-democratic polity.

9

Rights as Political

9.1. INTRODUCTION

The course of history makes plain that human beings are prepared to use force to secure their needs. The great strength of liberal democratic thought has been to accept this natural fact while diminishing its social destructiveness by developing political systems in which persons can meet their needs by acknowledging a scheme of mutually acceptable rules and in which the use of force is devolved on agents charged with impartial enforcement of those rules. Thus, the natural reasons that individuals have to employ force—their strong natural desires to preserve their lives and liberties, for example—are acknowledged as permanent pressures on society which can never be suppressed though they may be civilized through the institution of rights.

In this chapter I make some general remarks about the connection between liberal democratic thought and a political understanding of rights, and pursue the bearing that has on belief in universal human rights, rights-scepticism, and talent pooling.

9.2. THE POLITICAL UNDERSTANDING OF RIGHTS

As I understand it, liberal democratic thought is best understood in relation to the social contract tradition. That constructs political arrangements as a scheme of co-operation the terms of which are laid down by free and equal persons. The significance of the contract tradition is that it points to the value of individual freedom which makes a place for the notion of a moral right or a justified limitation of one person's freedom by another's. In this way, social contract theorizing addresses the natural fact that humans use force or the threat of force against each other by translating the idea of justified coercion into the idea of moral rights and placing the power to enforce them in a legally regulated political system.

In the course of its development this notion of voluntary politics has been unable to sustain the distribution of freedoms of equal worth on which its claim to the allegiance of free and equal citizens rests. Liberty has come adrift from equality, because the boundaries of individual liberty have been set historically by private property rules. The resulting conception of rights as proprietary was doubtless facilitated by the fact that the disputers of doctrines of absolute power and the divine right of kings shared with their opponents a background understanding of self-command drawn from their theological view of a self-owning God in whose image humans are created as (dependent) self-owners. Add to that the development of market institutions for which the idea of individual labour power as an alienable commodity was highly functional and the proprietary conception could scarcely fail to have become the entrenched view.

But the theological background no longer has any purchase on the disputes about liberty and equality in modern constitutional democracies. And the play of proprietary rights has made for such inequalities in wealth and power that liberal democratic societies cannot meet the citizenship claims they generate. A revised theory of rights as political tries to reform this political tradition from within by reworking its basic elements under the organizing idea of self-government. The need for such a theory arises because proprietary rights cannot be seen as appropriate to the fundamental value of autonomy on which liberal democracy is erected.

By rights as political I mean a conception of rights developed for persons conceived as citizens of a modern constitutional democracy.[1] The rights of citizens are, of course, moral rights but their character is political in that they are powers that flow from political principles of the kind worked out in the tradition of liberal democratic thought. The fundamental idea is that of a

---

[1] Here I use the idea of a political conception of justice developed by John Rawls. See Rawls, 'Justice as Fairness: Political not Metaphysical'.

liberty–constraint system as an agreement made by free and equal persons. The need to base rights in agreement may be understood from the following which recapitulates points scattered in earlier parts of the text.

Given that to have a right is to have a moral ground for coercing another, one main concern of a theory of rights is to determine when coercion is justified. The answer might be taken from such sources as accepted authoritative readings of divine or natural law, intuition of the requirements of an independent moral order, or a putative agreement between persons concerned to ensure a certain distribution of liberty. Since the rights we seek to determine are to cast persons as citizens in a modern democratic regime we must adopt a version of the last answer. The reason is that citizens of such a regime have different, sometimes incommensurable, moral, religious, and philosophical views and associated modes of justification. Lacking agreement on such matters, citizens can share a scheme of rights only if they are prepared to forgo the conflicting deliverances of their independent moralities in favour of a scheme they all agree.

This last point arises because of the character of the right–duty nexus. There can be no imposition of a duty on another person in the absence of a principle which can be acknowledged by her as a free and equal person. No one can be conceived to have a duty under a principle she could not morally countenance. Given the existence of moral pluralism, rights cannot be taken from a theory, such as Catholic natural law, which marks off one set of moral beliefs and justifications from another in our polity. Even if we think such a theory is true, we cannot make it the basis of our politics, because it could not be the basis of moral acknowledgement by citizens with the variety of moral and religious persuasions to be found in all modern liberal democracies.

The same point comes through from a consideration of the analysis of a right as a justified claim. What this entails is that the ground on which the claim is made is one acknowledged to justify coercion in our community. The presupposition of mutually recognized grounds as premises for arguments about the legitimacy of particular candidates for rights is a matter of the nature of justification. Here I follow John Rawls's view that:

'justification proceeds from what all parties to the discussion hold in common'.[2] Accordingly, to justify a rights claim to someone is to give her an account of how that claim follows from a starting point we both accept. It follows that schemes of rights are social in that they presuppose shared values or interests and a common judgement that their importance justifies securing them by force or the threat of force.

Now in a polity of persons whose ends are heterogeneous no proposed scheme of rights can be shared if it presupposes meanings drawn from favouritism for one of its contained ends. In the circumstance of heterogeneous goods citizens can share a scheme of rights only if there is common ground in the form of a shared view of how they are to deal with their differences. There can be no a priori guarantee of the existence of such a common ground. Liberal democracies owe their existence to the contingent fact that their dominant moral and political traditions historically embodied a right of conscience which made possible a principle of toleration and development of a conception of persons as morally autonomous agents. These were enabling ideas for the political settlements that followed the Wars of Religion in Europe. The settlements helped to sustain peace by allowing for a diversity of religious doctrines and a plurality of conceptions of the good. The constitutional politics that subsequently flourished has always had to allow doctrinal diversity while bringing about social unity through expanding the understanding and enjoyment of the conception of autonomous persons underlying the principle of toleration. One main thesis of this book has been that autonomy leads to self-government or democratic citizenship, not to self-ownership. So the scheme of rights appropriate to the deepest commitment of our political tradition is developed out of the principles of self-government.

In developing our understanding of rights as political we need to keep in mind the fact that rights belong to that branch of morality which deals with the justification of force, and that for us the control of justified force is normally the monopoly of the state. So talk of moral rights connects with the framework that regulates state power. We talk of rights against the state as a

---

[2] Rawls, *A Theory of Justice*, 580.

way of making the point that it would be wrong for the state to do or refrain from certain acts given that its rationale is to realize the principles of autonomy. And we acknowledge that such rights presuppose autonomy as a social good without thereby assuming a spurious statist underpinning of individual rights, that is, one which makes them powers of individuals dependent on the pleasure of the state. The points at which coercion is thought justified are represented as determined by an ideal community on the basis of what all can agree. That reconstructs the civic identity appropriate to a natural individual capable of responding to others as members of a community of ends and furnishes her with justified claims on the design of actual political communities.

So it should be stressed that a conception of rights as political is not to be thought of as making rights the children of politics whatever the polity turns out to be. Political rights are those moral rights that define the fabric of the good polity. That is an ideal that may be more or less realized in actual states. As ideal it furnishes us with the critical tools, including the idea of rights, for assessing actual polities. However, the good polity is not some distant Utopia but one that is within our grasp because its values are presupposed, if not fully honoured, by our actual political practices and our allegiance to constitutional democracy. So it is liberal democracy at its best. That is why, in seeking a conception of rights that better meets the expanded claims of modern democracies than the proprietary view, we stay within the tradition of thought that gives rise to rights and re-examine the foundational idea of autonomy. The thesis of rights as political is the claim that the best understanding of autonomy is captured by the political rather than by the proprietary conception. And that also enables us to adjudicate the dispute between advocates of the minimal state and of a more extensive redistributive social democracy in favour of the latter.

One further point about this political understanding of rights is that it starts from the claim that autonomy is the value to be secured by rights. That is merely to claim that autonomy is the fundamental presupposition of our political tradition. There is no claim that it is a universal human essence. Nor need such a strong claim be made. Justification of the political conception of rights is fundamentally addressed to an adversary within our political tradition and needs only to proceed from a premiss that is shared by the adversary.

9.3. HUMAN RIGHTS

The contextual character of the problems and principles with which I have been dealing suggests that talk of human rights is a misguided extension of the values and practices of one political tradition to all. My view that rights presuppose a shared commitment to autonomy would appear to make the idea of universal human rights theoretically incoherent and practically dangerous.

The charge of incoherence arises because autonomy is a parochial commitment of Western moral thought. It does not make sense then to take autonomy for a universal criterion of moral community. Indeed it may be argued that there are no universal criteria, only ones internal to the traditions and ways of life of particular communities. In any case, it may be said, my argument employs a view of justification as proceeding from shared premisses which makes universal rights impossible except by agreement. And autonomy is not a universally shared principle.

The practical danger of a universalism of rights is that it encourages imposition of our ideals and standards on other cultures, sometimes to the point of political interference and often through 'softer' cultural denigration and replacement of local customary ways of being in the world.

These are weighty points but I think they can be accommodated in our understanding of rights as political. The first thing to be said here is that the theory is a version of political liberalism, a doctrine worked out for politics not the whole of life. So, talk of human rights expresses a universalist attitude to political values, not to the details of different ways of life. We are talking of an overarching framework within which many kinds of life may be pursued, and it really is largely silent on the substance of these. That is not to deny that some forms of life, those practised by intolerant evangelizing sects, for example, would be unable to flourish within that general framework.

To deal with the first criticism (the claim that universalism with respect to rights presupposes an unacceptable doctrine of universalism with respect to criteria) it is useful to distinguish between descriptive and normative versions of a theory of rights. The descriptive version of rights as political moves from the existence of a practice of rights to the shared presupposition that accounts for its character and intelligibility. Thus it may be said to describe our sense of rights. The normative version projects our practice as one that ought to have universal political embodiment, an aim that acknowledges current differences in political values while anticipating future agreement. This is the version that runs into trouble for implying the existence of universal criteria of moral evaluation. The claim is that there can be no such criteria for there are no universal shared under-standings in relation to which universal criteria make sense. And neither can such criteria be drawn from an 'Archimedean point' outside all societies for criteria drawn from such an external source could have no purchase on the understanding or moral consciousness of those addressed. Accordingly, the normative version of a theory of rights such as ours lacks a basis in social reality and should be rejected. Is this conclusion warranted?

The normative claim is one that we make because of the character of moral evaluation for us. To evaluate human relationships in terms of a standard such as autonomy-regardingness is to be prepared to apply the standard in all similar cases—in the case of autonomy, wherever people have the requisite capacities of moral personality. Hence our moral evaluations are inherently universalistic. And so our universal-izing of rights is part of our understanding of the logic of moral evaluation. For this reason we inevitably find ourselves dis-posed to criticize breaches of rights wherever they occur.[3]

However, this argument only shows that we cannot reason-ably be expected to refrain from declaring the rights of people. It does not show that this local practice is a proper basis for intersocietal evaluations. Why should members of other cultures or societies find the practice intelligible and desirable? I think the answer is simply that in the case of political morality there is much more shared understanding than in other areas. This is

---

[3] Cf. Jeremy Waldron, *Nonsense upon Stilts*, 169.

because the international community has come to share a practice of intersocietal evaluation in human rights terms. This is manifest in reasonably widespread international subscription to the terms of the international code of human rights. Although this does not entail that states recognizing the international code hold themselves committed to the underlying values associated with various versions of liberalism, the fact of their subscription to the international code grounds the claim that a universalizing liberal theory of rights is intelligible to other societies and can find a foothold in their political moralities from which to proceed in moral/political justification. In sum, there is already a practice of intersocietal human rights evaluation and this can form the background that gives sense to the normative version of rights as political.

The desirability of a practice of evaluation in terms of human rights has much to do with the facts of near-universal political organization and the tendency of political power to enlarge itself and corrupt those who wield it. The near-universal repetition of the political form that we call the nation state, sometimes collected into larger blocks, evidences a world-wide political modernity that flies in the face of assumptions of massive diversity and incommensurability. For good or ill, the pooling of power that characterizes political organization is a world-wide phenomenon. And that means that people under political power share the problem of how to secure themselves from tyranny, dictatorship, and incompetent and unaccountable bureaucracies. This is no theoretical problem but one that has surfaced throughout political history and has been given contemporary immediacy by the events of 1989–90 in Eastern Europe. Any people which has suffered political corruption and incompetence or which is alive to the rich possibilities for internal oppression of the well-armed modern state has reason to consider the kinds of restriction on political power which a system of democratic rights installs. Thus, the urgency of the problem of limiting political power brings considerations of prudence, as well as local morality, to the selection of political values of the kind epitomized by human rights. To the extent that a system of democratic rights is adopted and acknowledged before other states the range of shared political meanings is enlarged. Of course the adoption of rights in non-liberal societies must be justified in terms of their mores and the overlap of their rights and ours will inevitably be incomplete and subject to differences of interpretation.

Here I want to recall that my overall aim is to develop a theory of what it is to have a right for the case of liberal democracies. That is the context of my claim that the best interpretation takes autonomy as the foundation of (liberal) rights. I do not say that all rights are liberal or that autonomy is the foundation of all rights. My present argument is not that there is a shared basis for a universalism of liberal rights. Instead it is the argument that the shared practice of human rights evaluation makes universalistic evaluations in terms of our theory of rights intelligible to others even if they disagree with us. This shared practice is then the basis for another—a practice of intersocietal debate about rights in which various theories are pitted against each other. This latter practice is an aspect of one of the central practices of our tradition—the practice of debating and contesting theories of justice. So we can see how our local practices can come to be shared once some suitable bridgehead to another culture is established.

The practical danger with any moral theory arises from the fact that its followers may be impatient to apply its prescriptions wholesale to an existing unjust or only partly just order. While the recent dramatic events in Eastern Europe have shown us the reality of radical revision of political orders, history teaches that wholesale transition to a new order is frequently accompanied by horrific deeds of retribution and purging of opposition. It may be hoping for too much to think this is less likely in a transition towards a polity based on respect for individual rights. But one advantage of a theory of rights is that it allows a creeping moral imperialism. Rights can spread piecemeal in an unjust or partially just regime thus reducing the risks of a Terror. This is because, as Jeremy Waldron has observed, a theory of rights is 'a series of discrete moral constraints on power and politics'.[4] Each constraint can function independently of the others. So we can fight issues as they arise. Censorship, torture, internment without trial, and so on, may be worked on one by one. This piecemeal approach has the

---

[4] Waldron, *Nonsense*, 172. I owe the point made in this paragraph to Waldron.

additional advantage of allowing practical problems to raise the issue of introducing rights, thus avoiding introductions which are unintelligible apart from their role in resolving concrete social issues.

In all of this I am not suggesting that normative claims such as: 'All human beings are born free and equal in dignity and rights' express a commitment to rights that everyone *must* share.[5] The framework of rights is not a necessary one. But it is a good and useful way of distributing power in the extended Humean conditions of limited affections, material scarcity, and moral pluralism. Nor am I suggesting that the only rights worth having are liberal rights. These are particularly appropriate in our political tradition. But there would be no point in wishing them on a tradition which had some equally satisfactory way of its own of instituting respect for persons or which was far removed from the Humean conditions.

9.4. RIGHTS SCEPTICISM

By a metaphysical understanding of rights, I shall mean one which holds that rights emanate from the requirements of a moral order that is independent of us. Since our society disagrees about whether there is such an order, or if there is, about what its requirements are, a theory of rights for a modern constitutional democracy cannot adopt any of the contested interpretations. It avoids these in favour of a construction that can be agreed by protagonists of competing moral traditions provided each is concerned to find agreement with the others. In the following I want to show that this way of going about developing a scheme of rights rescues rights from the scepticism that was most powerfully expressed by Bentham and has lately reappeared in Alasdair MacIntyre's scathing likening of belief in rights to belief in witches and in unicorns.[6]

H. L. A. Hart has usefully identified Bentham's complaint about moral rights as a matter of their criterionlessness.[7] What

---

[5] *Universal Declaration of Human Rights*, art. 1; see also *European Convention for the Protection of Human Rights and Fundamental Freedoms*, Preamble; and *American Declaration of the Rights and Duties of Man*, art. 1.
[6] Alasdair MacIntyre, *After Virtue*, 67.
[7] H. L. A. Hart, *Essays on Bentham*, 82.

this means is that there is no principle for the identification of such rights. Consequently they lack sense. Protagonists of natural law might disagree. But Bentham denounces them:

Right . . . is the child of law: from *real* laws come *real* rights; but from *imaginary* laws, from laws of nature, fancied and invented by poets, rhetoricians, and dealers in moral and intellectual poisons, come *imaginary* rights, a bastard brood of monsters.[8]

To understand why Bentham thinks that the idea of a moral right is unintelligible we must keep two aspects of his jurisprudence and political theory in view. The first is his view that right, obligation, and law, belong together in the sphere of sanctionable acts. Obligation is the primary notion and its criterion is the existence of sanctions. These are set by law, which Bentham sees as the command of a sovereign. Rights are then connected with law and sanctions by being reduced to obligations: to have a right is to be the beneficiary of an obligation.[9] Thus there is an unbreakable connection between right and law.

Rights are the fruits of the law and of the law alone; there are no rights without law—no rights contrary law—no rights anterior to the law.[10]

The second aspect flows from Bentham's command or imperative theory of law. It is that law is what the sovereign or lawmaker commands. So, no sovereign no law. On this view, an appeal to natural law to found rights makes no sense unless natural law is seen as the command of a divine sovereign. But, Bentham observes, natural rights

are of all things the farthest from divine rights. For in no mouths are they so frequent nor so much insisted upon as in the mouths of those by whom the existence of a divine law and a divine lawgiver are equally denied.[11]

So he sees the doctrine of natural rights as an essentially atheist one. That is why he sees it as incoherent, for lacking the support of a lawgiver there can be no natural law, without which there can be no rights.

---

[8] Jeremy Bentham, *Anarchical Fallacies*, 69.
[9] See Waldron, *Nonsense*, 35.   [10] Bentham, *Works*, 3, p. 221.
[11] Bentham, *Anarchical Fallacies*, 73.

One interesting aspect of all this is that Bentham concedes the principle of rights anterior to positive law as long as we are talking of divine rights. His denial of moral rights does not touch the claims of those who assert rights on the basis of divine law. Of course, that does not help liberals for they forswear any theologically based theory of rights as unsuited to the needs of citizens who disagree in their theology. But we should observe that the core of Bentham's demand on a theory of moral rights is the demand for a criterion, a way of identifying such rights. He thinks that there cannot be a criterion in the absence of a lawgiver. The response is to give him a conception of persons as lawgivers (that is, as autonomous), from which we generate a moral law, the system of principles of self-government. Rights as political takes these for the principles of right and so meets the demand for a criterion.

A Benthamite may still refuse to concede that moral rights have sense. He may object that talk of moral law is not talk of sanctions so it is not real law and any rights that flow from such alleged law are therefore vacuous. I want to make two points about this, a very general one about the connection between law and sanctions, the other about the law as the source of sanctions for rights as political.

While there cannot be law without sanctions, these do not presuppose the existence of civil law. The connection between the idea of a sanction and the ideal of civil law is, I believe, a contingent one, a feature that may be masked for us by what I call the assumption of civility. This is the assumption that civil or political society is the context for all morally rightful coercion. Now, to have a right, that is, a moral justification for coercion, it is necessary for that justification to be recognized in one's society. But, contrary to the assumption of civility one's society does not have to be a state. Imaginative constructions of intelligible social conditions without law, states of nature, show us that there is no necessary connection between rightful coercion and civil law. We can envisage a social situation which recognizes each individual as the sole executor of her rights, or one which permits individuals to call on others to secure their enjoyment of rights. What we cannot envisage is such a pre-political society giving some of its members a monopoly on the defence of rights without reconstituting itself as a state and making some response to the question of who controls monopoly power. The social contract tradition has taught us to see civil society and law as answers to the problem of how to ensure against over-enthusiastic exercise of moral rights. These are anterior to positive law and provide its justification. The right of resistance which Locke insists on is the standing reminder of the logical independence of justified coercion from positive law. I think that it is important to make this point about the independence of civil law and sanctions because a great deal of influential opposition to rights is based on what I identified earlier as the assumption of civility. But rights have sense apart from that assumption.

My second point is that rights as political holds that moral rights license us to call on the resources of the state to defend them, since that is the social form that defence of rights takes in our tradition. For rights as political, the state exists to vindicate moral rights, so the connection between right and sanction is preserved without supposing that all moral rights flow from legal rights, or are embedded in them. While the independence of legitimate coercion from law gives moral rights an insurrectionist cast, the theory of rights as political is able to draw that sting. It is a theory which draws on liberal democracy in its best light and so regards democracies as there to vindicate our rights and best kept to that purpose by our readiness to stand on our rights against the state.

Like Bentham, Alasdair MacIntyre takes the view that rights presuppose law: 'a socially established set of rules'.[12] Such rules, he insists, are in no way universal, but historical and local. It follows that the notion of a *human* right is empty. Responding to Alan Gewirth's attempt to derive human rights from claims to necessary human goods, MacIntyre comments that recognition of a good, even a necessary good, carries no obligation to secure another's enjoyment of that good, whereas recognition of a claim of right does.[13] Plainly, MacIntyre is here following Bentham in connecting obligation with coercive sanctions and these with law or social practice (what Bentham describes as 'something to which the force of law is given').

[12] MacIntyre, *After Virtue*, 65.
[13] Ibid. 64 f. Alan Gewirth's argument may be found in his *Human Rights*, h. 1.

MacIntyre wants us to realize that these are located within the domain of concrete historical social forms, for then we should see that talk of human rights is vacuous.

From what I have said in the previous section, it should be clear that MacIntyre's point that claims to the possession of rights presuppose social practice or institution is well taken. But from the fact that such claims are not intelligible apart from social recognition it does not follow that they have merely local significance. For, that conclusion would require us to deny the evident fact that people can and do construct relevant rules and sanctioning bodies on an international scale. Peoples or states are not closed societies whose social meanings remain purely local because unexposed to outside influences.

Nevertheless, MacIntyre's point stands against the view that moral rights are presupposed by liberal democratic institutions. Why not talk here of legal rights and be done with it? My answer is that legal rights presuppose social acceptance of law as a source of justified coercion, which in turn reveals social acceptance of coercion for certain very valuable social ends. The fact that we institutionalize coercion under law *is* a contingent fact of the kind that so impresses MacIntyre. But the criterion of morally rightful coercion is not the presence of positive law or civil society but of the moral principle a society takes to generate coercive obligations. How a society decides to manage the administration of coercion is a logically separate matter. The good reasons we have for declining anarchy for democratic law should not blind us to the latter's artificial and historically local character.

These explanations will scarcely satisfy MacIntyre because he recognizes, as many do not, that belief in individual rights cannot be sustained without belief in a certain conception of persons as autonomous agents. This conception of persons is criticized by MacIntyre and other communitarians for the way it represents 'man' as an individual prior to and apart from all roles.[14] The claim is that the idea of an autonomous agent is incoherent. It portrays a person as capable of choosing her own ends. The suggestion is that what that means, is that a person must be thought of as split into a metaphysical and an empirical

---

[14] MacIntyre, *After Virtue*, 56.

self. The metaphysical self is a constituting subject that is undefined by any aims and attachments (hence its priority or logical independence), precisely in order that it may create its empirical *alter ego* by choosing its allegiances. Of course, in the absence of any identifying features, we cannot attach any sense to the claim that such a metaphysical self exists.[15] But on the present account of autonomy (and all others known to me) there is no metaphysical self lurking in the depths.

Let us state at the start that autonomy *is* an ideal of self-creation. So an autonomous agent is regarded as capable of detaching herself from the ends she finds herself implicated in as a member of *this* family, tribe, or clan, a citizen of *this* state, an inheritor of *this* set of stories, of *this* way of doing things, and so on. And in this possibility of detachment lies liberation from the limits imposed on persons by socially given roles and expectations. But for this possibility of detachments to be castigated as leading to the metaphysical self we would have to suppose that autonomy requires a person to stand apart from all her existing ends at once. It does not. There is no wholesale choice of ends. They have to be assessed one by one because some must always be held stable to give us the identity that keeps us afloat as empirical reflective beings. Like Neurath's mariner we are never able to return to port to rebuild ourselves from scratch. We must be content to take out one plank at a time until the whole is re-created to our satisfaction.[16]

This idea of piecemeal assessment of ends preserves moral independence without presupposing a logically independent self. But talk of the self as prior to its ends needs explanation if it is not to point to a vacuous metaphysical self. The phrase was first introduced by Rawls to express the idea that parties in the original position are excluded from knowledge of their final

[15] There must be an answer to the question: 'What is it that chooses (or moves or sleeps . . .)?' As David Wiggins puts it: '. . . for each compliant of a predicate like "moves" . . . there exists a known or unknown named or nameable kind to which the item belongs and by reference to which the "what is it" question *could* be answered. Everything that exists is a *this such*' (Wiggins, *Sameness and Substance*, 15).
[16] Cf. W. V. O. Quine on rebuilding our talk of physical phenomena, 'Our ɔoat stays afloat because at each alteration we keep the bulk of it intact as a going ɔncern' (*Word and Object*, 4).

ends and attachments. In response to Michael Sandel's accusa-
tion that the original position involves a metaphysical conception of self 'shorn of all its contingently-given attributes' Rawls
claims that this is a misunderstanding, 'an illusion caused by not
seeing the original position as a device of representation'.[17] The
idea is that the original position models a point of view from
which a fair agreement between free and equal persons can be
reached. The model is designed to represent our sense of what it
is for persons to be situated fairly for the purposes of coming to
a binding agreement. So it excludes all the factors that bias
parties to an agreement in the real world. The exclusions are
represented in the model by the restrictions enumerated and
collected in the metaphor of the veil of ignorance. That is an
attempt to simulate the force of our convictions about the
circumstance of a fair agreement. When we reason in accordance with these restrictions, Rawls insists, 'our reasoning no
more commits us to a metaphysical doctrine about the nature of
the self than our playing a game like Monopoly commits us to
thinking that we are landlords engaged in a desperate rivalry,
winner takes all.'[18]

Against this background of explanation, we understand the
priority of the self over its ends to stand for a set of restrictions
on our reasoning for political principles. The restrictions are
designed to operationalize for practical reason the intuitive idea
that the point of view of the citizen in a modern pluralist
democracy must be transpersonally valid. So it must be drawn
from a conception of persons that they can agree for the purpose
of politics and which has precedence over their other differen-
tiating alliances.

Rights as political favours an Ideal Discourse situation over
the original position. Within this argument the priority of the
self over its ends is articulated in the restrictions of Ideal
Discourse but it is not caught in a global metaphor such as the
veil of ignorance. Instead, the force of the restrictions is
expressed by their monopoly position with respect to selecting
political principles. But on neither approach does autonomy
depend on the spurious doctrine of the metaphysical self.

[17] Rawls, 'Justice as Fairness', 238. For Sandel's interpretation of the Rawlsian
self see *Liberalism and the Limits of Justice*, 93–5.
[18] Rawls, 'Justice as Fairness', 239.

9.5. TALENTS AND BODILY INTEGRITY

In an earlier chapter, I elucidated the idea of self-ownership in terms of an analogy between absolute sovereignty and personal self-command. Absolute sovereignty, as Locke observed, is a despotism, the political expression of the master–slave relationship. A slave-owning master has full rights of disposal over the life and powers of the slave. He may not employ the slave's services to harm others, but he owes none of the slave's services to others. If this image of power organizes our thought about self-command, we will think of ourselves as having full rights of disposal over our lives and powers. We will think that we may dispose of our lives at our own discretion, that we may sell or lease our bodily parts, and that while we may not use our powers to harm others, no one else is owed any part of the use of our services. Thus self-ownership rights are strong on liberty and on the absence of forced contribution to others.

One attractive aspect of these rights is that they block social claims on our bodily parts just as much as on our labour. No one can demand the sacrifice of a kidney or an eye by another in order to save a life or improve its quality. A human cannot be bred in order to be cannibalized for spare parts for others, however many lives may be saved as a consequence. Bodily integrity is thus provided with a principled basis.

Now, bodily integrity has to be saved in any theory of individual rights, so the theory of rights as political has to provide a principle of preservation which is as effective as self-ownership. The trouble is that the principle of self-government or autonomy yields duties to contribute to others that go well beyond guarantees of non-interference. The conditions of autonomy cannot be satisfied unless the natural distribution of talents and powers is, in effect, treated as a collective asset of society as a whole, subject to the same principles of distribution as worldly resources. Perhaps the easiest way to understand this point is the following. If there is a duty to contribute to the well-being of others, they have a moral claim on the service of our talents and powers, so these cannot be under our exclusive individual control. We cannot be self-owners. In that case, the fact that talents or powers come in such-and-such individual parcels has to be treated as contingent from the point of view of justice. The natural facts of individual possession do not prejudice the question of who gets what under justice. Accordingly, and from the point of view of constructing entitlements only, we are to regard the distribution of individual possessions as common assets. This simply means that the question of entitlements is not automatically settled by the fall of talents.

Now, one worry about failing to regard natural endowments as owned where they lie is that society might be thought to own them and have, therefore, full powers of disposal over them. This prospect activates fears that the powerful would see no moral constraint on strip-mining the bodies and talents of the weak. The argument is that such proposals cannot be countered by individuals unless bodily integrity is protected by a right of self-ownership. The implication is that talk of individual rights to the services of others is incoherent and dangerous. It is incoherent because the aim of a theory of rights to protect individuals from being treated as mere means to others' ends cannot be met if all talents or powers are treated as distributable. No redistributions can be effected without violating bodily integrity. It is practically dangerous because redistributivism desensitizes our politics to personal violation.

It should be pointed out at the start of a reply to these charges that, for the purpose of devising a theory of justice, the device of regarding personal powers as a collective asset is not tantamount to treating them as owned by society. Ownership, whether private or social, is not yet established at the stage of theorizing where we locate the subject matter of social distribution. At this stage it is an open question whether talents should be owned by their possessors, or owned at all, and this is what the talk of collective assets is insisting. While there is a propensity to think that the protection of bodily integrity favours instituting ownership to coincide with natural possession, the connection can be made good only if there is no alternative.

The drift of my argument in this book is that talk of ownership of oneself makes very little sense. My preferred kind of talk is of capacities to act in accordance with principles or rules one has selected for oneself and which can be acted on by all others. The question is: how can bodily integrity be guaranteed by suc talk? Or, how can we construct a set of rights that both defend bodily integrity and the claims of the needy for the prerequisites of autonomy?

We should be clear that this problem of compossible rights exists for any theory that both sanctions redistributions as a matter of social rights and aims to be loyal to the notion of individuals as ends in themselves. The latter notion outlaws forced labour as immoral so if the benefits of natural endowments are going to be subject to redistributive principles, redistribution must stop short of conscription of bodily parts or talents. But given the fact that talents or powers come in bodily parcels and the value that bodily integrity has for a rights theorist, there is no alternative to the Nozickian intuition that violation occurs if someone else is at liberty to command all or any of my bodily resources. The rights that attach to the notion of autonomy or self-rule, whatever they are, must pair each individual with her own endowments and with no part of anyone else's. It follows that transfers must be freely made if bodily integrity is to be preserved. Accordingly, redistribution is justified only if it can be represented as founded on consent. In Chapter 8 the principle of strong social provision was shown to meet this criterion. In the Ideal Discourse situation it would be concluded by all as a requirement of autonomy for all.

But this abstract derivation of strong social provision leaves unclear how its operation is checked to conform with bodily integrity. I suggest that the appropriate check is built-in by the interpretation of strong social provision as a duty of care. While public care cannot reproduce the psychological feelings of mutual affection felt by people in intimate caring relationships, it can reproduce the other-regarding principles that govern the interactions of friends, lovers, and affectionate family members. The respect and concern for one another's well-being which characterizes those caring relationships is reproduced in the master principle of the public system—that it should embody only principles that can be adopted by all. In adopting the principle of strong social provision, a duty to aid the needy is undertaken. But as a principle of care which reproduces the other-regardingness of mutual affection it looks to the well-being of donors as well as recipients. The use of talents or powers in the service of others cannot be committed, even through voluntary self-sacrifice, to the point of destroying, disabling, or undermining the present or future autonomy of donors. Their entitlement to respect and concern means that their obligations to the needy can be no more demanding than what a needy loved one who cared for their well-being would be willing to accept in aid.

This approach helps us to identify appropriate interpretations of the principle of strong social provision. It does not lay out exact demands on talents and powers. These vary with social circumstances. For example, very little redistribution may be called for in regimes where wealth in natural resources and native talent combine to assure a commodious living for all. In other cases, a small working population may have to support a great number of dependants. There is no algorithm for settling the point at which the social demands threaten the inviolability of the workers. That remains a matter for local deliberation and practical judgement.

9.6. RIGHTS AND SOLIDARITY

Three main features characterize the outlook on rights I have been advocating against the self-ownership view. First, rights are seen as justified because they promote and protect autonomy, understood as the ability to devise and implement principles of action that all persons can accept. Second, the setting in which the principles that distribute rights are identified is a debate not a bargaining game. Participants want to arrive at the most reasonable interpretation of autonomy, not the most advantageous outcome under the assumption of each as out for herself. Third, rights are seen as positive as well as negative, reflecting their basis in autonomy as positive freedom.

The emphasis on the need for a shared basis for rights, the historical and culturally local character of the moral valuation of autonomy and rights, and the discursive setting in which the principles of right are identified make the outlook advanced here much closer to some communitarian doctrines than the traditional understanding of liberal rights. However, the autonomy-based community that is advocated does not lead to a common communal identity, nor to a common tie in 'brotherl love. The connection between autonomy and moral pluralism generates a demand for cultural diversity which undermines the case for defining identity in terms of a single communal goal and its associated system of affections and virtues. The liberal polity is an association in which many forms of flourishing and their associated virtues co-exist.

Since 'fraternity' is based on affection and shared ends, the factors of scale and moral pluralism in most contemporary democracies preclude trying to tie citizens together by a bond of love. The outlook advocated here would have civic friendship constituted in the collective process of defining and developing the social framework in which members advance their capacities for autonomy. That framework provides the institutional language in terms of which individuals identify their own autonomy interests and recognize others as deserving of respect and concern.

We might think of it as a kind of moral grammar that structures the political conversations and debates of citizens who are more often strangers than brothers and sisters. The possibility of civic dialogue observing such moral grammar makes the facts of our natural and social interdependence on strangers a good deal less threatening. Instead of trying to escape into forms of atomistic independence, we can accept our mutual dependence within the basic moral structure established in Ideal Discourse.[19] And the autonomy-regarding conversations and debates that citizens continue under the basic structure continues a collective process of self-understanding in which existing dependencies are continually scrutinized and restructured.

9.7. SUMMARY

In this chapter I have argued that rights are political in the sense of being moral powers which are specified by the political principles of a voluntary politics. I have argued that we should not be expected to refrain from asserting human rights generally, despite the parochialism of liberal theory, and that there is

---

[19] For a similar point see Bruce Ackerman, *Social Justice in the Liberal State.*

sufficient intersocietal evaluation in human rights terms to warrant our universalizing practice. I have addressed the issues of criterionlessness and the metaphysical self which lead to rights-scepticism and argued in each case that the belief at the root of the scepticism is unwarranted. I have argued that bodily integrity need not be violated under the principle of strong social provision. Finally, I have distinguished a fraternal from a solidarity-based civic association of the kind that develops under the ideal of autonomy.

10

Conclusion

10.1. MAKING SENSE OF RIGHTS

This has been an exercise in reconceptualizing the notion of rights against the state. The project was to examine the general framework of our thought about rights. I wanted to answer one main question about rights. This is the question of sense: 'What kind of claim does a proposition of moral rights make?' This question is closely related to two others. (1) The question of procedure—'How do we go about determining what rights we have?' And (2) the question of background conditions—'Why do we need the institution of individual rights?'

The received answer to the question of sense is that a proposition asserting a moral right is a species of proprietary claim. Such a claim is assertible just in case it is derivable from or constitutive of a person's status as self-owner as recognized in the social institution of private property. I have argued that this answer is mistaken. On my account a proposition of rights is a political claim which gets its sense from the status of persons as self-governing members of a liberal democratic polity. The shift from a proprietary to a political conception makes for dramatically different interpretations of the content of rights. Under the proprietary conception a question of content is answered by determining whether the putative content flows from self-ownership and the associated rules of private property. Under the political conception a question of content is answered by determining how it serves the interests of citizens who view themselves as self-governing in morals and politics and who understand self-government to be specified in principles of the sort I elucidated in Chapter 8. A good index of the rights that fall under such principles is given in documents such as the *European Convention on Human Rights* and the *American Convention on Human Rights*. The political conception of rights assesses such proposed schemes of rights by testing their role in securing the self-governing interests of persons.

10.2. DETERMINING WHAT RIGHTS WE HAVE

How do we go about determining what rights we have? Or, as this question may be put in view of the place we give to autonomy as the foundation of rights: how do we show the connection between autonomy and particular rights? This is a question about how we get from the general idea of autonomy to more determinate conclusions about rights. In Chapter 6, I presented this move as a form of social contract theory. Now the great historical paradigms of social contract theory presented contract as an agreement to protect antecedent rights. My approach departs from the assumption of pre-established rights. Instead rights are treated as the outcome of contract. My approach also departs from the common interpretation of a social contract as the outcome of a process of bargaining. As I see it the relevant process is one of rational debate. So my 'original position' is specified as an Ideal Discourse which is autonomy-regarding in observing constraints that reproduce the elements of personal and political autonomy identified in Chapter 5. The parties to Ideal Discourse are concerned to formulate political principles that all have reason to accept. The concern for principles that all can agree arises from the motivational assumption that the parties take autonomy for their social ideal and recognize their interdependence for its pursuit. Consequently, there is no need for a veil of ignorance to shroud the deliberators from knowledge that might bias their judgements. Bias is corrected by the requirement that every person be included and that all proposed principles pass the consensus test.

The Ideal Discourse models a way of thinking and talking that is available to anyone who accepts its constraints. Sometimes we may find it useful, although merely as a manner of speaking, to talk of partners in Ideal Discourse representing the voices of real people. But we should avoid taking this device too literally. It is developed to put before us in a vivid way the mode of thinking yielded by a coherent employment of our most central moral and political ideas. I have employed the device to identify the institutional principles which make autonomy-regarding discourse possible. These are described as the objects of agreement in the sense that they are principles which all agree in Ideal Discourse. The device mediates between the notion of autonomy and the set of institutional principles. Its purpose is to show how a proposed institutional principle meets or fails to meet some feature of autonomy. There is no suggestion that Ideal Discourse can take place independently of installation of appropriate institutional principles. Rather, we imagine such a discourse in order to work out its institutional presuppositions. In so far as these institutions can then be installed in the actual world, actual political discourse can realize the ideal. We will have a framework in which autonomy can be realized in speech and action. Once we have the principles of self-government we have the generative source of a unitary and intelligible scheme of rights. Bundles of familiar rights fall under each principle. And the content and limits of each right is determined by its justifying principle/s.

10.3. WHY THE INSTITUTION OF RIGHTS?

Our account of the sense of rights is incomplete without an answer to the question: 'Why rights?' This is really a question about the reasons for having a system of enforceable claims on each other. If social co-operation is necessary, for, let us say, the benefits of peace and security, or the economic and cultural achievements that result from co-operative effort, then its burdens and benefits must be distributed in a way that people accept as fair. Suppose then that fair principles of distribution are to hand. People may implement them by automatically adjusting their behaviour to each other so as to conform to the principles. But if they do not, if the Humean circumstances of justice obtain, then people need mutual assurance of one another's likely conformity to the principles. This assurance is provided by assigning each the right to compel others to give justice. Naturally, the assurance must be seen as something to fall back on when things would otherwise go badly from the point of view of justice. If assurance had to be cashed all the time there would plainly be insufficient interest in justice for its practice to survive. The institution of rights can underwrite the practice of justice only because most people most of the time are prepared to observe its requirements without coercion or the threat of coercion.

There are two possible explanations of general conformity to what justice requires. One is that it is in individuals' self-interest. This is often the case. But if it is the only motive then individuals will have less mutual assurance of compliance than it is in their interests to have. And it seems likely that the additional motive supplied by sanctions for non-compliance will be set aside as much as possible by strategies of evasion. A second explanation of conformity to justice is that individuals are also directly moved by the desire to give justice. At any rate this motive is operative if individuals value autonomy. For in doing so they endorse diversity and this further commits them to institutional arrangements that all can acknowledge as fair. Of course, the autonomy interest in abiding by fair terms of co-operation with others cannot be assumed to guarantee full compliance. That is why rights are part of the trussing that sustains social co-operation.

10.4. CONCLUDING REMARKS

The materials for the political understanding of rights which I have mapped out have been made available by recent developments in liberal theories of justice. Using a positive notion of freedom or autonomy, the idea of constructivism, the assumption of moral motivation to come to an agreement with others, and full information, a theory can be developed which differs in structure and content from the Lockian one. Whereas the Lockian view sees rights as primitive, a natural moral fact, perhaps ultimately founded in creation, the structure of a political theory of rights sees them as the products of a consensus among autonomous persons. So while the derivation of rights is a theoretical construction rather than an actual agreement, the construction allows us to see rights as social products rather than as brute moral data. This, in turn, allows us to think that rights might be devised for the purpose of defining citizenship for a plurality of people who differ in their substantive conceptions of the good. And so, given that citizens can view themselves as autonomous, a scheme of principles can be constructed for the basic framework of their common life.

The content of Lockian rights is notoriously limited to rights to be let alone and to be compensated for past violations of rights. Locke was free to supplement his freedoms from interference with a theologically based duty of charity. But that has no place in the Nozickian version. We are, indeed, commended to give to the needy as a matter of uncoerced morality. But we are not supplied with any motivation that would make that likely, or make it right for the needy to help themselves from the plenty of the rich.

The content of autonomy-based rights is a great deal fuller. Autonomy requires that people should have available to them many forms of living, and should be sustained in their efforts to live their chosen life. This calls for a pluralistic culture, for redistribution of resources, and for a more than minimal state. At the same time, the role of government is confined to sustaining the framework for autonomous life. So the question of whether to take rights as proprietary or as political has practical consequences relevant to contemporary arguments about the role of government and the character of the liberal-democratic state.

This book is offered as an attempt to show that the difference between a libertarian and a social-democratic liberal state is not merely a matter of differences in the packages of rights associated with each. The content of the package differs in each case because the *structure* of the rights is different. I have elucidated the structural difference as the difference between owning and governing. And this difference affects the structure of the state. Where rights are structured as proprietary claims defined by the terms of full liberal ownership their defence requires a minimal state. Where rights are structured as political claims defined by the terms of self-government as set out in Chapter 8 their defence requires a much more extensive redistributive state.

The restructuring of rights I have been proposing is thus not merely of theoretical interest but has clear practical political implications. It also shows that it is a mistake to try to defend self-ownership on the ground of autonomy. The conditions of autonomy require a social structure which recognizes rights and duties going far beyond those provided under self-ownership. Autonomy and self-ownership are incompatible. I should like to believe that I have shown why this is so. I also hope that I have succeeded in developing a conception of self-government which replaces self-ownership to mediate between autonomy and the political conception of rights.

References

ACKERMAN, BRUCE A., *Social Justice in the Liberal State* (New Haven, Conn., 1980).

—— 'What is Neutral about Neutrality', *Ethics*, 93 (1983), 372–90.

African Charter on Human and People's Rights, in Brownlie (ed.), *Basic Documents on Human Rights*; and Sieghart, *The Lawful Rights of Mankind*.

ALEXY, ROBERT, *A Theory of Legal Argumentation: The Theory of Rational Discourse as Theory of Legal Justification*, trans. Ruth Adler and Neil MacCormick (Oxford, 1989).

American Declaration of the Rights and Duties of Man, in Brownlie (ed.), *Basic Documents on Human Rights*; and Sieghart, *The Lawful Rights of Mankind*.

AQUINAS, THOMAS, *Summa Theologiae*, trans. of the Dominican Fathers (London, 1963).

ARENDT, HANNAH, *The Human Condition* (Chicago, 1958).

ARISTOTLE, *The Nicomachean Ethics*, trans. Sir David Ross (London, 1954).

—— *The Politics*, trans. Sir Ernest Barker (Oxford, 1946).

BAKER, JOHN, *Arguing for Equality* (London, 1987).

—— 'Arguing for Economic Equality', *Center for the Study of Ethics in Society*: *Papers*, 6 (Kalamazoo, Mich., 1992).

BARRY, BRIAN, *Theories of Justice: A Treatise on Social Justice*, i. (London, 1989).

BEER, SAMUEL H., 'The Rule of the Wise and the Holy: Hierarchy in the Thomistic System', *Political Theory*, 14 (1986), 391–422.

BENN, STANLEY I., 'Human rights—for whom and for what?', in Kamenka and Tay (eds.), *Human Rights*.

—— *A Theory of Human Freedom* (Cambridge, 1988).

BENTHAM, JEREMY, *Anarchical Fallacies*, in Waldron (ed.), *Nonsense upon Stilts*.

—— *The Works of Jeremy Bentham*, publ. under the superintendence of John Bowring (11 vols., Edinburgh, 1838–43).

BRINK, DAVID O., 'Rawlsian Constructivism in Moral Theory', *Canadian Journal of Philosophy*, 17 (1987), 71–90.

BROWN, K. C. (ed.), *Hobbes Studies* (Oxford, 1965).

BROWNLIE, IAN (ed.), *Basic Documents on Human Rights*, 2nd edn. (Oxford, 1981).

CAMPBELL, TOM, *The Left and Rights* (London, 1983).

222   *References*

CHRISTMAN, JOHN, 'Self-Ownership, Equality, and the Structure of Property Rights', *Political Theory*, 19 (1991), 28–46.

COHEN, G. A., 'Nozick on Appropriation', *New Left Review*, 150 (1985), 89–105.

—— 'Self-Ownership, World Ownership, and Equality: Part II', *Social Philosophy and Policy*, 3 (1986), 77–96.

—— 'Capitalism, Freedom, and the Proletariat', in Ryan (ed.), *The Idea of Freedom*.

COHEN, JOSHUA, 'Deliberation and Democratic Legitimacy', in Hamlin and Pettit (eds.), *The Good Polity*.

CRAGG, W., 'Two Concepts of Community or Moral Theory and Canadian Culture', *Dialogue*, 25 (1986), 31–52.

CRANSTON, MAURICE, 'Human Rights: Real and Supposed', in Raphael (ed.), *Political Theory and the Rights of Man*.

CROWE, MICHAEL BERTRAM, *The Changing Profile of the Natural Law* (The Hague, 1977).

DAY, J. P., 'Locke on Property', *Philosophical Quarterly*, 16 (1966), 207–21.

DEVLIN, PATRICK, 'Morals and the Criminal Law', in Dworkin (ed.), *The Philosophy of Law*.

DUNN, JOHN, 'Justice and the Interpretation of Locke's Political Theory', *Political Studies*, 5 (1968), 68–87.

DWORKIN, GERALD, *The Theory and Practice of Autonomy* (Cambridge, 1988).

DWORKIN, RONALD (ed.), *The Philosophy of Law* (Oxford, 1977).

—— *Taking Rights Seriously*, rev. edn. (London, 1979).

—— *A Matter of Principle* (Cambridge, Mass., 1985).

—— 'Why Liberals Should Care about Equality', in *A Matter of Principle*.

—— 'Liberalism', in Sandel (ed.), *Liberalism and its Critics*.

—— 'What is Equality?: I. Equality of Welfare', *Philosophy and Public Affairs*, 10 (1981), 185–246.

—— 'What is Equality?: II. Equality of Resources', *Philosophy and Public Affairs*, 10 (1981), 283–345.

—— 'What is Equality?: III. The Place of Liberty', *Iowa Law Review*, 73 (1987), 1–54.

—— 'What is Equality?: IV. Political Equality', *University of San Francisco Law Review*, 22 (1988), 1–30.

—— 'Liberal Community', *California Law Review*, 77 (1989), 479–504.

—— 'Rights as Trumps', in Waldron (ed.), *Theories of Rights*.

European Convention for the Protection of Human Rights and Fundamental Freedoms, in Brownlie (ed.), *Basic Documents on Human Rights*; and Sieghart, *The Lawful Rights of Mankind*.

European Social Charter, in Brownlie (ed.), *Basic Documents on Human Rights*; and Sieghart, *The Lawful Rights of Mankind*.

FILMER, ROBERT, *Patriarcha and Other Political Works*, ed. P. Laslett (Oxford, 1949).

FINNIS, JOHN, *Natural Law and Natural Rights* (Oxford, 1980).

FRANKFURT, HARRY, 'Freedom of the Will and the Concept of the Person', *Journal of Philosophy*, 68 (1971), 5–20.

FREEDEN, MICHAEL, *Rights* (Buckingham, 1991).

GAUTHIER, DAVID, *Morals by Agreement* (Oxford, 1986).

GEWIRTH, ALAN, *Human Rights: Essays in Justification and Application* (Chicago, 1982).

GIERKE, OTTO, *Natural Law and the Theory of Society 1500 to 1800*, trans. Ernest Barker (Boston, 1957).

GOLDING, M. P., 'Welfare Rights', in Raphael (ed.), *Political Theory and the Rights of Man*.

GRAHAM, KEITH, *The Battle of Democracy: Conflict, Consensus and the Individual* (Brighton, 1986).

GREEN, T. H., *Lectures on the Principles of Political Obligation* (London, 1941).

GUEST, A. G., (ed.), *Oxford Essays in Jurisprudence* (Oxford, 1961).

HABERMAS, JÜRGEN, *Theory and Practice*, trans. John Viertel (London, 1974).

—— *Legitimation Crisis*, trans. Thomas McCarthy (London, 1976).

—— *Communication and the Evolution of Society*, trans. Thomas McCarthy (London, 1979).

—— 'Towards a Theory of Communicative Competence', *Inquiry*, 13 (1970), 360–75.

HAMLIN, ALAN, and PETTIT, PHILIP (eds.), *The Good Polity* (Oxford, 1989).

HART, H. L. A. *The Concept of Law* (Oxford, 1961).

—— *Essays on Bentham: Jurisprudence and Political Theory* (Oxford, 1982).

—— *Essays in Jurisprudence and Philosophy* (Oxford, 1983).

—— 'Are there any Natural Rights?', in Waldron (ed.), *Theories of Rights*.

HELD, DAVID, *Models of Democracy* (Oxford, 1987).

HOBBES, THOMAS, *Leviathan*, ed. with an introduction by C. B. Macpherson (Harmondsworth, 1968).

HOHFELD, WESLEY N., *Fundamental Legal Conceptions as Applied in Judicial Reasoning, and Other Legal Essays*, ed. by W. W. Cook (New Haven, Conn., 1919).

HONORÉ, A. M., 'Ownership', in Guest (ed.), *Oxford Essays in Jurisprudence*.

INGRAM, ATTRACTA, 'The Perils of Love: Why Women Need Rights', *Philosophical Studies* (Ireland), 32 (1988–90), 245–62.

224   *References*

INGRAM, ATTRACTA, 'The Empire Strikes Back: Liberal Solidarity in a *Europe des Patries'*, in Karlsson, Jónsson, and Brynjarsdóttir (eds.), *Law, Justice, and the State*.

International Covenant on Economic, Social, and Cultural Rights, in Brownlie (ed.), *Basic Documents on Human Rights*; and Sieghart, *The Lawful Rights of Mankind*.

KAMENKA, EUGENE, and TAY, ALICE ERH-SOON (eds.), *Human Rights* (London, 1978).

KANT, IMMANUEL, *The Moral Law (Groundwork of the Metaphysics of Morals)*, trans. and ed. H. J. Paton (London, 1956).

—— *The Metaphysical Elements of Justice*, trans. John Ladd (Indianapolis, 1965).

KARLSSON, MIKAEL, JÓNSSON, OLAFUR, and BRYNJARSDÓTTIR, EYJA, *Law, Justice, and the State* (Berlin, 1993).

KERNOHAN, ANDREW, 'Rawls and the Collective Ownership of Natural Abilities', *Canadian Journal of Philosophy*, 20 (1990), 19–28.

KING, DESMOND, and WALDRON, JEREMY, 'Citizenship, Social Citizenship, and the Defence of Welfare Provision', *British Journal of Political Science*, 18 (1988), 415–43.

KONTOS, A. (ed.), *Powers, Possessions and Freedom: Essays in Honour of C. B. Macpherson* (Toronto, 1979).

KURLAND, PHILIP B., and LERNER, RALPH (eds.), *The Founders' Constitution*, 5 vols. (Chicago, 1986).

KUKATHAS, CHANDRAN, and PETTIT, PHILIP, *Rawls: A Theory of Justice and its Critics* (Cambridge, 1990).

KYMLICKA, WILL, *Liberalism, Community, and Culture* (Oxford, 1989).

—— *Contemporary Political Philosophy: An Introduction* (Oxford, 1990).

LARMORE, CHARLES, *Patterns of Moral Complexity* (Cambridge, 1987).

LESSNOFF, MICHAEL, *Social Contract* (Basingstoke, 1986).

LEVY, MICHAEL B., 'Freedom, Property and the Levellers: The Case of John Lilburne', *Western Political Quarterly*, 36 (1983), 116–33.

LINDLEY, RICHARD, *Autonomy* (London, 1986).

LOCKE, JOHN, *Two Treatises of Government*, ed. Peter Laslett (Cambridge, 1960).

—— MS The Lovelace Collection of the papers of John Locke in the Bodleian Library.

—— 'Venditio', repr. as app. to Dunn, 'Justice and the Interpretation of Locke's Political Theory'.

MACCORMICK, NEIL, *Legal Right and Social Democracy: Essays in Legal and Political Philosophy* (Oxford, 1982).

—— and BANKOWSKI, ZENON (eds.), *Enlightenment, Rights, and Revolution: Essays in Legal and Social Philosophy* (Aylesbury, 1989).

MacIntyre, Alasdair, *After Virtue: A Study in Moral Theory* (London, 1981).
—— *Whose Justice? Which Rationality?* (London, 1988).
Mack, Eric, 'Distributive Justice and the Tensions of Lockeanism', *Social Philosophy and Policy*, 1 (1983), 132–50.
Mackie, J. L., 'Can there be a Rights-Based Moral Theory?', in Waldron (ed.), *Theories of Rights*.
Macpherson, C. B., *The Rise and Fall of Economic Justice and other Essays* (Oxford, 1987).
—— 'Human Rights as Property Rights', in *The Rise and Fall of Economic Justice*.
—— (ed.), *Property: Mainstream and Critical Positions* (Oxford, 1978).
—— 'The Meaning of Property', in *Property: Mainstream and Critical Positions*.
Maritain, Jacques, *The Rights of Man* (London, 1944).
Marshall, T. H., *Citizenship and Social Class* (Cambridge, 1950).
Martin, Rex, *Rawls and Rights* (Kansas, 1985).
Marx, Karl, 'On the Jewish Question', in Waldron (ed.), *Nonsense upon Stilts*.
McMurrin, S. (ed.), *The Tanner Lectures on Human Values*, iii (Salt Lake City, Utah, 1982).
Melden, A. I. (ed.), *Human Rights* (Belmont, Calif., 1970).
—— *Rights and Persons* (Oxford, 1977).
Mill, J. S., *Utilitarianism, On Liberty, Essay on Bentham*, ed. Mary Warnock (London, 1962).
Minogue, K. R., 'Natural rights, ideology, and the game of life', in Kamenka and Tay (eds.), *Human Rights*.
Nelson, William, *On Justifying Democracy* (London, 1980).
Norman, Richard, *Free and Equal: A Philosophical Examination of Political Values* (Oxford, 1987).
Nozick, Robert, *Anarchy, State, and Utopia* (New York, 1974).
O'Hagan, Timothy, *The End of Law?* (Oxford, 1984).
Olivecrona, Karl, 'Locke's Theory of Appropriation', *Philosophical Quarterly*, 24 (1974), 231–3.
O'Neill, Onora, 'The Great Maxims of Justice and Charity', in MacCormick and Bankowski (eds.), *Enlightenment, Rights and Revolution*.
—— *Constructions of Reason: Explorations of Kant's Practical Philosophy* (Cambridge, 1989).
Parkinson, G. H. R. (ed.), *Marx and Marxisms* (Cambridge, 1982).
Pateman, Carole, *Participation and Democratic Theory* (Cambridge, 1970).
—— *The Problem of Political Obligation: A Critique of Liberal Theory* (Oxford, 1985).

PETTIT, PHILIP, 'Habermas on Truth and Justice', in Parkinson (ed.), *Marx and Marxisms.*

—— 'The Freedom of the City: A Republican Ideal', in Hamlin and Pettit (eds.), *The Good Polity.*

PITKIN, HANNA FENICHEL, *Fortune is a Woman: Gender and Politics in the Thought of Niccolò Machiavelli* (Berkeley, Calif., 1984).

PLATO, *The Republic*, trans. Desmond Lee (Harmondsworth, 1974).

QUINE, W. V. O., *Word and Object* (Cambridge, Mass., 1960).

RAPHAEL, D. D., 'Human Rights: Old and New', in Raphael (ed.), *Political Theory and the Rights of Man.*

—— (ed.), *Political Theory and the Rights of Man* (London, 1967).

RAWLS, JOHN, *A Theory of Justice* (Oxford, 1971).

—— 'Fairness to Goodness', *Philosophical Review*, 84 (1975), 536–54.

—— 'Kantian Constructivism in Moral Theory: The John Dewey Lectures', *Journal of Philosophy*, 88 (1980), 515–72.

—— 'The Basic Liberties and their Priority', in McMurrin (ed.), *The Tanner Lectures on Human Values*, iii.

—— 'Social Unity and Primary Goods', in Sen and Williams (eds.), *Utilitarianism and Beyond.*

—— 'Justice as Fairness: Political not Metaphysical', *Philosophy and Public Affairs*, 14 (1985), 223–51.

—— 'The Idea of an Overlapping Consensus', *Oxford Journal of Legal Studies*, 7 (1987), 1–25.

—— 'The Priority of Right and Ideas of the Good', *Philosophy and Public Affairs*, 17 (1988), 251–76.

—— 'The Domain of the Political and Overlapping Consensus', *New York University Law Review*, 64 (1989), 233–55.

RAZ, JOSEPH, 'On the Nature of Rights', *Mind*, 93 (1984).

—— *The Morality of Freedom* (Oxford, 1986).

REEVE, ANDREW (ed.), *Modern Theories of Exploitation* (London and Los Angeles, 1987).

RIESS, HANS (ed.), *Kant's Political Writings*, trans. H. B. Nisbet (Cambridge, 1970).

RORTY, RICHARD, SCHNEEWIND, J. B., and SKINNER, QUINTIN (eds.), *Philosophy in History* (Cambridge, 1984).

ROUSSEAU, JEAN-JACQUES, *The Social Contract*, trans. Maurice Cranston (Harmondsworth, 1968).

RYAN, ALAN (ed.), *The Idea of Freedom: Essays in Honour of Isaiah Berlin* (Oxford, 1979).

—— *Property and Political Theory* (Oxford, 1984).

SANDEL, MICHAEL J., *Liberalism and the Limits of Justice* (Cambridge, 1982).

—— (ed.), *Liberalism and its Critics* (Oxford, 1984).

SCANLON, T. M., 'Contractualism and Utilitarianism', in Sen and Williams (eds.), *Utilitarianism and Beyond*.

—— 'Rights, Goals, and Fairness', in Waldron (ed.), *Theories of Rights*.

SCHAUER, FREDERICK, *Free Speech: A Philosophical Inquiry* (Cambridge, 1982).

SEN, AMARTYA, 'Utilitarianism and Welfarism', *Journal of Philosophy*, 76, (1979), 463–89.

—— and WILLIAMS, BERNARD (eds.), *Utilitarianism and Beyond* (Cambridge, 1982).

SIEGHART, PAUL, *The Lawful Rights of Mankind* (Oxford, 1985).

SKINNER, QUINTIN, 'The Idea of Negative Liberty', in Rorty, Schneewind, and Skinner (eds.), *Philosophy in History*.

STEINER, HILLEL, 'The Structure of a Set of Compossible Rights', *Journal of Philosophy*, 74 (1977), 765–77.

—— 'The Natural Right to the Means of Production', *Philosophical Quarterly*, 27 (1977), 41–9.

—— 'A Liberal Theory of Exploitation', *Ethics*, 94 (1984), 225–41.

—— 'Supernatural Powers: Can there be a Right of Bequest?', Political Studies Association Conference (Manchester, 1985).

—— 'Exploitation: A Liberal Theory Amended, Defended, and Extended', in Reeve (ed.), *Modern Theories of Exploitation*.

—— 'Capitalism, Justice and Equal Starts', *Social Philosophy and Policy*, 5 1987, 49–71.

—— *An Essay on Rights* (Oxford, 1994).

STRAUSS, LEO, *The Political Philosophy of Hobbes: Its Basis and Genesis* (Oxford, 1936).

—— 'On the Spirit of Hobbes's Political Philosophy', in Brown (ed.), *Hobbes Studies*.

SUMNER, L. W., *The Moral Foundations of Rights* (Oxford, 1987).

TAYLOR, CHARLES, *Philosophy and the Human Sciences: Philosophical Papers*, 2 vols. (Cambridge, 1985).

—— 'Atomism', in *Philosophy and the Human Sciences: Philosophical Papers*, ii.

THOMSON, JUDITH JARVIS, *The Realm of Rights* (Harvard, 1990).

TIERNEY, BRIAN, 'Tuck on Rights: Some Medieval Problems', *History of Political Thought*, 4 (1983), 429–41.

TÖNNIES, FERDINAND, *Community and Association (Gemeinschaft und Gesellschaft)*, trans. C. P. Loomis (London, 1955).

TUCK, RICHARD, *Natural Rights Theories: Their Origin and Development* (Cambridge, 1979).

TULLY, JAMES, *A Discourse on Property: John Locke and his Adversaries* (Cambridge, 1980).

228 Referenceз

Universal Declaration of Human Rights, in Brownlie (ed.), *Basic Documents on Human Rights*; and Sieghart, *The Lawful Rights of Mankind*.

WALDRON, JEREMY (ed.), *Theories of Rights* (Oxford, 1984).

—— 'Theoretical Foundations of Liberalism', *The Philosophical Quarterly*, 37 (1987), 127–50.

—— (ed.), *Nonsense upon Stilts: Bentham, Burke and Marx on the Rights of Man* (London, 1987).

—— *The Right to Private Property* (Oxford, 1988).

WALZER, MICHAEL, *Spheres of Justice: A Defence of Pluralism and Equality* (Oxford, 1983).

WIGGINS, DAVID, *Sameness and Substance* (Oxford, 1980).

Index